WHAT AN EXTRAORDINARY TITLE FOR A TRAVEL BOOK

by

P.J. EMERSON.

By the same author:

'Inflation?   Try A Bicycle'

'Northern Ireland - That Sons May Bury Their Fathers'

'The Dove of Peace a'learning 'ow to Fly'

First Published 1986
P.J. Emerson.
Rhubarb Cottage
36 Ballysillan Road
Belfast 14

I S B N   0   9506028   2   5

To Norah:

Who said
Yes
I could go

And
Like a fool
I went.

And my thanks are due to Dervla, who threw away the first draft of this book; to Amanda who ditched the second; and to Mary who proofed the third.

PREFACE

Time is cheaper than money.

CONTENTS

FOREWORD.

It is a relief and a delight to write a foreword to Peter Emerson's travel book.

In the 'fifties and 'sixties, I had a hope that a new Irishman would emerge who had noticed the existence of the rest of the planet and who would become useful to the other people on it. This Irishman would recognise his special position: he belonged to an island that had once been colonised and yet was part of the rich North. He could perhaps explain one lot to the other lot. He would be post-tribal and post-sectarian.

There were signs that this new Irishman was about. He provided soldiers for UN peacekeeping forces and a fresh voice in the European Community. He provided distinguished public servants such as Conor Cruise O'Brien and Sean MacBride. There were even signs that the world was aware of him. Colm Cavanagh, long-legged Derry man, was serving in the UN Development Programme in Dar es Salaam. He had two Indian colleagues:

First Indian: All the senior posts here are held by Europeans. Even the UN is racist.

Colm: I agree.

Second Indian: I've never heard a white man agree about that before.

First Indian: Colm's not a white man; he's an Irishman.

This new Irishman has almost disappeared in the selfish welter of this latest and longest round of Ulster Troubles, with its tribal killings, its genteel bigots and its impertinent churchmen.

But some have survived. Peter is one. He was in the Royal Navy for nine years, a submariner. He was a teacher in Nairobi for another three. He bicycled 8,000 miles in eight months, visiting most of the countries of Central Africa. In 1975, he came to Belfast. He has been a full-time youth leader in the Crumlin Road and a community worker in Ardoyne. He has stood unsuccessfully in local elections, on ecological and liberal tickets. He has written two books before this one. In 1979, he went travelling again, this book is the result. In 1980 he became very active in CND, and still is.

He is the kind of traveller who moves slowly along the ground, on foot or bicycle, and who does not bother where he'll be at nightfall. In this book, he meets people, notices things and draws deductions.

He is a pacifist, that brave stance. He feels strongly about the important things: the starvation, the cruelty, the disease, the slums and shanty towns, the destruction of trees and topsoil, the pollution of air and water, the arms race and the nation state.

Like all the best travellers, he is very funny about travel.

Harry Barton. 1985.

For reasons totally beyond the control of the author, the journey followed a logical sequence of events. But as the text doesn't even attempt to follow any (chrono-)logical pattern, perhaps I should just spend a few moments putting you into the picture before taking myself out.

From Belfast I cycled across Ireland, Wales, England, France and Spain, so Europe deserves a word or two. Yes; that'll do. The journey proper started in Morocco in the month of November and in the year of .... Well, in a wee mountain village, the new year was celebrated; new, that is, to the followers of Islam. Drums were beaten and songs were sung as we entered the 1499th year of our Lord in what was to a Christian reader still the 1979th year of the reputedly same Lord.

For six weeks I travelled from plain to mountain, enjoying wonderful hospitality, smoking too much hash and learning too little Arabic. In Marakech, in one of those extraordinary coincidences which, via methods unknown and for reasons various, bejewel the lives of us all, I bumped into a fellow lone cyclist who was definitely not a fellow - Amanda - and together we climbed in the snows of the Atlas. Then she went that-a-way, soon to cycle across the Sahara, while I ventured east with less adventurous frames of bike and mind.

On Christmas eve I entered Algeria, to share what should have been a silent night with a donkey; alas, this particular Allah-damned beast knew not the peace of the stable. Like Morocco, Algeria is also Moslem of Arab and Berber stock, and it too is a land of contrast between the empty expanse of the desert and the often rich and fertile slopes of the Atlas. The differences between the two countries lay mainly in their political leanings and in the fact that the latter is oil-rich. I spent a month in and around the more southern side of the Atlas, with one foray into the desert itself, to the oases of Ghardaia and Ouargla. And for a further four weeks, I journeyed in the last of the three countries of the Maghreb, Tunisia, another right-wing, non-oil-rich state.

To get into Libya is easier said than done but if done 'tis worth saying. Here too my sojourn was for a month, mainly because of restrictions imposed by petty officials in embassies and consulates. Much has been the abuse hurled at Libya by the western press and right-wing politicians - only some of it is deserved. As so often happens, however, the politics of a place is a mere veneer .... and the real character of the Libyan lies beyond the bureaucrat.

Despite a fairly tight schedule I still managed to be late on arrival at the Egyptian immigration control in Alexandria. And not least because the Libyan/Egyptian border was closed and under heavy military guard, and because I therefore had to go round what I could not go through, both the border and the law. In so doing, I lost my bicycle and gained a canoe. Yet all was forgiven, and a month in the land of Egypt was the gift of the state, giving what it had no right to possess.

It was nice for a change, but I couldn't take it for long. In Khartoum, I bought a bicycle recycled. My first machine, one of the old hand-made racers, was in sharp contrast to this brute of a bike - regal it appeared, ancient it was, and heavy beyond measure. To buy such a mode of transport in a land where there was virtually only one tarmac road was a little unwise; not so much for the infinite flatness of The Sudan perhaps, but certainly for the hills of Uganda. Therein, a number of bits of the bike fell into more bits; yet not for this reason did I stay for just three weeks. To be a mouth in a land short of food might not be right. And, as I'll explain in the text, to use the official exchange rate was financially prohibitive.

In earlier times, I had visited Central Africa. By now travelling across the North and up the Nile, I learnt of some of the ways of the Arabic speaking peoples, while in The Sudan I witnessed the steady but dramatic shift from Arab to Negro. Uganda I had wished to re-visit, to study the tragedy that has befallen that land. And in Kenya, where I had lived and worked in the early seventies, my journey came to an end. Ten months, two bikes and two diseases was the total.

*   *   *

Such a journey into the lands of another continent should give the traveller a chance to see not only what was and what was not in these foreign countries, but also the opportunity to contrast much with what may not be so right or what might be intolerably wrong with his own, his so-called developed civilisation.

There was indeed much to see; and sadly, there is a lot wrong in what might be the closing decades of the existence of our species. But the story of our human evolution does not have to end yet; it has been a fascinating one so far, and there's every reason to think that the future could be just as exciting, a lot more sophisticated and - well, maybe - a good deal less bloody. The purpose of this book is simply to point out a few observations, mainly of what was, partially of what was wrong, and just a little of what might be more right, both here in this country, and there in the vastness of Africa.

P.J.E.
Belfast
1.1.85

CHAPTER 1

A PART OF, OR APART FROM, NATURE, (PART ONE).

The disadvantage in giving a book an extraordinary title is that you, the reader, be you ordinary or otherwise, will expect the content to match the name.   It won't.   It will merely start by beginning at the end.

The first place I want you to visit is a farm in The Sudan.   Later on, we will look at other sectors of society: we will dine with no wine in homes, huts and hovels;   we'll work at a well, in a mill, down a mine;   we'll travel by bike, on beast, and in barges;   we'll learn about schools and care about health clinics;   and we'll bargain and barter in bars and bazaars.   We might even take a peep inside a mosque.   But first, let's go to a farm.   Well, it isn't really a farm ....

I want to take you away from the comfort of your railway station waiting room next door to the closed buffet, to the biggest country in Africa, a country where such vastness can only be accommodated in the seemingly endless flatness of the open desert;   to a land which only slowly moves from the emptiness of the Sahara to the semi-savannah of the south;   to a land scorched by the ceaseless rays of the sun;   to a land, hot dry and dusty. And in the south, in the unpolluted airs of the African night, the world was alive;   the distant horizon was blessed with the long awaited clouds, each in turn lit up in the excitement of silent lightning .... and somewhere was awash with the first of the rains.

There was a bog in The Sudan called The Sudd.   It was the size of Ireland, a massive area of swamp-cum-river-cum-swamp-cum-island-cum-swamp, into and out of which flowed the White Nile; by the time it emerged it had lost half of its volume through evapouration.   There, in teemimg humidity, were miles and miles of papyrus and a welter of wild-life.   This was the bog which had kept secret the source of the Nile, the quest of many an erstwhile explorer. Here, invariably, they'd got stuck; and once stuck they'd been bitten, several times certainly by the mosquito, maybe only once by the crocodile.

On this particular evening in May, I was just down south and up river of The Sudd, travelling on a road that hardly deserved the name, in this the beginning of the rainy season. Soon, much of it was to be transformed into impossible, impassable, black cotton mud.   On either side of the road were dark barked trees, a welcome change from the treeless horizons I'd just left behind me .... or so I thought!   And there, by the roadside, a young cattle herdsman bid me welcome to his 'farm' for the night.

Imagine, then, the scene.   Forget the world of straw manure and wellies if but for a moment, and focus in on what is, in a different part of the world, just a different way of doing things. The cows, different again from our fleshy freisans, wore the hump on the shoulders and that empty sack of skin between their fore legs; their torsos were skeletal, the rib cage of each clearly patterned in the sides of their hides; and on their heads were horns, huge and hemi-spherical, large enough to hold the sun at dawn, and such had been a deity in days of yesteryear. Just at this time, the cattle were coming back to the camp for the night. The camp itself was simply a patch of dry, cleared earth wherein many a stick was stuck, one for each cow, in circular patterns around the many fires. Each animal knew its own stick, and the young boys of the camp simply tied the beast to its pole with a short length of rope. To attach a cow to the wrong stake was regarded as the height of juvenile stupidity. We approached the camp, this young man and I, just as all this activity, these preparations for the night, were in full swing. The sun had just disappeared to leave an evening still; barely a breath of air disturbed the calm, and only a few wisps of cloud drew lines to frame the trees.

With all my worldly goods....

I, foreground stage left, sitting cross-legged on the fireside ground, was wearing my tailor-made (?) 1980-look, 1960 pair of trousers, a pair of flip flops and a ten-p-PT-t-shirt, bought in the previous year's jumble sales in Belfast. The fading grey of my slacks and my matching off-white shirt blended gently into the shades of the dusk made hazier by the pillars of smoke a'rising from those fires of dung and wood. Save for the soft swish of their tails and the occasional stamp of their hooves, the cattle were silent and, just like home, a quiet cow is a cow content. On the other side of the fire, stage right, sat my host and his companions, and all were dressed in uniform guise; typical of the Nilotic tribes, these folk were fine specimens and speciwomens of humanity, tall, well-proportioned, and every one of them fit and healthy - or so it did appear. They were wearing, in sharp contrast to my somewhat casual gear, in colours of deep black .... er .... nothing! Well one had a metal anklet, another a lion's tooth necklace and an ivory brace-let. Some had their hair dyed an orange colour with a prepara-tion made from cow's urine. But otherwise they were wearing nothing at all at all. I know that when in Rome one should do as the Romans - eat spaghetti I mean and not just go to chapel - but I thought I'd remain what only we would call decent, but that's just because we have a different way of looking at things. Mind you, I was trying not to look at things anyway.

The camp was for the young. A baby spent three years with its mummy, three with its gran, and then he or she went to spend his/her childhood and youth in the cattle camp. All the young lived together, learning together, each one teaching the next as his or her turn came along. Come adolescence, sex education was apparently learnt, not so much in theory, more, let us say, in the laboratory. Just as the craze for all things new has spread from mathematics to physics, so too institutionalised sex education might follow similar trends to become new sex - as old as the hills - of which there were none in this part of the world. Whether promiscuity existed, I knew not, but I did learn the price for a bride was forty cows or so, depending on inflation; the local currency was indeed the cow, though unquoted in the financial times exchange rates .... but perhaps that's because cows don't float too well. When a couple married, they returned to the village of their elders. Till then, the young men and their juniors went around naked, while the girls wore a simple length of cloth to cover most of their torsos .... thereagain, throughout the world, women have always tended to be more dignified than men.

The camp diet was extremely limited. I was offered a tin of milk, fresh from the teat, un-TT'd and untreated .... but nature's filters are usually the best. And that was all they had. The cow was rarely killed for its meat. A little fruit or fish would sometimes supplement the menu; in such circumstances, the very least I could do in return was to offer them, from the supermarket of my rucksack .... a packet of biscuits.

The dusk passed into night. And, as if from nowhere, the entire camp was suddenly all-covered with an all-pervasive almighty all-buzzing sound. Nothing could be seen; there was just this nasty noise as a swarm of the dreaded tsetse fly flew in for their supper of cow or human blood. They sucked with a proboscis in a similar manner to the mosquito, but these were larger brutes with a probe which felt like a pin-prick if not an injection; and that probe could quite easily go straight through a cotton shirt or a pair of flannel trousers. After some minutes, they left. Just as well. The cattle folk protected themselves from all these beasts of the bush, not by clothes which would have been useless anyway, but by covering their bodies with the ash from the cow-dung fire. Thus, so often, they looked like wraiths, grey or even white; and most of them survived, unbitten by the tsetse, unplagued by the sleeping sickness it carries. Herein, therefore, lay one of the reasons for their nakedness, and for the fires in such temperate climes. Their way of life, simple perhaps, had logic.

We chatted for a while before laying out on the ground for a good night's sleep. The bed was a straw mat; the pillow, a hollow tube of wood. The latter was portable and, with the spear, was always carried by these herdsmen. The spear, I was happy to note, was invariably held with its safety-catch on - the latter, a fluffy ball of white cotton, stuck onto the point.

At dawn, all were awake, and I was soon partaking of breakfast, another tin of milk. Now some girls had already started to collect all the dung into big piles, just beyond the camp perimeter, while others .... each with a tin .... were on their marks .... ready .... steady .... a cow started to piddle, GO! The tin was thrust under the upraised tail and, ah, 'tis done, a fine tin of mornin' fresh urine. Lovely day for a pee. What it was used for I was, as yet, uncertain; but I was a little concerned for the urine tin was just such a one as I had drunk my milk from. Yes - you're right - and just as we might add a dash of lemon to the sweet martini, so too they added a soupçon of cowpee to the milk. Sláinte. Milk, with that little extra something.

Well, too late now. Mind you, after six months in Africa, I thought my guts were reasonably tough. Most strange foods my stomach machinery digested without too many backfires or major breakdowns; indeed, such had been my success to date that I was happy to boast of bowels bionic. For cow's urine, however, I was totally unprepared. I was caught, as it were with my trousers down, retrospectively speaking, for two days later, I got the worst diarrhoea I have ever had .... oh, I was woe.

Before leaving this excellent hospitality - how were they to know my guts could only cope with pre-packed, processed, plastic peas? - I felt I should leave a little token of European civilisation. To you, mine host, a pair of shorts. Ooooh!

Now I am short and plump while these people were so incredibly
tall and thin.   Not a hope.   Like a lift out of control, the
shorts did fall straight back to the ground.   Never mind. They
were still pleased with the gift.   Gratitude is but one of the
many qualities of so-called 'primitive' peoples.   I hope in my
turn I was also grateful for their kindness - and cowpee!
        Such,   then, was the night of the Sudanese cattle herdsman.
His day was spent with his animals quietly wandering from here to
there in search of food in a land of no green fields, in a land
where vegetation was sparse, but in a land of no fences, where
freedom was limited only by the bounds of poverty.   In bidding a
temporary good-bye to the tribes of this area, it is interesting
to note that it was a process of evolution which caused them all
to be so tall, and it was a different process of the same
evolution which had actually caused the pygmies of the jungles
not far south from here to adopt a shorter stature.

                          *   *   *

        The North Sudanese sometimes criticised their southern
fellow citizens for their more naked ways, principally because
the former were Moslem and, in a manner not unlike that of some
Christians, governed by strict codes of (their sort of) morality.
From the cattle camps of southern Sudan, then, may I transport
you in an instant to Morocco, not to yesterday's Barbary Coast,
but to to-day's peaceful plains of the agricultural North and
West, and then to the silent valleys of the Atlas mountains.
        Firstly,   then, to Ksar-el-Kbir, to a way of life so
different from, yet in ways somewhat similar to, that of the
Nilotic peoples.   A small group of dwellings were clustered
together somewhat haphazardly in the middle of a number of fields
- there was none of the far from splendid isolation with which
we in Europe associate a farmhouse.   The buildings were simple,
one-storey affairs, built to enclose a compound which in turn was
in the centre of a small vegetable plot surrounded by a cactus
fence.   Beyond the cactus, the grazing and woodlands were
shared;   it all seemed to be a pretty good example of the mixed
economy, in which some property was personal and much was
communal.
        I arrived at the hour of sunset, one of the times when the
Moslem is called to prayer.   The father of the house, a
splendid old boy not least because of his white beard, had taken
off his shoes to advance a few steps into the garden to pray.
He stood; he bowed, he stood; he bowed, he bent, he stood;   he
bowed, he knelt and kissed the ground, he stood.   Such were the
exertions of the devout.   And during them all, prayers both
silent and spoken were offered to Allah.   His duty done, he
turned and our eyes met - yet our mouths were silent for I knew
not one word of Arabic, I'd only just started to learn the
alphabet!   The Moslem, however, is always quick to recognise

the traveller and minister to him or her, for so it had been written, and thus had spoken Mohammed, the prophet.

We entered the compound, slipped off our shoes and went into the one and only living room; it was simply lavish. Simple, certainly, for this was the bedroom, sitting and dining rooms, all in one. The furniture consisted of two beds, and they filled up the two ends, one couch in between the beds, and one small table in the little bit of floor space that was left. The walls of mud contained one no glass nothing window, and the door was of heavy, unpolished wood. But the bedspreads, the carpet, the cushions and the curtains were all of magnificent, richly embroidered and brilliantly bordered materials - in a word, lavish, in true Arab tradition.

Dad was wearing his **jeleba**, the everyday, all-purpose tunic which deserves a special mention. It was a one piece garment, not unlike the friar's habit, with an enormous hood which could be a rucksack for the shopping, an umbrella in times of rain, or a night simulator whenever the time for forty winks offered itself. In these hot and humid lands, such times were often nigh, and the landscape was spasmodically spotted with 'sleeping **jelebas**' as Amanda, my travelling companion in much of Morocco, used to call them. The **jeleba** had two very baggy sleeves, and its only other attributes were two slits in its sides so that, if you were caught unprepared, in a land where conveniences were few, you just had to crouch where you were and there you were, in your very own portaloo!

The Mark O Jeleba

The ladies of the house, alas, were not allowed into this one and only special room. They laboured in the kitchen, on an open fire on a mud floor, and they worked from a crouching position over yards and yards of delicate lace material bundled into their laps. The staple food was kous-kous, more pleasant to the palate than the pee of a cow. When all was ready, one of the women prepared a bowl of water so that the menfolk could wash their forks called hands and then, with a little Bismillah (a wee prayer of a grace), all in a circle started on the one great pile of food heaped on the one tray. On top were a few vegetables and perhaps a dash of meat - the mark of the comparatively rich family - and to each of us, Dad did apportion a hunk around the tray when the pile of kous-kous was nearly done. The climax of the meal, the climax of any Moroccan feast, was the tea. When all had had a sufficiency, the women came to take it away, not least because what we'd left behind was their supper! And in came one tea pot, a charcoal fire, a bellows, several glasses, an enormous lump of sugar, a metal club with which to smash it to sensible proportions, and a bundle of mint. The tea pot was an exotic little thing with its conical hat as tall as its spherical body. Dad became the cook, testing and tasting as we would a wine. Thus the meal was over: Hamdullah (thanks be to God).

And so to bed. The biggest and best was mine for the night - now where, in Europe, will the host give his own personal bed to the guest? Ummm .... perhaps that question best remains unanswered. Outside in the compound the goats and a horse passed the nocturnal watches by regularly dropping dung which, the following morning, the women did collect for cooking fuel. They rose at an early hour to immediately start baking, or rather frying, the bread for our breakfast; only then did the menfolk start the day's routine, dad taking the animals to graze, sons aspiring to something which they, and society, and the western world, pretended was better - urban, white-jeleba labour in the bureaus and banks of Ksar-el-Kbir.

The Berber village was a different affair. To the south of the mountains, they were constructed in a form which appeared to allow for military defence. The village comprised a sort of block, with the outer mud walls of adjoining houses forming the perimeter, and this was only broken in one or two places where all and sundry made their exits and their entrances. Each house retained a certain amount of individuality, however, for there was no centralised government agency restricting the designs to those of plans A or B. The corner houses were often of three stories, the corners themselves being surmounted by little turrets, and each wall was occasionally adorned by a window made of fresh air or perhaps of a metallic grill. Often, the ground floor was for the donkey or the goats, while the two upper floors were for the folks. One home, then, would perhaps consist of only two rooms.

Within the mountains, there was neither the space for such

a layout, nor would there have been the military need. The houses were sturdier, reinforced with strong timbers in readiness for the winter's snows. They consisted of one or two stories at the most, and togetherness was achieved by building each one very close to its neighbours. On the steep slopes that prevailed, they appeared to almost stand on each other, while each retained a view of the valley below.

And the

Berber's home

is also a castle

In the rough and rocky terrain of the mountains, the valley floor offered little, and every inch was used in a lattice of fields, all fed by the main river or from human-made canals held in place by the roots of the poplar trees, alive, and aglow in the yellows of autumn. To the south lay the vast expanse of the Sahara, and into this ocean of sand and stone ran a valiant river or few. Only some disappeared into the blue. Others, in the heat of the desert, never made the sea, and they made instead a "chott", a flat pan of salt, the creation of millenia. For as long as the rivers remained wet. agriculture flourished. The banks were marked by the frond of the palm, and the irrigated plots confirmed the belief that sandy soil - or is it just sand? - is good for carrots! Close to the river, in the mountains or on the valley floor, worked the Berber, for as long as the day would let him, in a constant struggle with nature, in a perfect love-hate relationship. All too often, the twentieth century and its fox has lured the young (men) away to the towns, leaving the old to care for the world's most precious resource, the land. And the old continued to work unto a ripe old age; they lived until they died; there was none of our western, geriatric decay.

*   *   *

One way of life, a wonderful example of ingenuity, definitely deserves a mention.   In the little town of Matmata in southern Tunisia, the local folk have built homes which are in absolute contrast to those ghastly high-rise flats of contemporary Europe.   Their answer?   The low-sink!   Indeed, they've built nothing up at all; rather, everything is down, and in a successful bid to escape the merciless rays of the sun, they've carved holes in the ground, each cylindrical room connected to the next by an open area, a sort of foyer, by which all received the reflected light of day.   It was a most sensible arrangement and sociable too, for all too easily the passing neighbour could indeed just drop in.

*   *   *

In but a line, the scene changes again, to Egypt, where the same common factors of human adaptability have ensured the ability to survive.   Here, nature has created a different world;   yet here too, homo sapiens has been able to work with what there was - and is - to produce a way of life that definitely was - but only maybe still is - sustainable.
       - Is there a river in Ireland? I was asked.   Egypt is the Nile;   the Nile is Egypt.   The huge river flows forever, slowly and steadily, regardless of catastrophe.   It is, as it were, independent of time .... or perhaps it invented it.   For once every so often in what became known as a year, in what was later called the month of June, the rains did fall, in Ethiopia. There, rivers swelled;   Lake Tana filled, and then the waters flooded over into the Blue Nile and so to Khartoum, 1,200 kilometres down stream; here it joined the White Nile, fresh from The Sudd;   here was the penultimate confluence of rivers before the Nile reached the sea;   yet from here to that sea, some 2,500 kilometres still remained.   Close to Egypt's southern border stood Aswan, only 100 metres above sea-level, a full 1,000 kilometres from the Med.   Over such a gentle slope, there was no cause for rush;   hush, then, was no noise as the waters rose to flood over all the fertile land of Egypt, over the banks of the Nile in Upper Egypt, and over the fields north of Cairo which form the delta, a fertile triangle in a desert dead, the over-populated green in an empty yellow, the Bangla-Desh of Africa. Every year, the waters covered everything, and thereby the fields were fertilised with another fine covering of best, imported, Ethiopian silt - or so it had been in the good old days.   Those days, alas, were now gone.
       Throughout its Egyptian journey, the Nile flowed north with only the barest of meanders.   Wherever the silt had been deposited, there the land was fertile.   Elsewhere, the bare and barren rocks of the desert forbade all but the most daring to

wander.   Water is the blood of life;   the Nile is the artery of
Egypt;   and   nearly all human life lived within walking distance
of its waters.   The houses, indeed entire villages, were built
on slightly higher ground, in between the fields of the delta, or
up-river,   south   of the city of Cairo,   on the very edge of   the
desert.

From the   river itself,   large canals fed smaller ones in a
perpendicular lattice until all the fertile land was irrigatable.
Water was transferred from one level to another with a technology
which   has   existed from (what a Christian might)   (but   what   a
Moslem   would   not call) biblical times.   A near naked   farmer
stood in the waters of the river,   in front of him,   a canvas bag
tied to a pole.   When full of water it was lifted by a simple
lever,   the other end of which was counterbalanced by a great big
blob of dried clay.   Simple.   But a little bit of technology
would   perhaps   have done no harm.   The other system was a   bit
more sophisticated; a series of clay buckets were strapped to the
circumference   of a large wooden wheel,   up to 4 or 5   metres   in
diameter.   The timbered teeth thereof interlocked with those of
a horizontal wheel,   to the axle of which on its upper side   was
attached a long long pole.   The whole creaky works was operated
by the donkey or the ox, encouraged if necessary by the child who
sat   behind   on an extension of that pole.   He,   with a   whip,
provided   not   the coercion of the carrot,   rather the   force   of
fear.   It was rather sad to see so many of these animals blind-
folded   on the theory that, if they knew they were going round in
circles,   they   would get bored and slow down.   Yet birds   fly
over   continents,   fishes swim the oceans and the   wildebeest   of
Africa   migrate   in   their thousands over distances   which   would
easily deter us humans.   No,   we underestimate both the ability
and the tolerance of the animal,   but we perhaps more so than the
Arab;   we call the ass stupid   -   they describe it as patient.

The staple   food,   in a national diet different by far   from
the   kous-kous of its western neighbours,   was beans,   beans,   the
shape of the broad with the colour the brown.   Beans were   the
chips of Egypt.   The basic meal was a dose of these with a dash
of olive oil in a small bun of bread.   Variety came with onions
and tomatoes, not to mention a side salad from a water cress type
plant.   Egypt was   a   haven for the   vegetarian,   though   the
predominance   of   beans did restrict the pleasures   to   those   of
sounder disposition. Alas,   the average Egyptian was vegetarian,
not through choice,   but through poverty.   Fruits,   grains and
sugar   cane completed the indigenous harvest   -   oh the land   was
fertile enough, so far.   But poverty remained, because of over-
crowding,   bad government,   and economic factors which   suggested
that food should be exported!   Do we blame those who owned the
food   for   selling   it abroad ....   or ourselves in   Belfast   and
elsewhere who bought and still buy it?

The corn was reaped by hand;   old men,   on their haunches,
spent   all day in the heat of the sun collecting little   handfuls
of   the   vital cereal.   The harvesting of sugar was done   by   a

group, for this was hot and dusty work.   The sticks were all
piled on top of each other .... and then the pile did rise, for
underneath was a camel!   The other animal often seen was that
cumbersome beast, the water buffalo, and it too added that little
touch of Asia.   It could pull a plough or turn a well, but it
preferred to spend the entire day in the cool of the river.
Wouldn't you?   Well, after a close inspection, you probably
wouldn't, for the waters of the Nile were not the cleanest.

The main canals were often protected from the noonday sun
by palm trees, and here in the shade the men did take a rest to
eat a bean, to smoke an illegal joint, or to manufacture rope
from the fibres of the palm by twisting these around those and
those around these on a strand held taught by the mighty big toe.
In both town and country, in the villages and amongst the fields,
water was always available;   under the cover of something, a
couple of earthenware jugs were there to quench the thirst of any
worker or passer-by.   In the evening hour, the womenfolk walked
from their desertside homes through the latticed fields to the
river to then return, laden, with water jars finely balanced on
their heads.

There are two words which the visitor to the villages of
Egypt will often hear.   The first is **fad'dr**, and its utterance
is invariably good news.   It could mean hallo, welcome, sit
down, come and have a glass of tea, won't you stay for a meal?
would you like a bed for the night? or simply whadaboutyer?
Here a **fad'dr**, a drink;   there a **fad'dr**, an edible stick of sugar
cane;   even a meal of bread in molasses, the thick black treacle
left behind from sugar processing - superb.   Sometimes the
fad'drs came so thick and fast that a few just had to be
declined, for if the day was full of **fad'drs**, I would ne'er have
got any "furd'r".   And all this kindness came from homes on the
very brink of abject poverty.   In the average one storey house
was the barest of furniture, an old heavy seat made from very
thick timbers and a bed or two of similar construction.   The
floor was earth, the air hot and dusty, and the water from the
river cloudy with heavenknewwhats.

Now, if I may digress awhile, I will talk of a **fad'dr** that
was odder than most.   The Mussulman, again not unlike the
Christian, had some extraordinary ideas in his head when it came
to matters of sex.   It all started like this: **fad'dr**, a group
of women, all dressed in black, bid welcome.   We sat and
chatted while a glass of tea was prepared.   Some were young,
others not so, and the talk was more of them asking me the
direction of my wanderings.   It was a good question.   Then
along came a someone - a feller - who said in English that I
should not be talking with women!   So I had to go on my way.
Later, as the sun set, a village was at hand.   I found a wee
café and ordered a meal of beans and beans - the menu was a
little limited. Fad'dr. Come and stay the night. Oh good.   We
chatted with others who were giving this beanhall continual
trade.   At one point in the middle of a sentence, my host for

the night said love.   Ah dear,   his English was not as good as
it might have been;   nor was my Arabic, of course.   No, I said,
you mean live.

Time   for bed.   In such temperatures,   I needed little.
The room I'd been given,   part of a school, was quite large.   I
laid out my sleeping bag and myself on top.   It was too hot for
anything but 'me' underpants.   Then in he came and said,

- My wife died two months ago;   can I make love with you?   I
immediately thought poor wife,   if that was all she had meant for
him.   Then I more immediately thought that I ought most
immediately to think of myself!

- No,   I said.   And, as always happens on these occasions,
the   requests   persisted until   they annoyed and   antagonised   and
aggravated and aaaaagh!   At last he went away;   and, ah well, I
couldn't complain.   Nothing was amiss.   Wrong word,   but you
get my meaning.

The   next   night,   I   stayed in another little   village in
someone's   timber-reinforced-mud home.   And,   courtesy of   the
Aswan   dam,   this   village now had electricity;   by   the look of
things,   it   had been one of the few advances since the   days   of
Tut-Ankh-Amun.   His   family   of little girls peered round   the
corner.

- What nice daughters you have.   Oh God!   Couldn't I even
compliment   a   little six year old on her smile   without   someone
thinking I wanted to copulate!   It took all my powers of Arabic
to get out of that one.   End of **fad'dr**.   The second word was
bucksheesh.   **Fad'dr** was spoken by the adult and it   invariably
meant   kindness in word if not indeed in deed;   bucksheesh came
from   the   lips   of   the young and it meant   the   very   opposite:
gi'eme! gi'eme! gi'eme!   The white man was money, and **bucksheesh**
was   the word of demand and demand they did,   damn them,   a   darn
site   too often.   In a way,   one couldn't blame them for   it;
they   had   heard   of and seen the disparities of   wealth   in   the
world,   and   my presence was perhaps an excellent opportunity for
some   international redistribution thereof.   It just so happened
that   I didn't wish to participate in such an involuntary   system
of   taxation   and   when three young lads started   to   attack   my
rucksack from behind,   I resorted to the use of non-minimal force,
wielding   a   blow with my sugar cane stick,   and yield they   then
did.   On reflection, I suppose I fell into the European trap of
thinking that property has rights;   on further reflection I
will   return to the subject of the Egyptian village farm.

Here,   in the fields on the banks of the Nile, was a way   of
life   which had been intimately,   but which now was no longer   so
closely   linked with nature.   In our more northerly latitudes,
we know the seasons of the year only too well.   In the tropics
of Africa,   time is governed not so much by the sun,   more by the
rains   and the seasons of wet and dry.   While in Egypt,   where
the   sun varies little from hot to just hotter,   where the rains
are almost if not totally non-existent,   time was governed by the
flood.   So   it was that the early Egyptians first   ascertained

the fact that 365 days are in the year. And it was they who first contemplated a move from the nomadic to the settled way of life, where animals were domesticated and cereals were grown, and where people first started to live in communities.

Some of the Egyptian villagers were still living in a comparatively undeveloped state, for the story of the evolution of our species moved from Egypt to Greece, from there to Rome and thence elsewhere. Though in those days gone by, everything had depended upon the flood, and every act of planting and harvesting had been timed accordingly. Now, they'd built the dam. The flood was no more. And the people were plagued with progress .... of which more anon.

*　　*　　*

As the fourth and final example of a way of life close to nature, may I now cast your mind to the farmstead or **shamba** of East Africa? Here again there was a marked contrast with the monoculture so prevalent in European farming, let alone those vast areas of the American prairies which produce only maize and cornflakes.

On the western side of Kenya's rift valley, in the hills near Kapenguria, sat the simple home of a man, a woman, and their kids. The sun had set, leaving in the glow of dusk a silhouette of blue satanic hills. The cows were 'in' for the night, in their protective hedge of thorn tree cuttings, and over a hole in the ground in a hut called home, mum cooked the evening meal: ugali, the staple diet prepared from maize. By the time it had been stirred with gusto and a mwiko - a large wooden spoon the size of a small spade - it would perhaps be ready. To test the putty like substance - or so rumour had it - you got a small portion in the hand, rolled it into a ball, and threw it at the side of the hut. If it bounced back, catch, 'twas under-done, bung it back in pot; if it stuck to the wall, ah, parfait; but if this thick stodgy food was overdone, the ball might be hard indeed, and excessive cooking would be confirmed by a hole in the wall!

A large hemi-sphere of ugali was served with a much smaller plate of greens, the most common being a spinach like vegetable. And all of us, adults and tiny kids alike, sat around the mound and ate with our fingers till all was gone. It was a food the nutritional value of which was found only if sufficient - nay, huge - quantities were eaten; huge, that is, in the eyes of this European not used to only one main meal of one main course a day. When supper was over, bed was called for; the kids and I slept on just straw mats near the dying embers of the fire, while mum and dad enjoyed the one and only piece of furniture in their possession; happily, it was a bed. Unhappily, this family had no lights let alone books, sewing machines, games of kiswahili scrabble .... or contraceptives.

In the morning, I saw more of the **shamba**. Everything was as it were on top of everything else, the broad leaves of the banana protecting the young shoots of maize which in turn gave shade to the groundnut. More luxurious protection was underneath the mango tree, while the paw-paw gave little or none. If the harvest was plentiful, food was stored in small huts on stilts, protected thereby from the attentions of snakes and adders. If the harvest was not so full ....

*   *   *

In the West, not least by an excessive dependence on energy intensive machinery and oil based fertilizers, we have managed to achieve that which can ensure that mass starvation is a fact only of the historical past and not of the European present, namely, a food surplus. Sadly, the human race still hasn't been able to work out how worldwide hunger can be eliminated, even though it knows how to produce enough for everybody. We have achieved this European surplus in a way totally inappropriate, perhaps to ourselves (who now suffer from structural unemployment and not least because of the excessive mechanisation of the agricultural sector); perhaps to our own descendents (who may well inherit land from which all the goodness has been extracted); and certainly to the poor of the third world and for two reasons. Firstly, the people there can perhaps exist in independent poverty, but they would be totally unable to survive if their independence was sacrificed to the multi-national companies which control the petroleum and oil based fertilizers. And secondly, because they would not be able to afford, in terms of land or work, the huge quantities of animal feed which our animal-intensive monocultures have made necessary. In Europe we buy and feed to our animals that which, in more enlightened times, could feed the victims of drought and disease who continue to die in their millions.

*   *   *

They used to have rather a nice policy on land in Libya. In the regions near Tobruk, there wasn't an awful lot of rain, yet everything depended on it. So a joint system was devised and it basically worked like this. The land was not owned collectively or individually; the land just was not owned at all .... but it was used by everyone. With bated breath, the rains - or perhaps only the rain - was awaited. One good storm cloud or less might have been the all of it. Ah! There it was .... over there. All then disappeared in the direction of the damp to plant in those areas now moistened. A great system, given the restrictions of the prevailing climate. Alas, in the name of socialism, Gaddafi had now ordered that each farmer should have his - oh in Libya it's all 'hises' - his own fields. It could work, but in the absence of a decent irrigation system, there remained a most pressing need for rationalised, nationalised rain.

In the Atlas mountains, in the fertile fields of the Nile basin, and in the vastness of the southern Sudan, land was not possessed by an individual or corporate group; it was simply used by the present generation which had succeeded its forbears and which would, in turn, bequeath that land to its children. In irrigated fields, land was at a premium; while in the grazing lands of the savannah, there was enough for all as long as no-one wanted all. The systems were sustainable as long as the net population growth exceeded not the capacity of the land. Just as too great a number of elephants killing too many trees will in effect cause a decrease in the total elephant population, so too there may be a perfect balance between a society and the land which sustains it. And, of course, there must be a balance between the entire population of this planet and the planet itself; if at all we aspire to the adjective civilised, that balance should be neither hunger nor war!

Yet at home in the west, people own land. They think. By what right? For who was the he who first said this was his, who then built fences to demarcate it and weapons with which to defend it? Thus began a long and sorry tale. Perhaps it should be possible for people to own certain things, not least of course the things they help to create; but surely, it cannot be right for any one person or institution to own land or any other natural resource. To rent, yes; to tenant, certainly; but to own, never; for "we do not inherit the world from our parents, we borrow it from our children". Ummm .... interesting. But before I go on to talk of the changes necessary in our western society for that philosphy to become policy, I'll first talk of the way the people of Africa travel hither and thither, and of how we in the West seldom dither.

*   *   *

Back to the land of Egypt; therein I witnessed the days of sail, days that will not completely go before at least in part they do return. In Cairo, I ventured onto the Nile, this most ancient of rivers, in a nasty little rubber canoe. One or two might have thought I was going to paddle to Aswan and beyond .... but no; I merely wanted to travel for a day or two, to acquaint myself with the waters, and then to cadge a lift, illegally as it transpired, on one of those gorgeous old sailing barges which forever plied the slow and gentle river at a slower more gentle pace.

Beyond the western bank, towering over the fields and houses of Cairo, towering over centuries of human endeavour, stood the pyramids, powerful, majestic, silent, timeless .... yet these pyramids were a good couple of hours older, and so was I, by the time I'd managed to paddle sufficiently far upstream to get out of the city and into the country, delete country, insert desert. Sometimes, the yellow sandstone rock came right

to the very banks;   elsewhere,   it did retreat,   leaving a small
plain of those fertile,   alluvial deposits,   watered as always by
many a human-made canal.   In those parts, soon to be plains, the
papyrus reeds were numerous and huge, especially from the vantage
point of a canoe.   The thick blades shot 3 - 4 metres into the
air,   and within this acquatic forest lived divers ducks whose
noise   was   intense,   their bill of music a permanent variation on
the noted theme of quack.   I stayed just for a quick
quack, however, for there was my barge .... and for the next four
days, tranquility was mine.

          The good ship whatever it was, was about twenty metres long
and   of metal construction.   They'd all been made of timber in
the good old days of course, even as long ago as the first Middle

Avast the mast

East political crisis when Moses .... oh we'll leave that one,
shall we?   Happily, some boats were still of wooden construction.   In the boatyard in Alex, all the timbers were cut by
hand.   The log to be planked was plonked on a trestle some two
metres high;   then, with one atop and one below, two sawsmen
progressed from one end to t'other, twice in this plane, twice in
that;   hence one plank!   The ship's mast was of solid wood, as
was the even longer gaff attached to the masthead.   It was
difficult to get spars of this length, so invariably it consisted
of three or four bits of wood, bound and nailed together with
copper strips.   The result was a long sweeping curve from which
the heavy sail did hang, while at the bottom was another wooden
bulk, the boom.   The one and only sail was of canvas, patched
with old jute bags and other odds and ends.   The weight of
everything was excessive, but nature was kind. The wind usually
came from the North, the stream always from the South, so passage
either way was fairly easy, especially so because they went up
the river empty to return, full, laden to the gunwhales, with
rocks and boulders from the desert.   It was nice to know the
latter were useful for something.   Needless to say, the Nile
Delta, consisting as it did only of alluvial wastes, possessed
neither pebble nor stone.   The entire construction industry
depended on these quiet masters of the waters, these geriatric
swans of the Nile.

The barge was manned by just two men: Ahmed, the captain,
and his mate, in the nautical sense of the word, Ali.   When just
sailing along, one man on the heavy wooden tiller was enough.
But when action on the sail was required, like when the ship was
going under a bridge, many a muscle was needed.   The great gaff
had to be lowered to the horizontal only to be re-hoisted once on
the other side.

Now most matelots of the world have, or certainly had,
fairly limited diets.   The mariners of Egypt were no exception.
Bread was the staple food.   A whole pile of it was in the
corner of the one and only below decks compartment, each loaf a
hollow of dried out crust.   To liven it up a little, or to
prevent our teeth from cracking up a lot, Ali used to throw some
good fresh Nile water over them just before meals were served.
With the bread came the cheese of the water buffalo, if we were
lucky.   Sometimes, we just had bread and tea.   And once a
day, perhaps, there would be a cooked meal, a soup job, made of
course, from bread.

River water was drunk straight.   It didn't look very nice,
it certainly wasn't very clear, but I always had a look up
for'ard first, just to make sure no-one was carrying out some
other sort of personal routine and .... och well .... I was still
alive.   I worked on the theory that if it was good enough for
them, it was good enough for me.   As long as the waters were
alive, as it were, as they were, as long as fishes and things
still lived therein, then I felt sure that nature could manage
the recycling process without me worrying too much.   It was oil

and chemical discharges I feared the more. Still, at least there was this one advantage in sailing upstream: the waters were getting cleaner as each day passed - in theory; not that I noticed much change.

Lavatorial facilities were few. A metal plate with a hole in it was hooked onto the gunwhale of your convenience and thereupon you balanced and performed, rendering unto nature that which was natural. The Egyptian always preferred the crouching position; the long-standing European custom of the vertical pee was not considered polite. For my part, I thought one habit of the Egyptian was a little rude. He spat. With enthusiasm, vigour, determination and zeal, he spat. With the frequency of the chanting imam, he cleared his throat, gargled up spit from the depths of his gut, and out would come saliva with a speed and accuracy second only to that of the cobra. That long established British invention, the spitoon, had lost its prominence at the same time as its protagonists.

Now many a time and oft during the previous few months, I had received advice about my beard: shave it off! Many North Africans had moustaches, but full grown beards, no. Well, I'd had that advice in Belfast too, but within half the world of Islam, the advice was given with a little more vehemence. Islam, like Christianity, like any institutionalised religion or political philosophy, has its sects, in this case the **Sunnis** and the **Shi'ites**. The **Sunnis** of North Africa didn't like beards, the **Shi'ites** from the more eastern countries of Iran and Afghanistan were rather fond of them. And in Saudia Arabia, where lived together the factions of fiction and friction, the beard was often the mark of distinction between the two. Occasionally, inter-denominational tensions escalated to the point of bloodshed and at these times, the beard might not be a good passport. The Sunni interpreted the **Qur'an**, not only to the detriment of beards: underarm and even pubic hairs, all had to suffer precision incision. To counter this argument, I used to say my beard was a gift from **Allah**; that seemed to work quite well. But when the time came for a bath in the Nile, both Ahmed and Ali could not resist the temptation, just to see, did I actually have real and genuine Anglo-Irish pubic hairs. N-sha-Allah (if God so wills).

Unfortunately, the prevailing wind did fail to prevail, and my last two days were spent becalmed. **N-sha-Allah** again. The sun shone mercilessly down onto the hot tin deck and we could only sit, and wait, with a patience this European did not possess. I decided to give it another day but then, if no wind did blow, I would up and go. I said farewell. Ahmed and Ali were both genuinely sad at my leaving; the eyes were wet with sorrow; I was surprised they felt so much friendship had been established .... and I then realised that, my hosts, I understood them not.

There, then, was one mode of transport ideally suited for the purpose for which it had been invented and built. Its only disadantage was, perhaps, its speed .... but what need is there of speed?   Time is only money for those who wish to buy it; and the 'virtue' of punctuality is the converse of that of patience.

On either side of the mighty river were two and sometimes a few more roads;   on them, everything noisy did travel with little sense of purpose and occasionally even less of direction.

A more modern - but only just - form of river transport I encountered further up the Nile in The Sudan.   At the time, I was travelling on a road of dust and sand, and it was incredibly hard work.   The wind and heat were intense, and but for the former, the latter would have been unbearable.   Even with the blustery breeze, the haze of heat hovered on the horizons, while every so often the dust of the dry dry earth was sucked up into the excited spiral of a whirlwind.   I was only totally exhausted.   But in a little town called Renk, there sat a boat and there stood a sailor and

- Excuse me, captain, but ....
- **Fad'dr**.   And there was I, resting and travelling in, well, a style of sorts.

The vessel was designed specifically for the river, and so it had a reasonably shallow draught and a broad beam.   Usually, it travelled with at least one if not two barges tied up for'ard to the blunted butt of a bow.   It was a slow but steady form of transport and, in a land where there was virtually only the one tarmac road, where the river was the highway, it was a most sensible one.   The river was navigable from Khartoum to Malakal and, in the wet season, it was also possible to sail through The Sudd to Juba.

The old boat had not been painted or otherwise maintained since before the last Sudanese slump when the bottom had fallen out of the camel market.   Only one engine worked, but ....   The loo was inhabited by the most enormous cockroaches, a bad inch long and a good centimetre across, but water was everywhere which was delicious;   and, under a bucket and a rose, there was even a shower!   On the bridge, an earthenware pot of water was cooled by its own evapouration, and here we did all congregate for meals, crouching round a huge plate of kisra - a putty-like hemisphere of cooked **dhorra** wheat - and a small one of meat, fish or beans.   Meanwhile, down below, they were loading the boat and an adjacent barge with grain.   Lorry after lorry load was manhandled by the hands of men;   fellers of all ages formed a continual circle, throwing sacks into stacks as if they were half the weight.   While some women were continually sweeping the jetty for dropped grains - that was the level of poverty.

On the water's edge, the lonely fisherman cast his net by hand.   On shore, the donkey forever pulled its little cart containing an ex-oil drum to town and back for yet more water. While those who were not engaged in labour took rest in the shade of the banyan or schizophrenia tree, as I called it.   Never was much good at Latin.   A large, knarled trunk quickly dissipated itself into diverging branches, and fromto these wentcame more branchestrunks backintooutfrom the earth.

The cruise was most relaxing. On either side sat the occasional settlement. On board was many a chat. By night, I slept on top of the hatches, while by day, I always sought the shade of the bridge. It was 'ot. We were going south; and the sun, at this time of year, was northward bound for the tropic of Cancer. At noon, at its zenith, the sun was directly overhead. Under such conditions of heat, some candles stowed in my rucksack down aft melted, the wax seaped through the canvas and then did drip amok.

Malakal was journey's end, as far as this boat was concerned. The port was an administrative centre, though whether or not such had been, or was still, necessary was debatable. God's gift to the world was freedom; man's curse is governmental controls. Malakal had a district headquarters, a police station, a town council, a prison and various ministerial offices for education, agriculture and so on. Yet literally within sight of the authorities, a farmer irrigated his plot from the Nile by use of a bucket! What more need be said?

*   *   *

Oh quite a lot yet, for right across North Africa, especially in the three countries of the Maghreb, the basic mode of transport was the donkey. No matter how huge the Arab, his arse would sit upon his ass. Thus the master did travel, the hood of his jeleba up over his head, his legs sticking out so as not to hit the ground, and with his weight firmly placed in what was now the concaved back of his burdened beast. With tiny steps as if constrained by a mini skirt, 'the donkey trotted homewards into the sunset at a slow and noisy pace.

Along with the camel and the mule, the donkey provided the entire non-car-owning fraternity with the means of getting both the owner and his produce to the market place. Not in comfort perhaps. And certainly not at speed. But certainly nevertheless. And cheaply too, for here was a machine that not only cost little to maintain, but it also reproduced itself at no extra charge. Furthermore, whether at work or rest, it occasionally dropped one or two waste products that were more than useful for both land and fire.

The car, of course, has made its impact. In Morocco, for instance, there were two types of automobile: grand and brand new mercedes-benzes parked outside the various government buildings and major banks in the capital; and clapped out jobs, only the silhouettes of which retained the mark of the original merc, and these were the cars which took you and everyone else to the city and nowhere else .... these were the taxis which only travelled if they were at least full .... these were the machines which their European makers would have sent to the scrapheap, oh years previously.

In Libya, however, the car had not only arrived, it had not only overtaken everything on four legs, it had taken over. Perhaps it was unfortunate that there was virtually only one road in Libya, apart that is from one or two off-shoots that disappeared south into the yonder beyond yer, for it meant that everybody was going to where everybody else was coming from. Socialism, according to the gospel of Gaddafi, was capitalism for everyone, and even fourteen-year-olds were driving six-cylinder saloons around - I mean along. And in the rush to replace the natural, the carcases of camels, dogs and donkeys littered the roadside, victims of a mad matrerialism, dead.

But who are we of the West to criticise, we whose capitalism is the expanse of some at the expense of others, we who have built motorways by the dozen, to go the way everything else goes, achieving in total just as much as the one and only artery of Libya, namely, not very much. In the dawn of our paleolithic past, members of the human race learnt to communicate by sound and sign; thus was language born. Alas nowadays, the return of our species to its primitive ways is indicated by the habit it has acquired of communicating with its fellow human beings by the simple noise sounds like beep and honk. In traffic jams throughout the world, we witness the decline of our time.

In the last few decades, the West has devoted much of its energies to the creation of inter-city motorways, inter-city railways and inter-city airways, always inter-city all ways. Meanwhile, the cross-country routes have declined. Such are the ways of an over-centralised system. Every new road, be it motorway or by-pass, was meant to satisfy a demand; rarely was the correctness of that demand questioned; and never was it officially admitted that the very construction of that road would increase the very demand it was meant to satisfy. Thus society has 'progressed' from single lane bottle-necks to two-lane and now motorway traffic jams. We have, or so it would seem, gone mad, and the net result has been increased pollution, an increase in lead levels, an increase in our already excessive consumption of a finite resource, and greater levels of atmospheric carbon dioxide worldwide.

The governments of no matter what persuasion seem to do everything which will satisfy the material wants both of the majority of the electorate and of the major concerns in world business. And they do little to promote the more ecological forms of transport - barges on canals and rivers in Europe and Egypt are considered slow; bicycles in Britain and Uganda are too working class; horses mules and donkeys shit, whether they're British or not. Excuses are found, and 'they' continue to promote the more expensive and consumptive forms, because a 'good' level of consumption is 'good' for the economy .... so they say.

*   *   *

As the transcendental journey of the mind consumes not a drop of petrol, let us return to Morocco, once more to the Atlas mountains, to talk of amps in electric lamps, and to think in terms of therms. The hills were rocky, and on the steeper slopes only cactus and a wild sort of coffee could grow. Mounds of red and yellow rock, difficult to describe in the finiteness of black and white words, resembled huge loads of deposited waste, left behind in the process of evolution. And on the southern side of these hills, more evidence was seen of the patient work of the forces of nature: a river, red with the rock it carried in its waters, forced and forged its way through the gorges above the finest of waterfalls - Les Cascades d'Ouzoud. First, there were the gorges, wherein the running water was trapped between vertical, bare and craggy walls of rock. Then the river calmed, and flowed at a more gentle pace through an acre or two of flatter land .... before it reached the falls. Over it tumbled, to send forth a permanent cloud of life-sustaining spray and on either side of this second gorge, within spitting distance of a permanent rainbow, vegetation was plentiful.

Now the local farmers had constructed, on the very edge of the falls, rather special little mills for the grinding of their grain. A technical description is appended hereto:-

In a wee hut, formed out of the red rock, were two compartments - the turbine room and the mill itself. In the upper section or the mill, the all-weather, dual-tone, mono-purpose, automatic grain-feed regulator was a bit of ol' wood. Because the mill wheel was not exactly smooth, this stick bumped up and down as the wheel went around to give periodical thwacks against the bag of wheat, so to deliver more grains. The bag thwacks, t, were directly proportional to w, the angular speed of rotation of the mill-stone; truly, it was automatic. The rust-proof, precision-grown, maintenance-free, individually-engineered turbine blades were all bits of equally ancient timber attached to the turbine shaft by a certain amount of faith and good luck. The productivity and profitability of the machine were adjusted by the two-position, hand-operated, velocity control lever which dictated that either it went or it did not, and this was done by lowering or raising the entire contraption into or out of the water. And the emergency brake was another old stick which if necessary was thrust between the blades like a spanner in the works. In the lower compartment, having been ducted via a little channel from further upstream, the descending waters rushed through at speed before rejoining the main flow by cascading over the edge, their work done. In the upper compartment again, the mill operator BSc, AMITechE, sat on his haunches, awaiting the next full bag of grand ground grain.

Now the efficiency of such a system could be questioned. By the definition of the contemporary western engineer, efficiency is the ratio of work got out over work put in. (Just by the way, our western society is dominated by a myriad of

inefficient devices; helicopters are the worst offenders, but
electricity generators and motor cars commit the venial
equivalent of the same crime. Convenient they may be;
efficient they are not.) The European technocrat, on coming
from Oxbridge to Ouzoud, would quite possibly recommend a bigger
dam to generate electricity which could then provide power for
the relocated mill which, as a result, could cater for a much
bigger turnover and so on.

Yet those little mills, for what they did, were perfect.
Work was not put in, it flowed in. Work got out, therefore,
was as it were for nothing, or, in the language of the
mathematician, the mill was infinitely efficient. Its further
advantages were legion: it was labour intensive, for each little
mill provided work for one little person or one big hunch-back,
not that he had to do very much save sit there, peruse the
Moroccan stock market reports and keep an eye on things. Secondly
it consumed not one drop of the world's finite resources - that
is of the most fundamental value to all of us (yet it features
not in the equations of the mechanical engineer or civil
contractor); and most important of all, it gave to the local
people of Ouzoud control over their own resources. For as long
as their basic needs are not subject to multi-national or
governmental controls, then is there much hope for development.

The technocrat, of course, has his or her place; but, well
let's put it this way: it's not in the grain industry of Ouzoud
or anywhere else which has developed its own perfectly adequate,
ecologically sound system. So along comes the economist. A
quick glance at these mills suggested that capital expenditure
was nil and that running costs were also nothing (that is, if the
operators were also the owners, individually or collectively).
Therefore zero was the reading of all those standards by which
the economist measures what he or she calls viability - return
and turnover on investment after due account has been taken of
interest charges on capital expenditure, depreciation of fixed
assets, and the annual rate of inflation.

A further example of Moroccan ingenuity in the field of
energy creation was along a river below (to the South of) and
above (in the hills behind) Marakech. The entire stream had
been channelled into a concrete duct, and every fifty metres or
so, there was another little mill, similar in design and patent
to those in Ouzoud. Instead, therefore, of having one big,
western-type dam, they had opted for lots of little ones. Many
small can achieve the same as one big; the widespread
application of micro-economics has the same benefits, but few of
the dangers, of the big stuff; small is indeed beautiful, and
macro is aggro.

In Morocco, as in most countries of the third world, there
was no unemployment benefit. But with the labour intensive
grain production techniques as in Ouzoud, coupled with local
control of industry and (extended) (family) job sharing schemes,
the need for same was less.

In this particular sector of the economy, then, progress and development might not see the emergence of the director of the Moroccan electricity generating board, the chief controller of the Ministry of Agriculture brackets grain and cereals, the government's scientific adviser to the hydro-electric consortium of companies, the safety officer at the public health department and a host of assistants and administrators and assistant administrators and administrative assistants and secretaries for them all and full stop.   And, you know, on reflection in the waters of Les Cascades d'Ouzoud, the independent and self-reliant Moroccan, uncorrupted by the temptations of power of which centralised economics are infected, may well be better off. Unfortunately, the average Moroccan, on seeing the affluent European tourist taking photos of the falls on an automatic zoom, will probably think our side of the fence greener by far.

Before I go on - or have I done nothing else? - can I just suggest that the economist and the engineer would quickly point out that it's not only Ouzoud which needs a supply of mechanical energy to grind the grain etc..   (The economist and the engineer will, however, usually argue in their own interests as well; in similar fashion, there are few financiers who would fancy a formula which needed no finance!)   Indeed, to the North, there lie those flat and featureless plains where rains are few and rivers run slow.   But thereon, the sun does shine, rather incessantly, in fact; and near the ocean's shore, a breeze does often blow.   The chances are, therefore, that throughout northern and central Morocco, there will be indigenous sources of energy capable of supplying mechanical energy suitable for the grinding of grain.   (Throughout southern Morocco, of course, there just ain't no grain, save for the sandy ones.)   So too in Europe, it could be possible - via solar panels, heat pumps, wind generators and so on - to allow local communities the opportunity of creating their own energy.   The grid system of centrally supplied electricity could be there as a back up, and thereby, a marriage of both small and big industry could be achieved.   But no; governments like to control and institutions like electricity boards tend to seek their own aggrandisement.   A government which seeks more local community self-reliance will, ipso facto, seek less government.   There ain't going to be many governments that do that.

*   *   *

From Morocco, to the land of ancient and modern, the land of a thousand stars, the land of the eternal river: Egypt. From the little mills of Ouzoud to the vast contrast of the Aswan high dam.   The Nile was not only the source of life - it was and always had been a source of political power, not only via the fertile lands of the delta but also because of the numerous trade routes which linked the cities of Egypt with other world-

wide   centres   of   power.   The   importance   of   **Mes'r**   (as   the
Egyptians   called   their   own   country)   grew   even   more,   of   course,
after   the   Europeans   built   -   or   rather,   after   the   Europeans
hired   the   Egyptians   who   built   -   the   Suez   canal.

He   who   controlled   Egypt,   by   gad,   controlled   India,   it
was   said,   by   those   who   thought   it   necessary   for   things   to   be
controlled.   And   he   who   controlled   the   Nile   controlled   Egypt,
said   he;   and   so   it   was,   again   as   it   always   had   been,   that   men
dreamed   dreams   and   delusioned   delusions   of   grandeur.   Right
throughout   the   ages,   the   kings   and   emperors   of   this   world   have
sought   to   control   to   control   to   control   ....   while   the   poor,   who
fought   in   vain   the   wars   of   the   vain,   remained   and   still   remain
poor.   The   last   conquerors   of   Egypt   were,   of   course,   the
British.   They   only   took   Egypt   to   safeguard   the   route   to   India;
and   they   only   took   The   Sudan   to   safeguard   the   Nile   of   Egypt,   to
safeguard   the   route   to   India;   and   they   only   took   all   of   Uganda
and   Kenya   because   the   source   of   the   Nile   ....   where   the   hell   was
India   anyway?

It   was,   needless   to   say,   the   concept   of   power   which   had
given   such   impetus   to   those   African   I   mean   European   African
explorers   who   had   donned   the   pith   and   disappeared   for   months   and
years   on   end   in   an   effort   to   trace   that   elusive   source.   How
finding   a   tiny   brook   deep   in   the   heart   of   the   (as   yet
undiscovered)   Mountains   of   the   Moon   was   going   to   give   them   any
power   at   all   remained   uncertain.

But   never   mind!   Who   are   we   to   understand   the   incongruous
ways   of   our   political   masters?   Power   was,   and   still   is,   the   name
of   the   game.   Just   as   the   twentieth   century   has   seen   so   much
political   and   military   power   come   within   the   hands   of   so   few   men
and   one   woman,   so   too   this   our   generation   has   witnessed   man's
control   of   the   Nile,   not   by   stemming   a   stream   in   deepest   Uganda,
but   by   blocking   those   waters   in   midstream.   The   question   is,   have
we   learnt   to   conquer   or   to   harness   the   Nile,   to   live   with   and
within,   or   to   live   with   not   and   without   nature?   (Perhaps   it
should   also   be   pointed   out   that   these   our   times   have   seen   man's
lust   for   power   and   control   reach   another   ultimate   stage,   for   no
longer   does   he   have   to   control   the   rivers   and   mines   and   other
natural   phenomena   which   he   may   decide   have   strategic   importance,
because   he   now   can   develop   nuclear   power,   placing   it   where   he
likes   and   controlling   it   as   he   pleases.   Indeed,   with   fast
breeder   reactors,   he's   nearly   at   the   stage   where   he   doesn't   even
need   the   uranium   mine;   and   with   fusion   power,   he   wouldn't   even
need   that   -   just   our   meek   compliance.   But   surely,   he   who
thinks   he   can   live   apart   from   the   world   of   which   he   is   a   part,   is
he   not   a   fool?)

Let   us   now,   however,   return   to   the   land   of   the   pharaohs,
where   all   agriculture,   nay,   all   life,   depended   upon   the   Nile,   its
fertile   banks,   and   the   lattice   of   canals   which   irrigated   them.
The   only   source   of   power   used   to   be   the   muscle   of   the   man   or   his
beast,   and   it   was   the   primitive   pumps   which   I   mentioned   earlier
that   lifted   and   spread   the   waters.   But   now   the   amps   did   flow.

Electricity had arrived, the result of the dam at Aswan, a dam which is but huge, a dam which has drowned the fields and villages of many, and some of the ancient treasures of us all.

Now the supply of amps not only to the inter- continental hotel in Cairo, but also to the wee villages on the edge of the desert, sounds like a good idea. But is it right to put so much effort into the macroscopic singular rather than the microscopic plural? the mono-use of the maxi rather than, as in Morocco, the multi-use of the mini? Would it not be wiser, instead of having one high dam, to have lots and lots of paddle wheels all the way to the sea? And is it sensible, in a land of almost ceaseless sunshine, to place so little emphasis on solar sources of energy?

And what of the side effects? Now if side effects there be, then are these not an indication in themselves of how far we have removed ourselves from the earth, the very womb of our creation and the bosom of our existence? Firstly, the flood, the annual heartbeat of Egypt, has been stopped, and all the fertility which pours out of Lake Tana reaches Egypt no more; alas, it sits at Aswan, to rest unused at the bottom of a huge huge lake. The farmers of Egypt, previously independent and self-reliant if only to a limited extent, are now dependent on artificial fertilizers and the multi-national companies which make 'em. Admittedly, lake Nasser might have increased the amount of evapouration that takes place in a part of the world where the annual rain fall is nothing - so that certainly can do no harm. But the dam has caused harm in a different though totally unexpected way: the absence of Ethiopian silt has allowed the mosquito to flourish in Egypt like never before. Admittedly, malaria is now nearly under control, but is it really wise for us to interfere with the preventative medicine of nature?

Just a few miles downstream, at Luxor, are the ruins of a bygone era, the temples of the pharaohs, the enormi colossi of Ramses, the obelisks of the queens and, on the west bank, in the land of the dead, the valleys of the tombs. There they found the sarcophagus or gold embossed tomb of the boy-king Tut-Ankh-Amun. There, everything is a monument to the skill and care with which the early Egyptians built to last. Alas, in these modern times, we live only for the present; motor cars are constructed with 'built-in-obsolesence'; and office blocks are no sooner up than the planners talk of demolition. Is it wise, then, given our impatience, given our titanic finiteness, to build such a dam as Aswan? The temples of the God Amon at Karnak are up to five thousand years old. One day, many years ago, within that hallowed shrine, a statue did tumble, a wall did collapse, and a pillar in the hypostyle hall did fall to the ground. And one day, the Aswan dam will cease to be. Will it be phased out, silted up, sabotaged, or damaged in a geological disturbance? How it will die, we cannot know. But that it will die, we can be sure. Is it sensible, therefore, to store so much water at the head of a densely populated valley, 1,000 kilometres long?   Would it really not be better to have ten thousand paddle wheels, no matter how primitive, merely sitting in the current, generating what little mechanical energy and/or electricity they could for the use of the most immediate neighbourhood, and affecting the natural ecology of the river not at all?   If something goes wrong with a paddle wheel, few would have cause for concern.   If but one block of the Aswan dam ....

Coming closer to home, there is talk of dams, barrages and the like.   Some say they could supply the energy needs of so many.   Others talk of considerable damage to the natural environment.   And the advocates of nuclear power rub their hands with delight at the dissension.   Yet just as in Morocco, just as not in Egypt, the construction of several paddle wheels in the narrows of Strangford Lough, for example, would not only do minimal damage to the environment and that only on the tiny area on which they were built; would not only cause minimal obstruction to the free flow of shipping; would not only help to ensure the survival of the mud-flats and the wild-life which inhabits them; but would also produce as much electricity as any ecologically destructive tidal barrage.   Now there's a thought. And I'll leave you with that unless you'd like to join me, this time to travel out of the land of Egypt which boasts of not one drop of oil, to the land of OPEC, wherein and whereout it flows like milk and honey.

*   *   *

Algeria and Libya are the two countries baptized certainly but blessed, well, perhaps, with the oil well where all is oil but where all is not well. In theory, this is a source of energy. But unlike the mills of Ouzoud, it could also be and indeed is a source of international and strategic power. Like the black gold of the North Sea, the stuff is assumed by this generation to belong to only itself as defined by national borders. The fact that it took millenia to make, the fact that the borders between Algeria/Libya and their neighbours did not then exist (and the fact that no part of the North Sea is any more intrinsically British than it is Argentinian) apparently matters not. And all the efforts of the day are devoted to exploring, drilling, piping, shipping and exporting the precious liquid in exchange for the dollars and the yen of the international market place.

The uses to which all of this energy is put we in the West know only too well, for it all helps to fuel our economy. Whether that helps us, or whether it it just an end in itself, is debatable. (So we'll debate it .... though not yet.)   Not much of the desert oil is used locally, but it is only fair to add that a lot of the earnings therefrom are being used to increase the standards of living of large sectors of both populations, while further sums are being devoted to the future in such projects as the re-afforestation of the Sahara.

Now is the energy crisis insurmountable, or is it a problem much of its own creation? The governments of the West argue, as you know, for nuclear power, because they are only able to think on the macroscopic level. The big nuclear power station could replace the big coal-fired one and still leave the control of energy firmly in the hands of the central authority. But if the widespread application of the small sources of energy was implemented, if we managed to apply Moroccan ingenuity to our own energy problems, if we allowed or encouraged individuals and individual farms, factories, villages and communities to develop their own watermills and things and things, then could we move forward to an era wherein unemployment would be reduced, pollution would be much less, and the conservation of our finite resources would at last become a realistic goal.

But the only way centralised government can exercise control of the energy supply is by concentrating on the centralised sources thereof. The governments of the West don't mind whether or not they use coal, oil or atomic power (unless they need that plutonium for their bombs, in which case all the 'logic' of the day will be devoted to the nuclear option), and they will probably vote for the most economical (as per their definition of the word). They might even be persuaded by environmental arguments about the less limited and more indigenous supplies of coal. And they might, at a later stage, even consider investments in huge devices like the Severn barrage, multi-acre lattices of wind generators on the Yorkshire moors, or vast wave machines in Galway Bay. What they will rarely consider, however, is the alternative way of producing alternative energy, namely, through that widespread application of the small, just as in Morocco.

CHAPTER 2

A PART OR APART, (PART 2)

'Tis time to talk of commerce and trade, and first of all in Uganda, where not only were the codes of industry disobeyed, but so too were the very rules of physics and the theorems of science. The civil war had caused considerable bloodshed, though not yet will I talk of the human suffering involved (see chapter 5); it also meant that a lot of equipment was damaged, that maintainence schedules had gone completely astray, that the supply of spare parts had dwindled to a trickle and that the finance to fund such works had all but ceased to exist. On the upper reaches of the Nile, in the game park of Kabalega, were six motorboats. All had suffered varying degrees of direct damage and indirect neglect. Five had since been cannibalised beyond doubt and repair, and one remained in, well, sort of working order. The machine was started by a combination of skills: those of the amateur mechanic and professional donkey handler. It was primed, pumped and pummelled into starting, yet start with a kick and a fart it did; and it would almost certainly continue to work for as long as its African operators so wished.

The bicycle repair yard, in a small town just beyond the game park, was in the shade of a mango tree and thereinunder, many an old fashioned bicycle was looking very dead, upside down in the manner of a tortoise, its wheels in the air like legs akimbo. There was no welding or anything like that there, so many a task was simply a case of brute force and intelligence. My bicycle frame, after a sojourn in the hills of West Province in and around Arua, had just snapped dirty in two. So a bit of old tubing was put inside the frame, a nail was banged through the middle of it all to keep everything in position, and then a three man heave made the frame a two-dimensional object once more. The bike also needed some new brake blocks. Well, there are many of you, I'm sure, who believe passionately that if the world is to be saved from suicide, swords must indeed be turned into ploughshares. Take comfort, then, from the re-cycling cycling industry in Uganda, where high quality brake blocks were moulded from the tyres of Russian mark two comeongetov armoured personnel carriers, the wrecks of which littered many a quiet little shamba as a reminder of their bloody civil war. Such, then, was just one section of the commercial sector of the industrialised economy of Uganda. Its contribution to the gross national product of the nation was minimal, but its assistance to the cyclists of this land was considerable, and sufficient unto the day.

*   *   *

Let's now return to Morocco, to view another aspect of the transport industry, the artificial life support systems of ancient autos. In an atmosphere which would make the more meticulous western engineer cringe, in a shakey wee shanty of a garage on the side of the hot and dusty road, the hammers banged and the spanners cranked. Each mechanic seemed to work almost on top of his neighbour and only a miracle - or so it appeared - was able to keep the dust and the rust from the grease from the oil from the petrol from the paint, for all had long since been covered over all the workers' overall jelebas.

In both Morocco and Uganda, indeed throughout the poorer countries, considerable recycling was part of their way of life. Machines, like their owners, were made to go for as long as it was possible for them to do so. One advantage of such ways was this: you could get anything repaired, some or any how, and instantly. Whereas, of course, we in the West are more often told oh it would take a week, or it would be impossible because they're not making spares for those anymore, or again that it would in fact be cheaper to buy the new model.

*   *   *

And so to the agricultural sector of Moroccan commerce, the food processing plant, the olive oil industry. The olive tree, that symbol of the Mediterranean climate, was first given a hearty shake. All the kids then helped to gather the fallen fruit into the baskets there a'waiting. The donkey then played its part, carrying two large panniers full down to the factory, and here the de-stoned fruits were cast by their hundreds into the one and and only trough, to be squashed by the heavy rock wheel of the press, slowly rotated by a second silent donkey. The vat-man, a more wholesome beast than our folk of the same name, loved it, as do so many who are allowed to work their own craft and rejoice in the fruit of their own labours - a far cry from the techniques of mass production. His feet were bare, his jeleba up around his knees, and everywhere was olive oil. With bread and honey, it made a superb breakfast.

Here, then, was the very simple case of one industry producing enough of one particular commodity for the entire community at the cost only of time which was free. Some oil, of course, might have been bottled up for export, for money is the grease of trade, and the Moroccan would probably get paid more for the pint of his produce from the rich European than he would from his neighbour, even though the former had to pay the additional costs of bottling and transport, even though the former considered it more a luxury, the latter a necessity. As with the olive, so with the almond and the tangerine. Was it another case of poor economics, wherein a poor country grows cash crops rather than the basic foods for its own population; wherein some go hungry so that others can earn the foreign exchange necessary for the imported car? Do we, in buying something special because we always have almonds at Christmas, share the guilt? It's not quite as easy as that, of course, because Morocco wanted to export its products in order to attain a certain measure of self-reliance (or to pay off its debts on previous international loans, or to buy yet more arms for its 'defence'). But it's worth thinking about. The subject becomes more serious if and when we buy Indian rice or some of those Egyptian onions, if only because the poverty of the east is more stark. But if we were as careful with our land as Moroccans and Egyptians were with theirs, then perhaps we would be more agriculturally self-sufficient. Such is the pre-requisite of (human) development in any (third world) country; such a goal, therefore, should also be ours; and when we've erradicated hunger, when we're all reasonably well self-sufficient, then can we swop a few goodies, at Christmas, Id-ul-Fitr, or indeed at any time.

Here at home, of course, industry has adopted a different mode. Because the 'economies of scale' favour the bigger enterprise, because the big government adopts policies which enhance those so-called economies, and because the 'philosophy' of growth almost insists that a company must expand every year if it is to remain in business, industry has suffered from a policy of centralisation, of mergers and take-overs, and of corporate conglomerates. There is a sort of natural, or should we say unnatural, tendency for the big to look after the big, and for the big to see their own vested interests in the success of their fellow big (as long as the latter aren't too big, of course). And many a government, capitalist and socialist alike, either rationalise big business or nationalise it, but either way they promote it, via taxes grants investments and subsidies, and via the construction of great big inter-city motor, rail and air ways, from which big business is the first beneficiary.

It is worth emphasising that the economies of scale only work for as long as only the economist is looking at the problem. As soon as the social costs of unemployment, for instance, are also taken into account, then the picture changes. And as soon as the consumption of finite reserves of energy and/or ores are also inserted in the balance sheet, then the position makes a drastic alteration.

The huge has replaced the small; human contact, social value and job satisfaction have faded; energy consumption has grown; unemployment has rocketed. And we in the West now suffer from a situation in which money, originally invented as a tool, has become the master; in which money can employ people but not the other way round; in which money can earn money by doing nothing, just sitting in a bank, while people who do nothing are considered to be, by the economists and others, a drain on our resources.

There is a need for a mixture perhaps, of some big industry and some small. You cannot, however, promote the use of both

in all sectors of the economy.   You can have the big to produce
kidney dialysis machines,   and the small to make wholemeal bread
so that folk don't get kidney infections so quickly.   But you
cannot have umpteen big energy producing power stations without
removing the need for the construction of smaller units.   So it
is that the ultimate big regards the success of the small as a
threat to its existence. And so it is that the capital and energy
intensive   sector   of a centralised economy is in   direct
competition with the labour intensive and diversified approach.
In a word, perhaps we should change the way we define what is and
what is not economic .... and quickly,   before the mistakes and
sadnesses of our own society are adopted by or imposed upon   the
countries of the third world,   where there is already suffering
enough.   We shall therefore do just that, in chapter 4.

                              *   *   *

        And so to the outlets,   the markets, where all the benefits
of   industry are said to become available to the public.   Away,
from the super- hyper- mega- markets of our impersonalised world,
not just to the Libyan equivalents,   not just to the city centres
of   those capitals like Nairobi which have become the suburbs of
the multi-nationals, but to the bazaars of Tunis and Marakech, to
the souks of Khartoum and Cairo,   to the sokoni of Kenya .... but
first to a stall in Uganda.
        He was only a little boy,   about ten years old I'd expect.
A wee line of cleared earth was the path which linked the dirt
road to his home, his parent's shamba.   By the side of the path
he sat,   all day,   behind a little table with one bowl of peanuts
thereon.   By the side of the path he sat, all day, waiting for
a customer,   to whom to sell this tiny surplus of food,   to earn
just   something as an income for his parents.   By the side of
the path he sat,   all day,   in vain.   In every Ugandan
village,   especially   those which had suffered directly from the
years of Amin and the wars which defeated him,   the story was no
less tragic.   The shopkeeper was silent, sitting now amidst the
walls of memories in his store in which nearly every shelf was
empty;   a box here and a bar there was all that was left from
what had been the general grocer-cum-hardware shop of every
'luxury' - cloth,   powdered milk,   saucepans,   cigarettes and even
margarine.

                              *   *   *

        There is,   in the old fashioned markets of both Europe and
Africa,   a certain common factor.   Whether you are walking
between   the piles of cassava and maize and paw-paws and
plantains behind which sit the women of whose labours these are
the foods and fruits,   or whether you are buying the winter

turnips and cabbages laid out on the barrow of your local market
gardener, the atmospheres differ only in part.   For the market
is the meeting place, where women meet women, where men meet men,
where business is shouted and scandals are whispered, wherein the
world goes round.   It is an atmosphere which is totally lost,
cut off, amputated by the automatic doors of the modern shopping
centres of Europe, killed by the beepboopbeep of the supermarket
till behind which sits the assistant, lonelier by far than the
little Ugandan and his bowl of peanuts, listening only to her
machine going beepboopbeepbeep, beepboopbeep.
    There were, of course, differences between the **sokoni** in
Kenya and those from which they took their name, the **souks** in
Khartoum.   In the former, the piles of passion fruits and
pineapples, guavas and bananas, mangoes and maize cobs contrasted
with the cones of dates and nuts and peppers and spices with
which the Arab relished her cooking.   In both were the
entrepreneurs of the age, standing behind their mats on which
were laid out transistors and torches, irons of steel, bicycle
wheels and spare parts for the 1954 model merc of which everbody
should have had at least one!   While in the latter were also
the camels, cows and goats; to get there, some of the traders had
walked for days, over miles and miles of desert scrub; this was
their only livelihood.

"Funny things, committees"

    In Swahiliphone Africa, both sexes competed for business,
the women trading in the traditional domestic sectors of food and
clothes, the men involving themselves in the more mechanical and
more lucrative ends of business.   In the Arab-speaking world,
the freedom of women so to trade and chat was more restricted,
and in the rural areas it was more the men who idled and
gossipped over countless glasses of mint tea.   But it was in
the **souks** of the cities that the Arabs really came into their
own.   In Marakech, the city founded by some ancient warrior to

be the centre of his empire, an enormous bazaar filled a large part of an area protected by the walled defences of the old fortress town. The tourist each trader tried to attract, and many a product was designed for his or her excessive needs. Different streets, as in any city, were given over to different trades; but all were twisty and narrow, and crowded with the wares of the labourer, the laughter of children and the hubbub of continual pedestrian and donkey traffic.

Here, the heavy banging and clanging as iron was moulded into gate and crate; next, the dying of clothes, as reams unseamed were placed into vast vats of every hue - all natural dyes I hasten to add, with the bigotry of the convinced conservationist. Further on, cloth was being spun, a little lad yards down the alley-way slowly returning to base. In one back yard, sheep were being slaughtered; their throats were slit; their carcases immediately skinned; and the skins, equally immediately, were treated in some vile concoction by the near naked slaughterers who were covered in the spatterings of what had been flesh, what was stink.

Back to dead still life: the artisan was adding the final touches to a most ornate saddle, fit for a prince or anyone else who could afford it. In a quiet corner sat the smith, working patiently with his tiny hammer, carving yet another Arabesque design into an enormous brass tray or silver tea-pot. All this metalwork was soon in the bazaar, glistening under the rays of umpteen electric lights. Next door, there were trinkets, jewellery, swords and knives, coins and old hats - everything one needed for the pre-plastic era. Other stalls in the main street offered every gourmet's speciality. How he had got there I knew not, but there was the merchant, sitting cross-legged in the middle of his angled kiosk as if on the mountain slope, surrounded by piles and piles of nuts, dates and figs. His neighbour was another escapologist, and he sat amidst multi-coloured cones of powders, each one a pepper or a spice. Then came the cobbler: every shoe a yellow slipper with no back and a slightly pointed toe. There were avenues and avenues of clothes shops, and great lengths of coloured material hung to the ground from every square inch of ceiling. Finally came the chemists: jars upon jars of powders and juices and .... what on earth were those?

    - Dead phosphorescent beetles.
    - And what are they for?
    - They're aphrodisiacs.
    - I see. They were for men. The ladies version was a more innocent looking powder. Other drugs included bones and other bits of dead animals, all guaranteed to cure the most unpleasant of ailments, either by getting rid of them or by giving you something much worse to worry about. And so it went on, arcade after arcade, everywhere the talk of trade.

Outside in the square were the cafés, more stalls and a few odds and sods: snake charmers with non-spitting spitting cobras;

musicians on flute and drum; and young acrobats of amazing dexterity. Everything was a shilling, but it was all worthwhile. And in came the coachloads of tourists to question the price of this or the hygiene of that. From a roof-top bar, one of the rare buildings to reach the exotic height of three stories, Amanda and I watched the packed crowds of shifting humanity. The sun did quietly descend, the smoke from many a hot fat pot rose steadily to the stars, and o'er the noise of it all hung the peace of a crescent moon.

*   *   *

My other example of a souk was in a more divided metropolis, where many activities were diverted beyond the market place, and where many of its citizens were just temporary visitors. Tunis is a city which should be approached from the sea. On your right, the ruins of Carthage. Ahead, the harbour, and in its calm waters the reflection of this ancient city, its old mosques and minarets, and its medinah in which still thrived the bizarre bazaars of the bey. Tunis was a city I approached from the west, so my first sight was the shanty town, a human excess clinging like a leech onto one side of the country's prosperous - for some - capital. Sanitation, as ever, was poor, and a shallow lake nearby was alive with festering pollution. The centre of the city boasted the usual run of formica-tipped banks, and to the north were the rich suburbs, houses of a distinctly Mediterranean flavour, with their little porticos of wrought iron, their little shades of green tiles and their beautiful flowers in bloom. Pretty indeed; yet the shanty ....

But, to the souk. The old medinah was squashed in by the city's ancient walls; the market inside was a maze. Shopkeepers, hoteliers, street pedlars, and schoolboys who had already embarked on a career of economic survival, competed with each other for custom; the little cul-de-sacs were crowded indeed, the claustrophobic effect exacerbated by the roofed arcades from every beam of which hung more goodies, clothes saucepans tea-trays and samovars. Alley-ways went this-a-way, and others went like that; yet all were hidden from the bright Mediterranean sunlight by the produce of thousands, and it was with relief both for the soul and the pocket that one emerged, intact, and without every souvenir.

Elsewhere in North Africa, that same magic bustle was a feature of many a crowded lane and multi-coloured line. In Libya, alas, all was changing, as the bazaars of yesterday were rendered obsolescent by the automated supermarkets of our mad to-day. And in Kenya too, there existed rather an odd situation. I speak of Nairobi, the East Cheam of Africa, the Dundalk of the dark continent, the African antithesis of Africa. Now if, my reader, in your local Belfast shopping centre, you one day found no spuds, no cabbages, no sausages and no cornflakes, you would be

shocked.   And if,   instead,   the shelves   were full of cassava,
maize and millet,   you would be altogether shocked   -   indeed, in
order to describe your state of surprise,   you would probably   be
tempted to employ the expletive.   In Nairobi,   where everything
was   designed   more for the rich white   tourist (and the   equally
rich   black bureaucrat) and less for the overwhelming majority of
indigenous Kenyans,   African foodstuffs were in desperately short
supply.   But in   the   downtown   upmarket super-stores,   every
European   taste was catered for.   Nairobi,   1,600 metres   above
sea-level, was upside down.

    But is not also our society?   The local shop   and   the
village   store are gradually being squeezed out by the big; as a
result, unemployment in the retail trade is rising; and secondly,
shoplifting and other deeds of a more wholesale less wholesome
nature are on the increase.   Yet again we may ask questions: what
is economic and what is its worth?

    Whatever   the answer,   it is not the superlativelyprefixed-
market which,   world-wide, is so dominant in this last quarter of
the twentieth century.   A combination of the good old-fashioned
market/souk/sokoni and the wee corner shop is probably   adequate
for most communities here and abroad.   For   therein   lies   a
social function,   more valuable than any economic gain.   And
therein,   too,   perhaps,   lies better produce.   That home made
bread of the village baker,   be it the wholemeal bap of home   or
the dated, peppered flan of Morocco,   is so often better   by   far
than   the   plainwhitesliced   of   the   automatic machine.   The
natural   varieties   of locally produced stuffs can never be   well
catered for by the large,   centralised,   energy-intensive,   mass-
production   factory.   In returning to the smaller shop   units,
however,   may   I   suggest we ask the butchers of Tunisia   to   no
longer hang the goat's head outside to prove its throat had   been
slit, and no more to spray the multitude of insects which forever
feasted on every joint,   all of which,   of course,   were displayed
in the front window that wasn't.   The diseases of flies were bad
enough;   but   those   of the multi-national petro-chemical   drug
companies' fly-sprays were much more expensive!

*   *   *

    The subject of flies and fleas leads me to talk of bugs   and
beasts,   and   leads us both once more to the cradle of   the   Nile.
Before   contemplating their horrors,   it would perhaps be nice to
look at the more fascinating aspects of nature's minutiae,   some
of   which were far from minute.

    The   tropical dusk said a quick goodbye to the sun and   the
long   hours   of darkness were heralded by an army of midges   and
moths,   all   of   which flittered and fluttered round the one   and
only   light.   The larger ones were the more masochistic;   and
beasts the size of a big toe flew fast at the solitary light bulb
like kami-kaze pilots to then knock themselves out;   they crashed
to   the floor with a clunk;   they scampered around for   a   while

before resuming airborne travel to zoom around gathering their sexual senses while driving all humans senseless ... till at last they could re-focus for another quixotic charge at the sexless light.   Such were the soirées in The Sudan.   In Belfast, the grills protect some windows from the stones which fly in summer; in Juba, the same grills were designed to keep at bay the bugs of the night.

*   *   *

The waters of the Nile, as I mentioned earlier, were not clean.   Nor, indeed, could be the houses whose walls were of mud and whose floors were the earth.   In such circumstances, hygiene was at least difficult.   The little girl sat in the shade of the palm tree hour after hour, waiting only for the night.   The flies in her eyes were too numerous to count, yet continually did they suck from the juices of her cornea, and not at all did she try to brush them away. How could she? And why would she? Too quickly they would have returned.   Only after the sun had set would the festering flies disappear ... to be replaced perhaps by the infuriating whine of the mosquito.   This little girl, like so many others throughout the villages of Egypt, would almost certainly go blind before the age of forty.   The eradication of this disease depended on one factor only: the provision of clean water or, to put it another way, the re-diversion to that provision of only one day's worth of the international arms race.

*   *   *

Once more - if you are still with me - to The Sudan.   I was, at this time, in the area just east of that swamp of The Sudd, and just north of the cattle camps.   The wet season was just starting, literally, this very day.   I had been reasonably content - well, most of the time - going along the hard though sometimes very sandy road.   But when this great wall of water approached from the East to give me my first drops of rain since Libya, further travelling became impossible.   No sooner did the torrents fall than the frogs did start to croak with an intensity almost deafening.   And no sooner was the ground a'wet when, as if from nowhere, the termite flies arose out of the ground, like so many bodies on the final day of judgement. Few made the ranks of angels, however, for after only some seconds of resurrected bliss their wings fell off, and their wriggling torsos fell to the ground, there to be quickly gobbled up by the hordes of apocalyptic frogs.   Now as luck would have it - as luck always did, for how else would I now be here to write a couple of huts were near.   I pushed and squelched the remaining furlongs and asked for shelter from the storm and for the night.

Fad'dr.   In I wet went, through the tiniest little doorway, and there sat the whole family, perfectly dry.

A cut-away get-away

       This hut, my shelter from the thunder, resembled the conical hovel of the comical troglodyte;   it was quite big, a good 5 metres high and, on the ground of cleared earth, it consisted of three concentric circles of sticks.   The smallest one contained the tallest timbers,   each haphazardly climbing to support the roof; a ring of shorter branches held up the centre, while the largest circle was where the thatch reached the ground.

No one length of wood was straight, but from the outside, the entire structure formed a perfect symmetry. The tradition was to build in circles and curves; we Europeans, in comparison, are invariably rectangular, unless we're thinking of beans.

Inside the home, the centre circle was the larder, the middle one the sort of kitchen-cum-working area, while around the outside was the bedsittingdiningroom. The only furniture consisted of a few straw mats and funny little wooden things, the shape of a non-U 'U', which balanced on the ground, upside down, to form the smallest of seats or the hardest of pillows. Inside, little naked children hoped the rains would soon stop, while mum, on bended knee, prepared the **dhorra** and a spot of dried meat. The latter did not smell quite right, but, ach well. Dad amused the children with a guitarharp, made from wood and the shell of a tortoise. And last of all, granny, old, and with not much longer to live by the look of things, lay impassively in one .... well, there were no corners! Though she faced the prospect of a death without even an aspirin to ease the pain, at least she knew she would not die in loneliness. Furthermore, she obviously knew she was going to die, as did all the members of the family; and thus, even at this early age, the kids could learn in the most natural way that death is part of life.

*   *   *

While on the subject of medicine, I would like to talk a little more of the plague of the tsetse fly, that little beastie which in certain parts of Africa - or so I'd been told - made the existence of both human and domestic animals impossible. They were right. I was in the Kabalega game park again, on the slightly unusual safari vehicle of my bicycle. The head game warden told me I wouldn't be allowed to go and see the famous falls of that name on such a machine, but .... I crossed the Nile and headed south, as if making for the exit. I was soon out of sight, if only because too too often, the grass was way above my head. So when the time came, several miles later, I turned left, and my only company was wild-life. The prospect of elephants was a little daunting - the activities of my imagination positively frightening - and - good God! -

There on the ground was a tiny little insect which looked like a blade of grass, just as you would find on your front lawn. Only it moved. It was, literally, a ten-centimetre blade with legs on; so too the stick insect, a living twig on stilts, has adopted the perfect disguise. There were also some beautiful butterflies of every colour and design - only evolution can explain how different species have come to be what they are; but who can explain evolution? One was blue and black on top, green and yellow underneath; yet again, it had created its own colourful camouflage - perfect - if it flew upside down. And the birds: some were absolutely tiny yet in the brightest of shades, pale blues, sun yellows, and pillar-box reds - depending on which side of the border is your pillar-box.

My life was in little danger - and so said all of me! The leaping gazelle proved you don't HAVE to have porridge for breakfast, and the infinite variety of life was confirmed by the presence of the tsetse.   Oh thanks.

The falls.   I stood right above the gap, watching the roaring waters tumbling over themselves before crashing through and over the rocks.   Below, the turbulence gradually abated, the surf fading until once more the Nile was a tranquil lake of unlimited length.   Upstream, the length and breadth of the river was just one big bundle of liquid energy, the waves frothing over rocks and boulders as far as the eye could see - and sixty kilometres beyond that!

It was time for some mangoes and peanuts, time to repair a puncture .... and lots of time to worry about whether or not I'd be safe.   I was a little worried about animals;   I was actually much more concerned about men, poacher and patrol, a lot of whom roamed the park, the former in search of the elephant for its tusks, the latter in search of the former.   They all seemed to be rather trigger happy.   The African at peace is man at his happiest;   but at war, he is man most cruel.   If detected by either gang, I felt sure I would be food for the birdies, the maribou stork and the vulture.   I laid out my sleeping bag and tried to relax by thinking about .... d'you know, I can't remember.

Because of an extra day I'd spent in the park, my food calculations had gone a bit wrong.   Breakfast was a peanut.   I topped up with water - the Nile tasted little better here than it had done in Cairo - and I headed south once more.   Hallo puss, you might say, in the early hours of your day; but I said nothing as a herd of buffalo stampeded into the distance with the noise of rumbling thunder.   How I'd scared them I knew not; if only they'd known what they had done to me! But nothing else was around, save for a few tsetse which rapidly qualified for more adjectives.   They lived in trees, just as in The Sudan.   If there were no trees around, I could be sure there'd be no tsetse, to tease, torment and torture, and the trees they opted for were usually those same, small, black-barked ones.   A few were just above the falls, but then the track crossed over plains and the occasional river, so I was troubled no more.

Until ....   The track was little better but the trees got denser and denser.   Out they came, these tropical beasts, and they bit.   And they bit.   And bit by bit, I was bitten to perforation and desperation.   You could flick 'em, brush 'em off, swear at 'em; it all made little difference.   I'd long since lost my pacifist instincts in so far as the mosquito was concerned, to name but one of the more nasty of God's bright and beautiful perhaps creatures.   In similar fashion, I now felt little love for these bloody bastards!

I stopped in the tiniest of clearings and quickly put on

more clothes. Two layers of jersey and shirt, of trouser and short, was just about enough. The trousers I tucked into my socks. That was a little better. It was quite warm. And there, in this clearing, was the most extraordinary tree; covered, it was, in nests which hung like Christmas decorations from the very ends of the branches. The whole tree was just alive with twittering tits. I suppose it was not odd that, with all these trees available, a whole family lived in just one of them; in similar style, lots of folk have chosen to live together in cities like Belfast and Benghazi. 'Tis an avian and human habit. Just downstream from the falls, many mighty maribous had sat almost on top of one comparatively small thorn tree, ill-equipped to take the strain. In The Sudan, a whole host of white egrets had chosen one arboreal home to thus change the colour of the tree. And in Egypt, while most trees had been silent, the occasional exception had been a hubbub of chirping sparrows. But, to return to Kabalega where these yellow birds, I rapidly ascertained, were tsetse eaters. In the shade of their tree .... in the shower of their droppings .... I sought shelter from the sun and the fly, and I had a lunch of literally a chapter or two - I could read my book, but there was nought to eat.

Pleasant as it might have been, I couldn't sit there all day. Night time was no time for travelling in game parks! There were still some animals around, but these tsetse had my undivided attention. I moved on. Immediately, these malicious midgets returned to the attack. Yet more clothes were necessary. I even covered my head with my mosquito net, wrapping the rest of it round my body. Every inch of me was now covered. Especially that one. It was not a little hot. But I had no gloves and only one pair of socks. I pulled the sleeves of my jersey way down over my mits; alas, stretched wool is neither air-tight nor tsetse-tight. My hands were just covered in black, everyone a beast, everyone a blood-sucking needle. Waving, banging, rubbing, anythinging my hands .... everythinging was tried; nothing worked. After an hour or so of cycling like a spaceman under seige, I was at my wit's though not my journey's end. I gave up. I got out my anorac, curled up inside it and there, in the middle of Africa, I rested - not so much my legs, but my temper. And I sweated like a smelly cheese. They were right: the tsetse does indeed make life impossible.

The day progressed. The sun cooled. It was vital that I got out of this forest, for now my water was running out as well. It was not a happy day. Another hour or so passed and gradually the flies got fewer; by the time the sun was reddening, I was able to take my "hood-job" off and .... I saw a goat. Then a shamba. A human being. At last. Another mile or two, and there was this tiny hut of a shop selling some bananas. I bought and ate the lot! And there I rested for the night; that, thank God, was the end of that little saga. If you want to venture

into the tsetse belts of Africa .... well ... let's put it this
way: don't get diarrhoea!
    The tsetse fly, then, the bug which inhabits whole tracts
of the sub-Saharan savannah, is to be avoided like the plague
which it is.   Some might suggest it should be eliminated, but
humankind should be wary before it sprays the entire Sahel belt
with some vile concoction which might exterminate more than just
the nasty beastly tsetse.   It should nevertheless be said that
not every bite of the bug gives you sleeping sickness, for I was
bitten ten thousand times, and if each bitten bit had been
diseased, then I by now would be deceased, a'laid to rest,
sleeping in pieces.   Fortunately, I suffered only from a severe
rate of underkill, and here I am, alive am I.

                    *   *   *

    There are, of course, a number of other diseases in Africa,
many of them almost as bad as the ghastly cancers of Europe, and
with at least two of them I had personal acquaintance: the first
was malaria. It's a disease which by and large can be prevented,
but it is up to the individual concerned to take suitable
precautions. I didn't.   I did, to be fair, (if only to myself),
start on the right track, buying a packet of chloroquin before
leaving Belfast.   But when I got caught in the winter's snows in
Algeria, I somehow felt the chances of being bitten by the
malarial beast were nil.   Then, sad to relate as I will, my
tablets (and me!) all got soaked in seawater when crossing into
Egypt.   Only there did the mosquito commence the onslaught.
Sometimes in small doses, later, in Uganda, especially when close
to some still water's edge, they attacked in droves.   Something,
I suppose, was inevitable.   And thus I came to acquire first
hand knowledge of the medical services in the more remote areas
of northern Kenya.
    Close to that little Kenyan shamba I spoke of earlier, in
the hills of the western escarpment, I spent another night in a
village wherein the shop was what others in Uganda had been,
tins of this, packets of that, and a plentiful supply of clothes.
Not all the stocks were of good worth, however; tablets and pills
various were supposedly the death of numerous ills and ails,
while creams and cures were there to make you feel brighter and
look whiter at only vast expense. My host was the local
entrepreneur who owned this one and only store, and in a shocking
wee shack of a café, sitting on rickety benches by a solid
unpolished table, we shared a breakfast of smokey tea and buns of
dough.   The medicines, he stressed, were bad news really - but
not a little good for business - and even though I had a
splitting headache at the time, I felt bound to agree both with
his arguments and my sentiments: chloroquin yes, but aspirin,
well, two a year at the most. So, no pills, just another mug o'
tea, and off I went, into the forests above the rift.

An hour or two and a mile or more later, I arrived at a most picturesque spot where sat another wee village. All was in a valley just behind the escarpment, that wall of sometimes 2,000 feet which in a myriad of different .... but damn it, I was in no mood for the aesthetics of the place; I was ill. I went into a murky mud café and .... well .... I just suddenly felt all sort of shattered, my unaspirined headache was still throbbing in the brain, and I didn't feel like eating at all. I had a bit of a drink and then went outside to rest. An hour or so lying in the shade didn't help, so I decided to stay the night. Now I knew there was a mission in this village, but I did not think it right for people to tour the world by staying in different missions. So I asked at a thing which called itself an hotel; it was actually called the New Florida or the Park Royal or somesuch, the name roughly written in earth dyes on the outside mud wall .... yet inside, there was only a dirty mud floor, an old table, and, if you were lucky, some mbuzi na ugali (goat and maize meal). But of beds there were none. They told me to go to the mission which was, in fact, attached to a hospital. Well, there was no harm in asking.

- Karibu. (Welcome.) Temperature 104. Malaria; bitten, I had been, by a bug.
- We're a bit full, said the nurse, you don't mind sharing do you?

In nearly every bed there were at least two patients. There I lay, like a hot and cold running shower, sweating profusely. My bedmate, I'm afraid, sought drier climes .... which was a pity for, as a result, the one and only bed with the one and only occupant was the one containing only me, the one and only white man. Now the mission, like so many other similar establishments the other side of Bangor, just happened to be Irish.

- Which part of Ireland d'you come from? I asked.
- Galway.
- I'm from Limerick,
- And Oi'm from County Clare.
- I live in Belfast, I rejoined.
- Oh. No, I haven't been up there. No, I spend my leave touring the west coast. No, I wouldn't go up there.
- You should; the border marks no barrier of beauty.
- Well .... no.

So we talked about the mission instead. What a task lay in front of them. Parts of Kenya might indeed be 'developed', but the average wee home up here, perched high on the mountain side which rose several hundred feet above the mission, was still faced with the problems of old, like drought and disease, and these were now exacerbated by the tribulations of to-day, broken families and booze. So, in came the patients, many still wearing the traditional skins and beads of (to-day and) yesteryear. Menfolk carried the wooden seats/pillows as well as a spear or two, just like their cousins in The Sudan. Ears were

pierced   -   or   should   I   say   holed?   -   or   should   I   say
excavated?   -   for   the   extended   lobes   drooped,   way   down   to   the
shoulders.   Arms   were   ringed   with   amulets   while   ankles   too   were
noisy;   and   sometimes   the   spare   fly   button   for   the   flies   not   yet
invented   was   'carried'   or   'worn'   in   the   lower   lip!   The   women
wore   skirts,   also   made   of   animal   skins,   sandals   only   rarely,   but
always   an   enormous   mass   of   bead   necklaces   which,   sitting   happily
on   the   bosom   bare,   provided   the   perfect   rattle   for   the   baby   whose
thirst   was   now   quenched.   The   more   beads   they   had,   the   richer
the   husband.

Hospital   work   was   not   easy.   Visiting   hours   tended   to   be
all   day,   whether   the   nurses   liked   it   or   not,   and   sometimes   the
visitors   stayed   all   night,   sleeping   on   the   floor   and   under   the
bed.   Damn   it,   they'd   walked   all   day   to   see   the   patient;   one
could   hardly   expect   them   to   just   turn   round   and   walk   right   back
again!

It   has   often   been   said   that   the   only   advantage   to   Africa
accruing   from   the   advent   of   European   'civilisation'   was   medicine.
I   think   I   would   add   one   or   two   more,   like   the   ice-cream   machines
in   Khartoum   for   one   and   ....   and   ....   no,   that's   about   it.   All
the   other   by-products   -   industrialisation,   Christianity,
borders   -   have   been   at   best   a   mixed   blessing.   But   to   rid   the
continent   of   smallpox,   as   has   happened,   to   control   diseases   like
polio   and   cholera,   and   to   begin   to   reduce   child   mortality   and   the
birth   rate,   all   add   up   to   making   for   a   better   world.   If   only   the
industrialised   countries   would   stop   spending   money   on   bombs,   then
malaria   -   like   smallpox   -   could   also   be   eradicated,   cholera
could   be   controlled   and   so   on.

In   the   meantime,   one   can   only   suggest   that   the   application
of   the   advantages   of   medical   science   should   not   work   to   break   up
the   extended   family   by   the   institution   of   old   age   pensioners'
homes;   or   to   create   an   over-dependence   on   drugs   or   the   medicines
of   hypochondria;   or   to   allow   the   multi-national   companies   to
try   and   replace   the   natural   with   the   artificial.   A   prime   example
of   this   was   Nestlés,   of   course,   which   tried   to   promote   the   sale
of   powdered   milk,   not   by   directly   infering   there   was   something
inadequate   with   breast   feeding,   but   by   failing   to   understand   how
inappropriate   is   the   second-rate   artificial   stuff,   especially   in
the   non-sterilisable   world   of   the   shamba;   in   so   doing,   they
caused   untold   harm   and   suffering.

In   singing   the   praises   of   western   medicine,   one   should   add
that   it   has   become   an   exact   physical   science   whereas   in   the   East,
and   in   Africa   too,   there   existed   a   deeper   understanding   of   the
human   mystique   and   a   greater   awareness   of   the   forces   of   the   non-
physical.   In   adopting   the   practices   of   European   doctoring,
therefore,   the   thing   to   be   avoided   -   apart   from   the   tsetse   -   is
the   large   centralised   European   style   hospital   in   a   large
centralised   European   style   capital,   under   a   large   centralised
government   bureaucracy,   other   branches   of   which   try   to   set   up   big
energy   creation   projects,   big   transport   services,   big   branches   of
even   bigger   multi-national   companies   and   big   government   offices

to administer all of these schemes, with banks to finance them, and big car parks into which all concerned could leave their mercedes-benzes, safe from the little watoto, the kids of the shanties, who might come and .... well .... just have a look .... just for starters ....

* * *

To put everything into perspective, I suppose I should also talk of the second little disease I got, almost immediately after the malaria. After only one night in the hospital, I felt, despite the proximity of the equator, on top of the world. I moved out of the ward but rested one more day at the mission before bidding farewell. It was nice, I must admit, to catch diseases only when outside the up-country clinic.

Further down the ravine, along the banks of a river, through a gorge and then, there I was, in the Rift Valley. Ah; time for some aesthetics. Behind me, the escarpment. Here it was steep and sheer. Elsewhere, it was a little less pronounced, but this wall of land continued in high profile right through the centre of Kenya. In the cool at the top, trees could grow and vegetation was thick. Down the slope, they slowly thinned, and amongst them were the occasional hut and its shamba. The height facilitated crop cultivation, but it was also a form of defence against cattle raiders. Down and out across the plains, only a few thorn trees and vertical cacti survived. I travelled first along the bottom of the wall where the infrequent streams encouraged the more agrarian pursuits, and then across the plains, whereon the grass gazelle did graze .... well .... a few.

Now after my little bout of malaria, my mind had decided I was OK. My body, however, thought otherwise, and it I mean I was still weak. Somewhere along the lonely rift valley floor, just when I wasn't looking, a virus did enter my eye. Apparently, if I'd been in good health, a corpuscle or two would have gone along and with no principles of minimum force inhibiting action, there would have been a quick little battle and that would have been that. Because I was a little weak, alas, that was not that, and that virus set in and established itself, just like that. Thus, I could not see, neither that nor anything else. It wasn't particularly painful; it just kept watering and, certainly in bright sunlight, I just could not see at all. In such a lonely part of the world, however, I simply had to keep going; two days later I reached Nakuru, sitting happily at the foot of a 3,000 metre volcano and at the head of one of the many rift valley lakes. Around the shores of the latter stood those magnificient pink flamingoes in their thousands, all of them standing on one leg and .... well, wouldn't you, if you had to stand all day in your own droppings.

A visit to the local hospital gave me a little medicine, and I then caught a country bus. Thus, I came to Nairobi. My blinking eye did not get better, so I went to an optician.
- Go to this doctor, was the advice.
Oh dear, there I was making use of private medicine.
- Take this drug. It was only developed a few years ago by one of the leading pharmaceutical companies in America. But for this, you would have lost the sight of your eye. Two hundred shillings please.
Oh dear, there I was using the drugs of the multi-nationals.
- And come and see me next week. Yes, that's right; another two hundred shillings.
Oh dear, there I was forced to remain in Nairobi and to use the services only it and a few other centralised capitals of the continent could offer. My eye began to get better. Oh no dear. And there I was. N-sha-Allah.

*   *   *

There is one aspect of the lives of all of us which doesn't (or shouldn't) fall into the category of politics and economics, but nevertheless it plays a considerable part therein: institutionalised religion. Islam was an aspect of King Hassan's monarchy, of De Chablis's socialism (though here its influence was smaller), of Bourguiba's right-wing dictatorship, of Gaddafi's belligerent left-wing version of the same, and of Sadat's more peaceful whateveritwasism. It was also alive and well in The Sudan, but so too was Christianity and it was, as we shall see, a divided nation. Any criticism of the rôle of the mosque, therefore, should perhaps be tempered with a critique of the institutions of Christianity. So maybe it's just as well that I have lived in Belfast.
In December 1977, long before I started this journey, President Sadat of Egypt, a Muslim, met President Begin of Israel, a Jew, on the Christian feast of Christmas. Hope was alive, dialogue was possible and compromise was promised. They spoke of peace. It was a most moving occasion, and the ripples of reconciliation were felt world-wide, even in the Irish Sea. In the Belfast sermon at midnight on that Yuletide morn, the priest referred to this historic occasion:
- My dear people in Christ, said the cleric from the heart of Northern Ireland, where inter-denominational hatred has left hundreds dead both in recent years and in earlier centuries,
- the solution to the Middle East crisis, said he, will only be found when everyone there is converted to Christianity! He did not specify which type!
From that subjective background, let us now look at how religion has affected the cultural heart and political head of North Africa. Just as the old testament goes into considerable

detail on how folk should live, so too the Qur'an speaks a lot
and not least on personal hygiene. It is the prophet who has
written that the body should be cleansed before prayer. At the
time of writing, he probably hadn't realised what a brilliant
ploy he had thus devised.

I must pause awhile to recall the one and only deficiency
of Arab and Berber hospitality: I was never, in any household,
shown to a loo. Sometimes, when I did ask, I was pointed in the
general direction of the great beyond, but never was I shown even
to a hole in the ground, be the home in a conurbation or in
isolation, in the mountains or the desert. Usually, I adjusted
myself so that my only overnight requirements were for a leak or
two, but even these were sometimes only achieved after the
exercise of much tact. The universal lack of a loo puzzled me,
especially as houses were always clean, and because the womenfolk
would surely have insisted on same. Only after umpteen weeks in
this land did I understand the reason: the washing and
lavatorial facilities of the entire village were in the mosque,
wherein, of course, no Christian was allowed to wander let alone
widdle. If you just happened to be Christian or Hindu, then
might I suggest you would be tempted to convert yourself pretty
rapidly, if only for the sake of your bladder! This does, I
suppose, give rather more meaning to the phrase "Muslims of
convenience".

This practice, and this is the point, gave to the mosque
the most wonderful means of retaining an influence over society.
The Catholics invented a fairly good rule when they said you must
go to church EVERY Sunday, and all Christian denominations got a
vice-like grip on society by starting schools, by getting a
virtual monopoly on them, and then by receiving grant aid for
such senseless sectarianism. Not satisfied with only this, the
Catholic Church in Ireland, in order to ensure it always got
government assistance, acquired very close links with the
authorities in Dublin. While the Anglicans in England went one
better by getting themselves established as the religion of the
state - only the Iranian system of Ayatollah Khomeini is more
primitive. Yet none of the churches, in all their political
manoeuvrings, achieved the power of the mosque in its monopoly of
the loo. In most villages and several towns right across North
Africa, they'd got yer, literally, by the short and curlies.

                         *   *   *

The daily life of the Mussulman is interrupted by several
of those calls to prayer, and any visitor will know that many an
urban mosque has this century been blessed with the megaphone.
The still of the night, then, was so often shattered by some
ancient imam who had bestirred himself to hobble along to the

mosque and there, before he'd cleared his throat or brushed his toothless gums, he would grab the mike and shout, with vocal chords of pensionable age and no talent, to the glory of God called Allah. More advanced techniques had pre-recorded the old boy, and the monotonous wail now emanated with a scratch and a scrape from what sounded like one of the original mono recordings. In theory, sleep or work did cease, depending on whether or not 'twas dawn or dusk, and all would heed the word of the prophet; in practice, ah well, they'd heard it all before.

In the country, as was to be expected, blind obedience was still strong. I stayed once with a very poor peasant, and he gave me a pretty good insight into the ways of the fervent. I had been welcomed, introduced to the missus and kids, and offered a small piece of carpet on the dried mud floor. Then, it was the moment for prayer. I sat in silence as he went through all these motions of bowing and bending to the East, of kneeling and kissing the earth. A noisy "Al - laaaaaaaaaaaaah Akbar!" was repeated so frequently that I felt sure Allah was getting bored of being told It was **Akbar**. Everything else was more silentjumbled, rather like the prayers of some old catholic priest who welcomes the faithful by saying,
- Eethenayovvefarveranovvesunanovverolyghoesamen.

In conversation, the fervent Muslim is as unsubtle as the fundamentalist Christian. Both contend that it is written and that that's that, and that's three thats. Neither of them think. They believe in a God, they believe God gave them brains, yet they do not think it wise to use 'em .... not .... if it is written. The fact that what is written here, in the book of Exodus or Al-Qasas, is not the same as what is written somewhere else, is apparently beside the point. The Moslem or Christian believer just chooses the quotations which he, or he or she, respectively, thinks justifies the deeds, and no more need be said, they say.
- But ....

The cry for logic is ignored. If only I was a Moslem or a born-again Christian, then I would understand. Until then, apparently, I can play in the pools of reason, but no depths of understanding will be mine.

A blind faith can make life a bit dull, though, can't it? In one lonely porter's lodge in Libya, I shared a particularly cold night with the gate-keeper; conversation was limited, but not only 'cos of my poor Arabic.
- It's not hot, is it?
- N-sha-Allah.
Oh.
- Thankyou very much for the kous-kous; it was delicious.
- N-sha-Allah.
Oh. Silence. Thinks ....   Ah!
- What do you feel about the socio-economic development programme put forward under the third comprehensive ....
- N-sha-Allah.

On Fridays, obedience demanded that each and every man should attend the service, up at the local mosque which, like the churches of Europe, was built to its own distinctive design, usually on some central piece of slightly higher ground. The main room was a square; the ceiling above was supported by pillars laid out at the corners of many much smaller squares all of which were carpeted; and in front stood the imam in his pulpit. Outside, on one or more corners of this central square of prayer, at least one minaret ensured that the mosque, again like the church, was the tallest building in town; and this gave the imam his platform for his daily daily wail. During the service, a pile of shoes remained by the doorway, and inside, row upon row of **jelebas** did bend and bow, in obedience to Allah and his prophet.

Just as we in Christendom vary from bare faced mission hall to glorious cathedral, so too do the Moslems have plain little mosques and beautiful big ones. In large measure, the Arab invented mathematics - that too could be described as a mixed blessing - and with such knowledge he was able to design and build with a skill that combined both science and art. The more magnificent mosques in Marakech and Kairouan, for example, contained amazing Arabesque designs in marble mosaics on ceilings, floors and walls. The stone was carved, the wood was shaped, the page was inscribed .... and every artist had the patience but not the booze of the medieval monk, who had the skills but not the women of the mussulman.

The world has inherited some superb souvenirs of a past still present. The grand mosques of Islam, like the cathedrals of Europe, are everywhere; the minarets dominate every city, and even in the smallest village, one building will be a distinctive white, or on it will stand the crescent moon.

Now each religion has its major denominations and minor sects, each considering themselves to be the chosen few, the ONLY ones who are right, the REAL lost tribe of Israel. The world of Christianity has the extreme protestants of Ulster from whom God protect us. And the world of Islam has, amongst other oddities, the Mozabites. They are known, affectionately, as the Protestants of Islam. You can't get much more fundamental than that.

*   *   *

They lived in a lonely part of the world, miles away from anywhere. Where the road to Ghardaia, their home, leaves the mountains, the view to the south contains nothing, just a flat horizon of endless desert. One hundred and fifty kilometres later, there is a wadi. Now wa'd is a wadi, you may ask. Well, I may answer; it's a well, an oasis or anything wet in a land of all dry. And what looks like a line across the desert turns out to be a valley, and only on arriving at the edge did I

see a village or two, and water gardens and palm trees.   Under
the blazing sun sat little clusters of small houses, every one
pure white or the lightest shade of blue or green   - thus was
all heat reflected.   The mosque, of course, was on the highest
point of what was still a sunken village, deep down in the wadi.
It was a most extraordinary affair: a structure, more like a
church tower than a minaret, emanated from the centre of the

The fanatical fundamentalist's phallus

roof and it leant like a weak banana in a symbolic deviation from
the normal.   It too was all in white.   The village appeared to
be just one dazzling detergent advertisement.   Here lived the
Mozabites as they had done for centuries, and here in this oasis
of fundamental fanaticism they practiced in peace what they
coinsidered to be the one true faith.

Their houses, one storey affairs of white-washed mud, were built in such a way that the entrance from the little narrow street into the foyer was at right angles to the entrance from the foyer into the main room of the house. Thus, in theory, it was impossible for a passing man to see or be seen by the woman inside. If she did venture out of doors - it would be for essential purposes only - she would be accompanied by a suitable aunt or grandmother. And the clothes that both did wear consisted of so much white cloth everywhere that only one eye remained naked. One little eye, in a shapeless cylinder of white, was the only indication of its human origins. (And it is very difficult, when eye-ing only an eye, to know if its owner is a nice bit of eye or an aged gran.) In silence, then, the pairs of wraiths walked on their journeys of brief necessity. Back they quickly returned, once more to be incarcerated in their own kitchens. And Allah, they thought, would be well pleased.

Such were the ways of the extremists, but even some of the more liberal Moslems were not a little chauvinist, if male; and not a little subservient, if not. Islam, as a religion, has given to a certain section of society - men - a most privileged position, and any threat to the religion would be interpreted by them as a threat against their vested interests. In such circumstances, the religion is more likely to last. Hinduism has survived mainly at the hands of the Brahmins; Islam will survive because of men. In both beliefs, a code of conduct deserving of condemnation is held beyond criticism by a religious linen which filters out logic.

*   *   *

There is another aspect of Islam which, especially in this nuclear age, is even more frightening; and it too has its parallels in Christianity. The Jihad of the Qur'an, or the philosophy of the holy war, suggests all who die for the faith in battle will go straight to the bosom of Allah. It was just such a belief which had led 17,000 Sudanese horsemen to their deaths in the battle of Omdurman in 1898. Wave upon wave of warriors had charged the British lines under the orders of the Mahdi, the 'saviour'; and wave upon wave had died, for the loss of but 48 British/Egyptian soldiers. Thus had the Christ of General Gordon been avenged; and thus, or so it had been said at the time, had a religious craze been eradicated. How wrong they were. The Mahdi remains to this day the natural hero of The Sudan, and his shrine in Omdurman is still reverred.

That belief in jihad is still very much alive; and the chance of another Mahdi in any Islamic country remains (there have, over the centuries, been more than one or two). On a more democratic front, there is the fanatical political sect called the Moslem Brotherhood - which also has its reflection in the extreme right wing of protestant politics - and it too was alive and kicking in The Sudan, Algeria and elsewhere. Indeed, in Egypt, it was they who killed President Sadat in 1981.

The parallel of the Holy War is, of course, the Christian philosophy of the Just War. The Moslem is not meant to kill his fellow Moslem; he's only meant to slaughter the other sorts in battle, if battle there has to be, and afterwards he is meant to be nice and forgiving. Alas, of course, it never quite works out like that; and Moslem killed Moslem on the Algerian/Moroccan border, and Moslem killed Moslem on the Libyan/Egyptian one, and the armies of states were a major cause of it all.

Meanwhile, in defence, they say, of freedom or some such other emotive cliché, Christians and Christians blessed the graves of Christians and Christians who had died fighting each other. The most recent example is perhaps the bloody little war in which the British - Allah I mean God not them again - fought the Argentinians in the South Atlantic. As the reader will know, however, Christians have done some pretty horrible things over the years, not the least of which, you will recall, were the crusades against the dreaded Moslem hordes of the infidel.

In Tobruk there laid the war graves of those who had fought these in the second half of a contest begun in 1914. The graves of all thesethose Christians were divided by nationality, no doubt to assist St Peter's filing system: here were the British, there the French, there the German cemetries - young men from all over the world who had fought and died over a miserable bit of desert. On the gravestones, all neatly laid out and beautifully tended, were the epitaphs, memoriams and the words of justification by which each nation thanked its dead. I walked, alone. I remembered Belfast, and that winter's day when crosses had been laid in the grounds of the city hall, one for each victim of the troubles. "Our only son" this cross of stone cried, from the solitude of a pensioners' home in Lancashire. "Known unto God" was the anonymous sign that here was the corpse of a young lad whose body had been blasted by shrapnel and twisted metal into unrecognisable flesh and spilt blood. Within yards of these graves, British, French and German arms were among the capitalist and communist weapons of Arabs and Moslems preparing to fight each other!

CHAPTER 3

REGRESSIVE PROGRESS

The excessive concentrations of power in spheres ecclesiastical are closely linked to those of other concentrations, the spheres economic and political. Perhaps the most obvious sign of this is in education, be it in the system of state subsidised segregation which the British government perpetuates in Northern Ireland, or be it in the Islamic schools and universities of North Africa. The influence of the imams was perhaps acquired unwittingly, for the Qur'an appears to have been the first book written in Arabic, so it is the source not only of words of wisdom, but also of grammatical construction and precise punctuation. It is, as it were, both the bible and the Shakespeare of the young mussalman. To learn two of the three 'r's', therefore, involves of necessity a pretty intense study of the fourth 'r'. So the whole education system, in the world Islamic as in the world Christian, is geared to the perpetuation of the state religion be it established or non-/dis-established, as indeed it is geared towards the economic/political maintenance of the state.

*   *   *

Now it would seem that from a number of points of view, there is a lot to be said for those indigenous ways and means of living which rely on locally produced materials and cost little. Furthermore, there is a lot more to be said - standby - for a way of life less dependent on and obedient to the institutions of church/mosque and state. Progress there must be, if only to alleviate the dreadful poverty which still persists in many parts of Africa; but progress must surely see a marriage of things African with those from elsewhere .... and perhaps Europe in time will be a more developed place if it too can learn of other cultures and ideas. Happily, not least through immigration, the possibilities exist.

In Africa, modernisation is the word by which much development must be achieved. Both words are part of our gradual evolution, and both involve both progress and pain. With both mine eyes I did see, and with the bias of one hand, I now record.

I want again to fling you to many a far flung corner of Africa, to look specifically at some aspects of what is sometimes inappropriately called development. First of all, I want to glance at the education systems, for it is these which seek to mould the youth to inherit a land from elders whose ideas may be fixed, whose ideals may be corrupt, and whose political philosophies they wish to perpetuate. Thus the incestuous status quo reproduces itself;   and education might hinder rather   than help evolution.   Let's have a look .... first stop, Morocco.

The primary school was just one room.   Therein were kids of all ages - though not so much of both sexes for, as so often happened and not only in Islamic countries, the boys got the preferential treatment - and they were copiously copying those extracts from the Qur'an which their only teacher had written on their only visual aid, a blackboard.   The hour was late, the light was fading, and thirty or more of them struggled to write by the light of but two or three paraffin lamps.   In the weeks and months to follow, some would be selected to go to secondary education, the rest would either return home for ever, or try again of another year.

Two of those who, in a former year, had qualified for that second stage of their education, were worried - as we all have been in our time - by a certain problem of mathematics.   They sought guidance, and the question concerned the expression:

$$f(x) \longrightarrow x/6$$

Now what, in the name of Allah, was the relevance of that question or its answer to the problems of an emerging nation? And what, for God's sake, was the relevance of either to the child of an industrialised state?   Would f be the answer, or would x be a lemon?

* * *

In the schools of East Africa, they have not only adopted a European way of teaching European subjects, they have also followed our habits of compartmentalisation and categorisation. The boys were here, the girls there, each sex wearing a brightly coloured cotton uniform for reasons unclear.   It was the first thing to hit this casual observer, and accordingly it receives the first comment. Why were uniformity and conformity needed in a process which was meant to encourage an objective analysis of the world we live in?   Why, in a process meant to enhance individuality were all forced into similarity? And wherelse were uniforms worn, save in the armed forces and other services which, in their overall need for discipline, inevitably suppressed a certain amount of individuality?

The European advocate of these European ways will point out that in the absence of such clothing and in the presence of widespread poverty, some of the children would appear in little more than rags and that, therefore, allowing the children to wear their own clothes would create an unhealthy competition.   Such, apparently, is allowed to continue unabated during the holidays.

At school, however, uniforms they wore, uniform they were, and thus it was possible to encourage the 'healthy competition' of athletics and academics, of good conduct badges, and of who would be the first to answer:

$$f(x) \longrightarrow x/6$$

if indeed it was a question.

The administrator's country pad

One night in The Sudan, on that very sandy stretch to the east of The Sudd, I met one of the so-called successful products of the system.
- Welcome to my village, he said, in greeting me to this small hamlet of huts, miles away from anywhere except other occasional hamlets of huts, close to the banks of the Nile.
- You speak very good English.

- Well, I'm a geography graduate on vacation from Khartoum university.

Ah, the very person to ask. Now there were trees to the north of this place, in the Gezira area south of Khartoum. And there were trees to the south, I later learnt, and increasing numbers thereof.

- Why aren't there any trees here? I asked.

- Er ....

Oh well, never mind. It was obvious he knew not why not and nor was he going to plant any. Time to change the subject.

- What do you hope to do after you've finished your post-graduate research?

- Work in administration.

Oh God - or Allah - (I was pretty near the 'border' in these latitudes) - may God and Allah help the world, for education won't!

There's the hub. Education, in so many countries, is a state run affair. Almost invariably, it will educate the sort of folk able to continue the administration of such a system, be it good or bad; almost invariably, the educational services are geared to maintain the status quo. And that which is meant to promote objectivity is by its funding (if not by its nature) a subjective institution.

Without a doubt, the simplest example of this is in the teaching of history or religion. Allow, please, this British (lapsed) Catholic (collapsed) to explain himself. For little Britons were (but I hope not are) taught to believe that Britain was Great with a great big "G", that it fought the wars of the just, that it abolished slavery and defended freedom and discovered Africa and invented physics and converted lots of pagans to Christianity and taught them all to play cricket and eat with a fork and wear long trousers and sit in parliaments. In similar vein, little Catholics were (but I hope not are) told they were made by God and that God loved them and more so than the Protestants and that all authority came from God and that we should all therefore be obedient to authority (especially that of parents and teachers) and that if we weren't good we'd go to purgatory and if we were very bad we'd go to hell hell hell!

The teaching of the rest of our education syllabus is also not a little subjective, as too it is in Africa. One of the main effects if not indeed one of the main purposes of the state run educational system is, yes, the maintenance of that state, which means the maintenance of the socio-economic basis of that state. In a word, education in a right-wing country will be geared to the economics of capitalism, in a left-wing one to socialism; but in both it is geared to the state. A child of such and such a nation will invariably grow up with a biased view, certainly of that nation's history, probably of that nation's predominant religion, and possibly of that nation's politics .... and most definitely of that nation's education system!

In the first two chapters, at least one of us saw how the centralised state will, as it were automatically, be tempted towards the more centralised system of energy creation, towards the promotion of a more centralised industry, centralised financial structures and so on. For similar reasons, not dissociated from the lust for power, the centralised government will forever favour a centralised political system and a uniform system for the police, the army and those other forces of the state which, in their very function, tend to both uphold the law (whether it's good or bad) and maintain the state. Now, if the government is going to centralise all this power and authority in a nice big capital city (and not least because the relevant government minister will be able to feel even more important and buy an even nicer and newer mercedes-benzez) then it will be necessary to compartmentalise the various functions of state. Centralisation can only happen with compartmentalisation, and compartmentalisation can only happen with specialisation.

Therefore the minister of education will either seek to adopt or unwittingly inherit an education system which runs on specialisations. Thus every subject is a discipline - that ghastly military word - so strict are the efforts to limit each subject, and within each subject the specialist.

The 'successes' of the system - the specialists - being beneficiaries of the system, tend to perpetuate it. The professional banker, let us say, might well be tempted to adopt a few specialist qualifications in order to boost both the ego and the salary - and it might give the job a bit more security as well, as an added bonus. From behind a pile of papers, (s)he will speak (in a jargon) with an authority that we, the mere lay persons of the street, are meant to admire. The whole process, needless to say, is mutually supportive, as specialists consult specialists, as professionals professionalise their professions. And, almost like the religious fanatic, it will only be the mathematics professor who, knowing and understanding both the 'f' and the 'x' of life, will be able to initiate others into

$$f(x) \longrightarrow x/6$$

In the more right-wing countries like Kenya, there has been almost a mad enthusiasm to adopt centralist policies, and not least because of the financial attractions that are invariably associated with big banks, multi-national companies, garden parties on the lawn at the British High Commission, and another brand new merc. Indeed, the situation has got so out of hand that a new word has been coined. In Swahili, the prefix **wa-** denotes the human plural - **wakamba**, for instance, are the people of the **kamba** tribe. Well, for all those ministers and bank managers and industrial directors who had been both advocates of and beneficiaries from a centralised system, for all those people who had indeed managed to get that very special saloon, there was now the new word: **wabenzi**.

Not only in Kenya did there exist an imported education system heavily biased in favour of the academic specialist. It was a system which fitted into a capitalist industrialised society very nicely but, like most other aspects of such a society, there were the waste products. There were many who, for reasons various, failed to survive beyond the primary level, some because they just never got there; there were others who dropped out in the exams at the end of their secondary schooling; and there were even those who despite getting all sorts of degrees and diplomas and doctorates, still finished up on the dole of which there was none. Indeed, it could be said that the system produced more 'failures' than 'successes', if any weight is to be given to the meaning of either word.

As if that was not bad enough, a more fundamental ill lay underneath. For when the various members of the **wabenzi** tribe made public pronouncements, all of them without exception talked of the development of the nation, of progress, and of that absolute pre-requisite of everything: agriculture. Back to the land, they said, **harambee** (a totally untranslatable word meaning - well, in some circles - something between "up the pope" and "pull your finger out"). All was in an effort to get people to work hard in the **shambas** of the nation, in an attempt to approach national agricultural self-sufficiency. That was the goal. But all the 'successes' of the education system were bank clerks and petty administrators in the city. It was the 'failures' who reaped the maize. The 'successes' enjoyed a guaranteed income, a pension scheme and a mortgage; the 'failures' prayed for rain. The successes merely administered the bureaucracies; the failures controlled the destiny of the country. Kenya, like many an emerging nation, was simply upside down. Development means political self-esteem, economic self-confidence and agricultural self-reliance; yet in opting for a centralised economic system, many a state has cut the rural throat to spite the urban face.

There were many examples to be found, especially in the more right-wing countries, where the education system had not only failed, but where it had also caused unnecessary hardship. In Morocco, I stayed on a simple farmstead where son number one was no longer at home. He'd gone to the city, to study. Meanwhile, his ageing father struggled to maintain the land, not only to feed the rest of his family, but also to pay the bills for the first son's accommodation in town. Whether or not the son concerned, having succeded at the expense of the failures in the classroom, would again succeed at the expense of others in the city, only time would tell. Until that day dawned, all that could be said was that he, like countless others, had been lured by the natural instincts of survival into the less healthy snare of the city, where rats did race, where a more cut-throat version of the law of the jungle did persist, and where, as it were by definition, some were bound to fail.

A centralised state both feeds and is fed by its

education system.   Furthermore, a centralised state tends to
become   more   centralised   than   it   had   originally   intended,
because for some of the failures there is no land,   and because
the city attracts both the successful and the unsuccessful alike.
(When the over-centralised city of Nairobi tried to de-centralise
itself   a   little,   it   was   the   richer   half   which   sought   to
repatriate the shanty, not because that was what they thought was
best   for   the   poor,   but   because that was what they thought was
best   for   themselves ....   for   the   shanty could be the   breeding
ground   of   cholera   or the hiding place of   thieves   and   Robin
Hoods.)   May I now look,   therefore,   at a   second aspect of
regressive   progress,   the growth of the city,   again both in the
various countries of Africa and in Europe.

*   *   *

The   urban   centres   of   Africa were very much alive;   they
served a hinterland a little, they profitted from it a lot.   On
the approach roads,   more and more traffic was heading for   town.
Carts,   each   constructed   from   the   individual enterprise   of   a
single craftsman within the confines of local resources   -   trees
and   wrecked mercedez   -   were pulled   by   donkeys   and   mules.
Pre-war   or   post-peace   lorries   fumed   and   farted   under
excessive loads.   Taxis,   the not quite so   wrecked mercedes of
Morocco and the peugeots or **matatus** of Kenya,   were both too full
and   too   fast.   And everything journeyed to   the   metropolis.
Within   each   city,   not only was there the   market   place;
there were also the trades and skills of former years,   sometimes
in tiny wee shops and crevices; there were   the noisy adaptations
of   western   industry   in   garages   and   scrap   metal   yards,   in
furniture   shops   and   hardware stores;   and there was   the   yet
noisier music of the transistor and the tape.   In   the   poorer
cities,   on the pavements of Alexandria,   in the bus stations of
Nairobi,   some   folk had set up 'shop' on a tiny little square of
pavement, selling a comb and a battery, a cigarette lighter and a
bicycle clip, and perhaps very little else.
In   every   capital,   not   far from   all   the   activity   and
commotion   of   so   many,   were the broad avenues   and   the   office
blocks   of   the few.   From the Cape to Cairo,   from Mombasa   to
Marakech,   the materialistic magnetism of the city had   attracted
those   who   have aimed for more,   and those whose lot   was   less.
Certainly,   those who had achieved a certain academic prowess did
almost   certainly   head   for   the   city,   for   therein   was   the
university, the civil service and the bank.   But there were also
those who,   for reasons of over-population or urban development,
had   lost their tract of land and for whom the city was the   only
source of refuge, though even then not a very certain one.
In third world countries everywhere,   there was the shanty;
a densely populated area of mud,   cardboard and polythene,   where
everything was used at least once;   a maze of little rooms   and

alleys, where women washed clothes and cooked food, where hundreds of children played with no toys; a mass of jostle and noise as yet more recycling industries made steady progress, banging tins into cups, cans into pans, and very very old mercs into very very odd bends.   A look at the rubbish of society is the litmus test of its wealth; in Europe, we manage to throw out vast quantities of stuff .... but in the countries of the poor, the piles were small, ash and dust were their content, and not even the chickens could find anything useful therein.

The worst slums were in Alexandria and Nairobi.   In the former, an over-crowded city in an over-crowded land, the scene was more oriental; humanity was squashed into the tenement flats of five or six stories, flats built in colonial times, flats which have seen litle maintenance over the years.   From every window hung line upon line of washing, though only the top level received the bleach of the sun. Alas, my days in Alex were spent in police custody of which more later, so I'll talk now of what my one eye saw in Nairobi.

Into the city had come thousands from the open spaces (and crowded villages) of its environs; and in the city, the wealth of the rich sat almost on top of the poverty of the slums. Both the proximity and the proportions of the disparities suggested the status quo would not last.

Nairobi, the low-rise shanty beyond the high-rise centre

Now parts of the Maghreb were just a teeny weeny little bit French.   Kenya was British.   The lord mayor of Nairobi wore the same robes as you would find in London at the show.   The judges used the same funny wigs that are donned in the Belfast courthouse. And the official opening was accompanied by the tune, "It takes a worried man to sing a worried song", played by the national brass-and-tin-amalgam-band.   The various institutions - police, armed forces etc. - were run on very British lines; and British exports.British investments were everywhere   - and Africa was not without its Irish multi-nationals either   - and English, that most unAfrican of languages, was far too widely spoken in a country whose official tongue was meant to be Swahili.   Meanwhile, Nairobi was full of my fellow continent-persons on short term contracts.   They ate the beef and the pud, they played the golf, and they went to the movies; and then they went home like me to write books about Africa.   They it was who shared a lifestyle with the blackwhitemen as they were called, the wabenzi.   Njonjo, the former attorney general, was the epitome.   A Kikuyu by birth, he had evolved into a pin-stripe-suited gentleman of the very best English traditions;   and he blessed his blessings in the good English church in which both his bride and his Christ were British.

The rich, black and white, had a good life, living at a standard few of them could have achieved in Europe.   The latter said they had come to teach, to help and to guide; would that they were as generous with their property as they were with their knowledge.   One of them put it like this:

- Everything goes down out here; your standard of honesty, your standard of efficiency, your standards of workmanship; everything but your standard of living!

They had servants and second cars, nice gardens and dinner parties, weekends down at the coast, visits to game parks and trips up Mount Kenya.   Almost certainly they were getting paid at least what they would have received back home, plus a little bit more as a gratuity or something, and yet the cost of living here was cheaper!   For as long as the rich whites were around, there would be a few rich black people; and that, so far, was what independence had achieved.   Meanwhile, hundreds of other Kenyans aspired to that wealth.   In they came from the country, no matter how slim their chances of success.   Everything told them to try the European-cum-urban way of life.

Nairobi offered some hope;   the shamba offered none.   So in they did come to the slum.   Therein, their fate was sealed. The Europeans in Nairobi, living at a standard grossly in excess of so many Africans, were part of the problem of Kenya.   Just as we, the citizens of Europe and America, are part of the problem of third world poverty.

Kenya, then, needed to change (its education system and) its economic ways to ensure that development took place right across the spectrum of society, but especially among the poor. Kenya, as a nation, would remain in more ways than one upside-

down until it righted itself .... by moving left. In the
meantime, the mixture of tribalism and capitalism would remain a
de-stabilising factor, and continuing disparities of wealth,
between city and country, between suburb and slum, would be the
measures of that instability.

*   *   *

     Urbanisation had sorely affected the right wing regimes,
but it had also played a part in the countries of the left, if
perhaps to a lesser extent. Urbanisation will in effect always
occur in those countries, left or right, which pursue the
policies of centralisation.
     It would be unwise to cite Libya as an example of socialism,
although its poverty had been almost completely eradicated. For
given the oil wealth of that country, and given its tiny
population, such an achievement was only too easy. Libya had
managed to bring together a number of policies in an unusual
concoction, the ideals of equality and the local control of means
of production were combined with the statist pragmatics of
centralisation, high rise urban flats in the suburbs of Tripoli,
and those vast supermarkets in which were sold both the plastics
of America and the electronics of Japan. Furthermore, just as
in Kenya, the education system had managed to produce an elite
which then supported the state. It was not the company
executive or business director who drove the car the make of
merc. Rather, it was that very special servant of the state,
not just the blindly obedient soldier, not just the sometimes-
law-abiding always-law-enforcing policeman, but the officer of
the special branch. A charming person he was and a devout
Moslem as any father of eight was bound to be for why else would
Allah have so blessed his seed; but the gun was in its underarm
holster, he was the servant of the state, and his salary was a
good bit more than that of the less equal farmer or common-or-
desert soldier. Though the disparities of wealth were smaller
and the abuses fewer, the spies and super-spies of Libya
nevertheless formed a sort of upper class, and they came to live
in cities.
     The socialism in Algeria, however, was more socialist; it
had certainly helped in the incomplete task of alleviating
poverty, it had succeeded in so far as it had given work to all
(and thus said those many folk who seemed to spend all day in the
market place, drinking le café français), and it had given to
each and every village a certain measure of local autonomy. It
seemed to me that the latter, combined both with an education
system which taught agricultural and not just the academic
subjects, and with the country-wide development of medical
services and industry, was the best way to avoid the creation of
shanties in the big cities, the iron filings on the magnet of

materialism.   Which leads me to talk and you to read of the next
facet of regressive progress, a facet which appeared to belong to
all the countries I visited;   for every one of them,   sooner   or
immediately,   had tended to opt for the projects   prestigious, of
which,   of course,   the broad avenues and the presidential palace
of the capital city were only the first examples.

*   *   *

I   suppose the process began when centralism first started,
when   as I mentioned on page 13,   our ancestors first   decided   to
hang up the spear,   to plant the cereal,   to domesticate the cow,
to   build   the home,   to set up villages,   to build   fences,   to
install   a ruler and to take up the spear again.   So much   for
civilisation!   It   was a process which led to an uncertain   and
temporary tranquility for the antelope and the zebra, bloody hard
work   for the camel and the cow,   and a mixed bag of culture   and
tax, auto- and demo-cracy, institutionalised religion, oppression
and war for the people who started it all.   The village,   which
no   doubt was peaceful enough,   led to the town,   the   city,   the
capital   and the nation.   It was part of a whole chain of events
which   affected our agricultural,   economic and political way   of
life.   Since   starting in Egypt,   this   process   has   come   to
Europe;   and   one doesn't   have to look too long at   the   world
before   concluding that both the policy and the   philosophy   have
gone west.

*   *   *

I will start,   in a most ordinary way,   where it all began,
in Egypt.   Soon there came the day when they did specialise, for
some did rule,   others were ruled,   and as a rule the latter worked
tooth   and   nail while the former sat in solitude, to contemplate
the stars, of which they felt they were part.   In the clear clear
nights of the desert airs,   astronomy was born,   mathematics   was
invented   and science was underuled.   There followed one of the
most prestigious government job creation schemes of all time when
the   kings built the pyramids for to bury themselves in.   The
biggest one,   for the good king Cheops,   is now some 4,500   years
old.   And in your by-gone days of your yore,   these 'primitive'
peoples   had   been able to measure out a square base accurate   to
within one centimetre measuring at opposite ends of the diagonal;
and   the   four   sides were lined up to the   four   points   of   the
compass   not   yet   invented with an accuracy of one   part   in   a
thousand.   (But   were   they   really   educated   mathematicians?

Could they have answered or solved or equated or have done whatever you do and I don't with

$$f\{x\} \longrightarrow x/6 \ ?)$$

Meanwhile, down at the social security offices, the workers of the day had carved, by hand, two million three hundred thousand blocks of granite, each 2.5 tonnes in weight. And these had been piled up on top of each other to form a pyramid of near perfect proportions. Inside, a long inclined passage rose up at a steep angle into the heart of the monument and there, at the top, was the chamber where once the body of a monarch had laid. Now it was all empty, for gold speculators of the pre-stock exchange era had long since plundered these pyramids, just as they'd done the tombs at Luxor.

The most prestigious project of them all was there, at Luxor, though within the dusty limits of to-day's town, few signs of civilisation were apparent. A long long time ago, almost exactly five thousand years before our own United Irishmen of the eighteenth century, a certain King Menon brought together the two lands of Upper and Lower Egypt - the latter was the Egypt of the delta, the former, the land of the river. The capital was first at Memphis, but after a dynasty or two, just as soon as outline planning permission was a royal thought, the city the temple and its God moved to Thebes, the first capital of the world.

I will pause awhile, no longer to complain about the ills of centralism in general and of prestigious projects in particular, but rather to stand in stupor at the deeds of our forbears, misguided or no. Let me describe the spectacle, just as it was for me as I stood in wonder, in awe, in amazement, in the temples of Karnak. I marvelled at all I could see - well, nearly all; for I also saw flies which also saw me and their continual attentions distracted my own. My diary makes bad reading.

I sat on the base of one of the 134 pillars which formed the centrepoint of the palace of the Gods. This, the hypostyle hall, was the work of Ramses the Second, the great, a king who had ruled in the year 1300 BC. Gigantic columns, so large in height and width they appeared to squash each other, covered more than an acre of land. On each of them, from the base to the summit, was a host of carvings drawings and hieroglyphics, while at the head were the lotus and the papyrus, the two symbols of Lower and Upper Egypt. The two lands were now one; for all Egyptians, here was their city, their temple and their God! But by that God called Amon amen, the presence of the deity had managed to attract hundreds of no doubt divinely devised flies all of which irreverently buzzed around out of bounds in the temples of others.

To my left was a courtyard, therein a statue of a pharaoh and his queen, therein a line of pylons had once stood as mighty edifices to a succession of monarchs, therein still stood an inner temple to some lesser God and another shrine from another king. Each pharaoh had felt bound to add his or her own personal monument to this magnificent and Godly home (though sometimes, in their enthusiasm to remember themselves, they'd forgotten their own predecessors whose creations they'd then demolished as we would a city centre). As a result, the entire structure had taken over a thousand years to build and bloody flies excuse me much had survived even longer than that. Beyond this courtyard was the main entrance, marked by a line of statues of rams. Here, amidst all these pillars, only the pharaoh, the queen and their priests had been permitted. Herein had been and remained the presence of Amon, the God of creation; for Thebes was God's land, the first land to appear after the

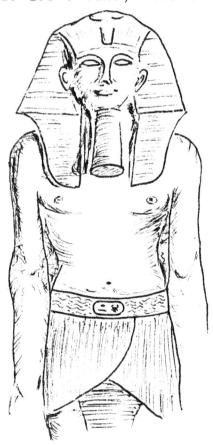

Daddy

bloody flies great flood had receded.

To my right was a second courtyard, surrounded by a great wall of carved stone, and herein stood further temples, more shrines and a great obelisk of granite, raising its point like the bloody flies phallus it was, needless to say the creation of a queen. Damn it, why were there so many bloody flies bloody flies. Question mark. Sorry, dear reader, I was bloody flies

interrupted.   To the south,   close to the sacred lake on   which
the   barque   of   Amon   had   always   been   moored,   lay   yet   another
courtyard with more pillars and monuments and shrines and bloody
flies.   Once   a   year,   along this route of curved   and   carved
column,   the   God   had travelled to Luxor where a   second   though
smaller   temple had awaited Him,   and from there He had   ventured
onto the Nile, His river.   The festival over, He had returned to
Karnak,   His temple,   the centre of His world,   the centre of THE
world.

Thebes,   the   city of the Gods,   sat entirely on   the   east
bank.   Villages a plenty to both north and south had kept it in
food,   and   the Nile had been the means of communication with the
outside   world.

At   sunset,   the   perfectly   calm   waters   of   the   river
reflected   the ever changing glows of the sun as it varied from
yellow   through   red   to gold in a cloudless sky.   Time was   a
friend,   and every moment offered another kaleidoscope of colour.
There   was   not a breath of wind.   Nothing moved.   It   was   a
perfect peace, the peace of the Nile, a peace which surpassed the
understanding of all those bloody flies.   The sun did set.   In
the west,   the world did die.   To the pharaohs of old,   the
opposite side of the river had been the land of the dead.

Their   lives had revolved round their   deaths,   and theirs
had   been   the only world civilisation to attempt a map of   the
world hereafter,   the book of the dead.   Great preparations had
ensured   - or they'd tried to - that the king and queen would
have a happy eternity.   Their entire lives they had lived on
the east bank.   Come death,   their last and final   journey had
taken them,   in state, to their tombs in the west, where life was
no more.   An entire village of workers, who probably had never
visited the eastern shores and its glories, had prepared the tomb
first by digging a tunnel deep into the rock of the mountains of
Thebes,   then by excavating a large chamber therein,   and finally
by painting a host of designs on all the walls and ceilings of
the vast sepulchre.   Meanwhile,   in the auric aura of the cold
catacomb, the artificers and artisans had created the cradle that
could never corrode .... for a corpse of ex-consequence.

All   the paintings told a story;   they showed the king
defeating his enemies,   being ministered to by his servants,   or
going on one of his great journeys, to the Red Sea perhaps,   or
even   deep into Asia.   Some rather weird creatures   were here:
human   bodies with animal heads of snake and ram grave in
countenance.   Birds and other animals of the erratic imagination
resulted in a gallery of glory,   and a continuous procession of
life in yellows, blues and golds led down down down, to where the
king had laid in peace .... for a wee while.   Having buried the
lord in a flood of gold,   the chamber had been sealed, covered
over and completely hidden.   Alas, of the many tombs made here,
all of them along with those in the pyramids had been ransacked
and robbed for prosperity, leaving but the pictures on the walls
for posterity.   All but one.   The tiny and magnificent tomb of

Tut-Ankh-Amun, who had died in the year 1352 BC; yet there had been enough gold in this little tomb to fill the entire top floor of the Cairo museum. (Some) God knows how much treasure had been stored in these other burial chambers.

My mind consumed a meal of aesthetics. The west bank also contained the Valley of the Queens - strict segregation still in force - the giant statues of Ramses II who had fathered some ninety plus sons (ah, the folly of ambition - how often do we die just before we succeed? Which reminds me, I must finish this journey pretty soon!) - and the temple of Queen Hatshepsut. All of them were mighty reminders of what had been superb edifices to the most imaginative minds of a most primitive age, during which so many had laboured and died. But many are the books which have been written on what has become the very science of egyptology, although a full treatment will only be achieved by a complementary visit to the botanical shelves for a detailed study of all those bloody flies. Suffice to say that the temptation towards the prestigious has survived the passage of time - the twentieth century Egyptian ruler has built the Aswan dam, and the lake thereby created carries his name; at the same time, however, the respect for our heritage from years gone by has actually grown, if only because nowadays there is less of it and more of them.

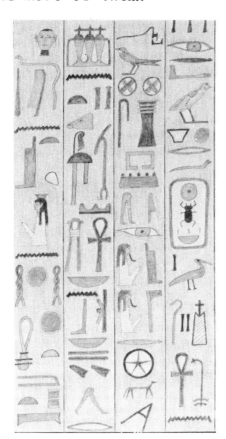

A word in your eye

Throughout the history of humankind, everything has had its good points, and while cities have indeed caused problems they have also led to blessings, not least in the form of museums. The contents of the sarcophagus of Tut-Ankh-Amun deserve more than the sentence received above; permit them please to have another below.

When I visited the British museum oh, many years ago, I found it full of Amonknewwhats from all over the place. Various Victorian gents had sailed the seven seas to countless countries which no-one else had ever thought of owning, and they had brought back umpteen **objets d'art** which they'd found, stolen or expropriated. Everyone had thought everything jolly jolly nice and, in exchange for a quick MBE or a peerage, gifts had been bequeathed to the British museum. Thus, within its confines, there were African masks, Chinese vases, Indian buddhas, oh, all sorts of stuff, all of which was fascinating, damn all of which was British. (Even in the Belfast museum, you'll find an Egyptian mummy, brought not bought in its first change of ownership.) (While on the streets of London, there stands an obelisk, hi-jacked from Thebes. One can understand the nineteenth century mind which stole it .... but not the twentieth century one which keeps it!) Meanwhile, dotted around the British Isles were many a retired crook, to each of whom had been donned a '-dom', of the earl or duke variety. They, too, could have filled a museum.

When I went to the Cairo museum, however, everything was Egyptian, which was as it should have been; I was in an Egyptian mood, I was ready for all things Egyptian and I was not prepared to see what treasures some Egyptian pirate had plundered from the post-historic sites of our demolished inner cities. It was, needless, to say, full of wonders: gigantic statues of pharaohs and their queens, great blocks of rock carved in the prolific hieroglyphic; wooden coffins by the dozen and mummies by the score. Folk had been pretty small in those days; it is extraordinary to see how the human race has got bigger and bigger and .... well .... looking at the size of some of to-day's American tourists, I think it's time to call a halt.

The burial chamber of the boy-king had been found, intact in fact, in the 1920's by .... och, the name doesn't matter that much; he could have been a she but but he was as it happened a he; he could have been Egyptian but actually he was one of those rare accidents of modern history called an Irish peer; and he would have been for a bit longer if he hadn't died of malaria.

Anyway, when they had first opened up the tomb, in a moment of emotion, they had found a large huge big enormous box made of gold, covered with carvings and engravings in a too beautiful two-dimensional relief work of animal goddesses and human princes. Portals were protected, corners were guarded, sides were adorned .... and each creature had a story to tell or a rôle to perform. End of part one. In a moment of expectation, the two mighty doors of gold had been opened, to reveal, inside, a huge big enormous box, of gold, again decorated by a host of drawings and diagrams. It too had been built with a double door and, after a wee cup o' tea and in a moment of excitement, these two had been creaked apart; inside, well well well, they'd found a big enormous box. Gold. Embossed. Beautiful. Commercial break. In a moment of exhilaration, two further gates of gold had been opened to expose .... guess what? An enormous box. The news. In a moment of exhaustion, this last pair had been carefully cranked open and, yes, they'd fount it, the sacred sarcophagus. A sarcophagus, I was told, was a box. Oh thanks. It was the one they actually put the body in, so perhaps it did deserve a special name.

The sarcophagus itself along with the mummy of Tut-Ankh-Amun and the magnificent blue and gold face mask which covered it, was still in its tomb, way down in Upper Egypt. All the rest of the stuff with which a king had been buried had been stored in these gold boxes; and all were laid out on display in the vast hall of the Cairo museum. Folding camp beds, golden thrones, gold walking sticks, 365 models of servants - literally one for each day of the year - and a whole host of little things and big, garments, cups, everything .... except a gramophone and ten discs.

The king's golden throne, beautifully embossed with a picture of him being perfumed by his young wife, was accompanied by a special step made, of course, of gold, and upon this did rest his feet. Now the ancient Egyptian had depicted an enemy by a decapitated body, and here, on this ledge in front of the throne was a line of such corpses, their flesh flush at the neck, tails, no heads. Tut-Ankh-Amun had, yes, made his enemies his footstool. Now, ding, I do recall such expressions occurring in the bible. Is it not possible, therefore, that the ancient Egyptians and Jews met, which they certainly did, and that their religious beliefs cross-fertilised? Or is it that Judaism is just a growth of earlier faiths, just as some consider Christianity to be a development of Judaism? What is true, however, is that the old testament is the human story of a human people written by human beings. God, if HeSheIt had indeed written a book, would not have had to travel to Egypt to clinch a cliché.

At Edfu, there was another similarity between these religions. Another temple, for this nation was just full of antiquities, greeted the visitor, as did another ticket collector. Inside, in a sort of side chapel there stood a special type of box ready, perhaps, to carry a God, and ready to be carried by the poles which supported it. The resemblance was striking. Was this the fore-runner of the Jewish arc of the covenant which in turn developed into the Christian tabernacle? Or was it just another example of how close a religion identifies and is identified with the state? For every city was/is blessed with the temple, the cathedral and/or the mosque, and only the shrines at Abu Simbel were now miles and miles from anywhere, on the shores of Lake Nasser, where the brightness of the blue meets the starkness of the yellow, without the softness of the intermediary green.

*   *   *

At the bottom of that lake was a little jetty, one rowing boat, half a wadi and a Sudanese Chief Harbour Commissioner brackets first class no less!   The place, appropriately named Wadi Halfa, is was and always has been in the middle of a Nilotic nowhere.   But, by gad and by God Sir, it was on the route to Godknewwhere and, like anything else which was on the way to somewhere else, it immediately assumed, in the minds if such they have of military men, strategic importance.   Thus it was that the British, who were of course the rulers of India, came, for the sake of that sub-continent, to Wadi Halfa.   It was a far cry from India - it was a far far cry from bloody well anywhere - but the British arrived and they stayed to build the prestigious project of their day, the Wadi Halfa railway.
Basically, Khartoum had become the gateway to yet another sandy somewhere else, it sat at, but could not influence, the confluence of the Blue and White Niles, and it too was of major strategic importance.   Why?   Because of India!   Oh yes, of course.   But how?   Why, because of India!!   Oh yes again, of course of course.   So the British had decided to by-pass that mighty sweepswoop of the Nile which is so plagued by the cataracts as to become unnavigable, by building one railway line right across the desert, just like that.   Basically, two British army lieutenants had managed to draw two straight, metal, British export lines across well over a hundred miles of sand - thus proving, of course, that nationalised industry is perfectly capable of not only the mundane.   It certainly was a feat, no less remarkable for its post-pharaohic vintage, and happily it was still in use when I came along.   Indeed, if suspicions served me a'right, it was still employing the original stock.
The joys of travel, few perhaps on this particular line, were enhanced by a game of chess with a fellow traveller from Munich and Europe and, oh yes, he also came from Germany.   The view to the right was sand.   The view to the left was sand .... and telegraph poles, standing like pawns .... oh, my move - sorry.   On each pole sat a hawk, the sea-gulls of the desert, ready to feed in the wake of the train on whatever the passengers threw overboard.   Umm - just lost a pawn.   Dust was everywhere, covering everything, he's got my bishop, coming in through every wooden shutter and every door, right, I'll bring out my queen.   The passengers, mothers, young children and all, just sat and suffered in silence, while the shades of dusk streaked skywards from the east.
- Check.   Hmm - these Germans don't say very much, do they? At night, game adjourned, two pieces one pawn down, and the third

class status of our carriage confirmed by the absence of any lighting, we sat, covered in sand and dust. The hours and the miles passed slowly, and all that was seen were the silvery sands silent in the light of a million stars.

If the train had been on schedule which it had been once the previous year, then it would have reached Khartoum within 24 hours. Ish. Well, dawn arrived and we did not, good morning, yes it's your move, but to travel quickly is to miss so much .... sand.

- Check.
- Check?
- Yes, check; I mean check mate.
- Lovely view, I replied, isn't it?

The train rejoined the Nile and we stopped for refreshments. Water! Everyone piled out of the carriages to spray and splash themselves with a bucket and aplomb - lovely word, that. And then to the stalls where we drank the iced juice of the pomegranate, ate the flesh of the banana and chewed on some nuts/beans which must have been beans/nuts 'cos they grew on trees. From henceforth, the train journey was not quite so dusty; not absolutely intolerable, just almost. A cup of tea in the restaurant car was the very relic of British colonialism,

- Would you like another game?
- Yes please.

Everything, including the waiters in their little white dickeys, were just as a 1903 BR would have wished. Only the slatted windows and the dust said this was not BR. And the prices charged said this was not 1903. But it mattered not, for no-one could hear above the noise of the 1903 engine! Your move! What? Can't hear you!!

Sooner rather than later, my opponent in chess enjoyed his second victory; and later rather than sooner, we arrived in Khartoum .... on the dot of ish!

In building this railway, the Brits had all the bits made in Britain. Once built, of course, it was able to assist the building of other outlandish devices in other outdesertish places, like the pre-fabricated gunships with which the British had fought the battle of Omdurman. Or, as another example, the passenger carrying cruise ship of the Mississippi mode, a wreck of which I saw on the Nile in Uganda! No matter how you look at it, to get ships 4,000 kilometres up river, above dams cataracts and swamps, to a stretch of water 600 metres above sea level was at least an achievement. For all their faults, the British colonialists had accomplished some mighty deeds .... if only because of the cheap labour .... which was one of their faults.

Before leaving the Wadi Halfa-Khartoum sometimes express, perhaps I may dwell a moment or two on the historical reasons for building what was not only a prestigious project. Just as with the Aswan dam, there was a further reason, associated with economic-political-military power. Basically, the reason was India and the whole business of empire building which not only the British were involved in.   Soon, indeed, there was to be the scramble for Africa as Europeans various decided which bits were to be which,   the which of which was not African, of course, 'cos damn it all they only lived there.   No, the which of which was British perhaps but European certainly.   For hot on the heels of the   former were the French,   the Italians,   the Portugese,   the Belgians,   the Spanish and the Germans - Christians all, of course.   The British,   then, were not only laying claim to the headwaters   of   the Nile,   for in the boardrooms   of   Whitehall, whiskers were bristling with the idea of drawing lines from the Cape to Cairo,   and moustaches were moistened with the thought of maps coloured in the bluish tint of colonial pink.

Meanwhile, in certain schools of learning, the British were producing   the   men   of noughtpointthreethree   calibre who were prepared   to face the unknown. Needless to say,   British public schools   had also produced their failures,   but they had   always been able to join the colonial service as administrators.   Now, unfortunately   for the courts of Victoria,   the French were   also drawing lines,   and off into the bundu had disappeared the French equivalents of British "chaps".   The whole process of colonialism was   actually quite easy: find it,   convert it,   control it and exploit it;   the only difficulty was in ensuring that   you   got there first.

So,   communications   were,   oh! absolutely   vital my   dear fellow,   absolutely vital! Charles? Sir! Build a railway, will you? Yes Sir. Small pause. Railway built Sir.   Alright boy, don't just stand there!

And up and down the Nile,   in the traditions of the Duke of York, marched the soldiers of the Raj.   Meanwhile, deep in that part of Africa which only the French called French, an expedition was   under way.   One French lieutenant   was   going to   walk eastwards from the Atlantic coast to lay claim to the **eaus** of the Nile - eaus or eaux, oh I don't know.   Now where he was going to hit the river was uncertain,   but it was quite a long   river; he was bound to hit it somewhere.

The   English   were marching down Africa,   the French   were marching across.   The race was on!

Act one - scene two - somewhere in the heart of deepest Africa - splash!   And on the banks of a tropical river,   one white man sat under a flagpole with a bit of red white and blue cotton on top while another white man sat under an adjoining flagpole with a different bit of red white and blue cotton hanging therefrom.   Then these two men, in a continent called primitive,   did speak of honour and dignity and other such like mythical figments of the patriotic imagination.   Statesmen did stutter.   Politicians did pontificate.   My God!   Mon Dieu. And Britain and France did bloody nearly go to bloody war because of it.   The place, Fashoda; the year, 1898.   But they didn't go to war,   so that was alright then wasn't it?   Well no,   not really, 'cos they went to fight the Boers instead.   Why? Because of India.   Oh yes, of course.

*   *   *

So much, then, for the Wadi-Halfa railway, a prestigious project of mainly military significance.   Alas, the twentieth century equivalents of the same have replaced them.   Take, for instance, the Nairobi to Addis Ababa highway, a road which north of a quarter way up or south of a quarter way down goes through an area of dead, volcanic desert .... though a little island of life at the half way stage could be converted into a more than reasonable motorway-service-station-game-park.

Now what was the purpose of the Wadi-Halfa railway save the expansion of the British empire?   And what was the purpose of a road across the Kenyan desert?   To help the nomadic tribes-people communicate with their own fellow citizens whom they regarded as foreigners?   To help them import the soap and powdered milk they could barely afford?   Or was it to form a strategic line of communication between what was and is (both before and after the coup 'cos the coup '82 failed) a right-wing Kenya, and what was but is not (before the coups of '74 and '77 which succeeded) a right-wing Ethiopia, against what was (before the other coup '69 did counter-coup the coup '78) and still is a left-wing Somalia?

May I digress awhile, from prestigious projects to politics - though all too often they are one and the same - and because it could be said, what with all these coups, that the politics of Africa are as noisy as a pigeon loft?   To put it in perspective, it is also necessary to have a brief glance at the extreme European (ie, American and Russian) influences in this area known as the Horn of Africa.

The aged Ethiopian emperor Haile Selassie, being the good old undemocratic reactionary autocrat that he was, was dearly loved by those upholders of democracy and freedom, Britain and the USA; while Somalia, under Barre, went socialist and received support from the USSR.   In the name of democracy freedom and socialism, the two contries went to war over a miserable bit of ol' desert called the Ogaden; in so doing, they were aided and abetted by the two super powers.

Then the Dergue took over from the emperor in that coup of '74 and three years later they went marxist.   Ah!   So Russia changed sides.   In the name of all that is pragmatic, so did the yanks.   Somalia was still socialist, of course, but apparently that didn't matter any more.   And in the name of democracy freedom and socialism, the two countries were still at war, over that same wretched piece of desert.

Russian warships sailed out of Berbera; American ones sailed in.   The big boys played expensive games, while the devastating famine killed mercilessly those who had already suffered enough the ravages of war.   The arms industries of the industrialised super-powers and death were the only winners.

'84 sees no end to the war, and on top of it all, a most cruel drought has compounded the misery.   Barre is starting to chat up Moscow again - how the Politbureau or the Pentagon gets out of that one, God alone knows!   And ghosts of the "shifta" wars between Kenya and Somalia are starting once more to stir the silence of those barren wastes of northern Kenya, where the only signs of any development at all .... is one tarmac road!

*   *   *

There is another prestigious project of a more peaceful nature.   To it, all third world countries have been tempted; and to it, all have succumbed. The national airline. So boeings fly here and boeings fly there and boeings are now being everywhere, in every airport in Africa.   Yet being independent should not mean going boeing, and nationalism should mean more than be the boeing be and how be the boeing seen, and whether its hues be of red and blue, or whether of black and green. Seeing, however, as the airports of Europe are being becoming to be being more and more boeing, then this is an observation which applies to us all.   Suffice to say that nationalisms can hardly be positive cultural values, if all they involve are the colours of our jumbos and the quality of our chips.

*   *   *

A more wholesome project of less prestige and of much more practical value was the development plan in Algeria.   No sooner had I left the cold of the mountains, no sooner had I arrived on the edge of the largest expanse of barren earth this side of the M2 roundabout, than I saw the creation of an industrial zone. Here, on the northern edge of the Sahara, the town and desert planning people had decided to build factories in the desertside. What made them put them there, on this flat bit, as opposed to over there, on that flat bit, or over there, or there, or there beyond the yonder there, on those there flat bits over there, I did not know.   There there, never mind, for who are we, mere mortals, to comprehend the machinations of the planner?
Nevertheless, it was there; it was part of the process by which each region was to have its own industry; it was part of the scheme in which Algeria would try to produce indigenously the greatest part of all her needs; it was a policy which accepted the intimate links which exist between economic and political independence; and it was a programme which sought first regional and then national self-sufficiency.   It was prestigious perhaps, but its purpose was sound, its effect was good.   In complete contrast, may I now take you to the southern side of the Sahara, where life was bad.

All along the southern half of the desert, there is what is called the Sahel belt. It is an area of semi-desert, where people struggle on arid plains in failing rains, just to survive. The belt is slowly moving south, slowly affecting more and more people. What was tropical forest becomes savannah; the savannah becomes scrub; and the scrub, in time, changes to semi-desert and desert. The whole process is taking place on a vast scale - the rivers in northern Zaire are at their lowest in living memory - and slowly but surely, an ecological disaster is destroying a continent. It is a disaster unprecedented in scale since the time of the last ice-age; its immediate effects are climatic - hence famine; its long term ones could be climaxial, as we in the North continue to produce more and more carbon dioxide, while the disappearing forests of Africa and South America become increasingly unable to re-convert it all; it is all the folly of man!

Sometimes, that disaster was more apparent in the west, sometimes in the east. At this time, its tentacles of tragedy were in the stony flats of Karamoja in Uganda. By 1984, as I mentioned above, it had moved to Ethiopia, but on such a massive scale that its effects are being felt in Kenya and The Sudan as well.

Now this drought in particular, and the whole southward march of the Sahel in general, was indeed the result of human error! In Gabon, the Europeans were raping the tropical forests and exporting the felled trees by the thousand. In exchange for which, the French have now offered Gabon a nuclear reactor!! Oh, what right have we Europeans to the word civilisation? In Cameroun, the sale of European hand-saws has encouraged the widespread destruction of trees to provide fuel for cooking .... yet every tree felled in the forests below the Sahara only accelerates its southward march. While in The Sudan, two prestigious projects - one ecologically disastrous, the other ecologically naïve - actually contradicted each other.

The Sudanese government had asked one European firm to build a canal to by-pass The Sudd, and a different firm of consultants to recommend ways of reducing the excessive vegetation which grows in the waters of the Nile. This vegetation was, admittedly, a bit of a nuisance. Whole islands of it existed in The Sudd, smaller clumps drifted into the swamp, and bigger ones came out the other end. Sometimes the stuff stuck to the bank and became part of it, but sometimes bits of the bank broke away to drift yet further downstream, great clumps of twisted weed and entangled reed, ready to foul the jetty and clog the prop.

In total, there was every economic reason for wanting to build the canal - better communications, cheaper transport costs and all that - and every every reason for wanting to control the reed. But was it wise to reduce such a vast area of evapouration? Was it fair to distrub the natural habitat of the hippo and the mosquito, for the latter would doubtless spread into the waters of the canal, especially in whatever still waters there might be in the locks controlling the flow.   The still waters would also aid the spread of the bilhertzia snail, the wee water-borne beastie which spreads the disease of lethargy known by the same name.   Whether 'twas 'tis or 'twould be wise, I'm not sure;   while I was there, they were definitely talking about it, but since then, the resumption of armed conflict in southern Sudan (see page 146) has led to its cancellation.   That may well be a blessing in disguise.   I have, as you now know, an antipathy to the ever-increasing big ideas of big finance and big government,   for   there must be a limit somewhere.   In retro-spect,   the Suez canal was a good idea;   the natural obstacle of the desert was overcome with the help of the natural rift valley and   the   lakes.   But   anything   which   only   exacerbates   the southward advance of the Sahel is surely to be avoided.

And so to the river-borne vegetation.   Well,   just south of Khartoum there lies another prestigious project of the colonial   era called the Gezira.   It is a large area of fertile land   on the banks of the Blue Nile and there,   the British had hoped,   would grow the cotton to feed the mills of Lancashire for generations and generations.   Well,   two anyway.   In those days,   the people had to export cotton from which to earn foreign currency   with   which   to   obtain   local cash   by   which   to   get transport via which to go shopping by which to buy which food why rich food;   nowadays, they were just growing food .... and a bit of cotton.   One must admit,   a self-reliant economy is blessed with a certain simplicity.

Now in the Gezira there was a problem,   they said.   The international   oil   companies   had   just   put   up   the   price   of fertilizers .... again.   Yet surely, all this natural greenery coming   down   the White Nile would make the most   virile   manure! Thus   one   if not two branches of high technology could be oh   so neatly by-passed,   not just for the sake of it, but in order that The   Sudan   could   continue to survive by making use   of   its own resources   rather   than   by being dependent   on   (multi-national) others.   While nature so often presents problems,   she usually also provides the answers.

                              *   *   *

So   that's the end of that little problem.   Next   please. Well one of the biggest reasons why all those twentieth century migratory   animals called tourists go to Africa is the   elephant; smaller reasons include the whole spectrum of wild-life from   the lion   to the lizard.   In hunting lodges and safari parks,   here was   ample scope for projects prestigious;   and a full report I could not possibly have given you without first paying a visit to at   least   one   of Africa's many   reserves.   There   had   been, of course,   lots of wild-life in Europe before 'civilisation' had killed it all, but for the four lions ensconced in concrete in Trafalgar Square; one blessing of the Sahara was that it had preserved the natural heritage of the jungle for at least a century or two.   Whether or not we are now wise enough not to exterminate it all is open to question.   In the meantime, however, what wild-life remained was a considerable attraction, and many a pound was spent for (or against) the rhino and the hippo, the geerenook and the gnu.

First of all, I am tempted to relate my own direct encounters with the weird and wonderful, the fierce and frightful of Africa.   I was in those arid parts of northern Kenya, where spasmodic thorn trees have as it were been lightly sprinkled on a dry and rocky terrain, and it was time to go to the loo.   The loo was just a great big hole in the ground with a wooden thunderbox construction on top.

The thorn tree

For very natural reasons quite beyond my control, I had chosen the hour of dusk.   With flies undone and naked bum, I crouched upon the hole.   Immediately, there were some strange underbum undercurrents which undermined I underline the owner of the aboveforementioned hithertoreferredto bum.   I understood not, over-reacted and stood to survey the scene.   Nothing.

Most odd, it was, and not a little eerie. I sat once more and
again these things, what e'er they were, fluttered and flustered
in flight at the achilles arse of my anatomy. I was determined
to get to the bottom of this - (sorry about that one) - if
only 'cos I was dying to .... to relieve my bowels as they say in
hospitals. I stood. Nothing. I sat. They returned. Curses.
I stood. Still nothing. What the bloody hell was/were it/them
this/those down there?   I thought .... ah yes .... so then
quickly .... IstoodIsatIstood!   Aaaah!   Bats!   Excreta!

Obviously, these beasts of the night which lived in this
pit of the shit usually decided that dusk was the time for a bit
of a breather.   Couldn't blame 'em for that, really.   Each
time I sat, thereby covering what for them was the only
source of light, they thought that night was nigh, only to find
on their little radars that a bum did block the way.   They
fluttered.   I stood.   Light shone.   So they returned inside
to hang around for a wee bit longer until, sun set and shit shat,
the silent night was theirs.

And that wasn't even in a nature reserve, so there was no
extra charge.   Nor was there in Uganda, where the post-Amin
chaos meant anyone who wished could enter the game park for nowt;
indeed, such was the chaos that on the average day, nowt wished
to enter.

Yet this was no average day, and I was no average nowt; in
I went.   (Please see map on page 100.) The road was not, but what
it was was a bit sandy till it rose onto slightly higher and
firmer ground.   A few skeletal trees, leafless, lifeless,
branchless and lossless, indicated that elephants had passed this
way, but the rest of the vegetation was the tall parched elephant
grass.   Now the commercials always try to tell us that Africa is
as full of wild-life as a television documentary is of truth.
Well, it was some time before I saw gazelle, though sure enough,
there were quite a few of them.   Sometimes they only realised
my presence when I was literally just a few yards away.   Immediately they would spring away, leaping over any obstacle of rock
or bush with a grace that was magnificent to watch.   When they
considered the range safe, they stopped to turn and just so many
heads, horned and hornless, appeared over the grass, looking my
way, a'wondering what I was.   Thus were animal curiosities
mutually satisfied.   Further along, a warthog or two also
decided I was too close for comfort; up went the tails, little
periscopes of hair, and off they scampered.   Towards the end of
the day, a herd of buffalo thought I was of no importance at all,
and a solitary monitor lizard completed this commercial.

I came to what had been a game lodge, what would be a game
lodge, but what was a ruin, though only superficially so.   Here
lived that warden, and he and his men operated those anti-
poaching patrols.   Now one of the easiest ways of getting rich
quick was through poaching.   The ivory of the elephant was big
money; among the not so horny of Asia, the horn of the rhino was
a much treasured aphrodisiac; and even the meat of the buffalo

and the hippopotamus provided a substantial source of income, especially in the Uganda of 1980.   Tusks and skins were smuggled out into Zaire and The Sudan, while meat was sold anywhere. Traffic through The Sudan was reputedly the worst, and it has been estimated that 1,000 tonnes of ivory have been exported from there during the last ten years.   Another ghastly abuse of 'economic sense'!   Killing was done by the gun or poisoned spear; of weapons, there was certainly no shortage in Uganda.

In 1960, there had been nine thousand elephants in Kabalega, and nine thousand colonialists in Kampala.   On the balconies and verandahs of government house, as the sun did set over the Mountains of the Moon, gins had been poured and fears expressed that the gins were too few and the elephants too many. Indeed, there had been considerable colonial concern that such a large number would kill all the trees, wipe out the vegetation and be the very death of the park.   So, along had come a bwanaman and he'd said that this was too much and these were too many and that 'market forces' should be allowed to control the situation.   He got a licence and then shot two thousand of them, wiping out whole families at a time, by the use of machine gun fire; he made his fortune and disappeared, the bastard.

There were now, twenty years later, just over an hundred elephants left, and the dangers of them becoming as extinct as the white rhino were very very real, in Kabalega if not else-where.   So, out went the patrol, into the bush.   They camped, and they awaited orders.   Up went an aircraft, looking for signs of illegal activity.   To catch them redblackhanded, in a park of four thousand square kilometres, was quite impossible.   But to have a patrol descend on a poaching gang within an hour or two was an effective deterrent.   If that was all there was to it, then it would have been fair enough.   But the gang was armed. The patrol was armed.   The pilot tried to insist on a pacifist policy but .... in a land like Uganda, in this immediate post-Amin era .... kill or be killed was the incentive.

- We shot three last night, they admitted.
- No, we won't bother reporting the incident to the police.

It was sad to see the bloodthirstyness of these warders; to not report to the police, however, was sensible enough, for within a day, the vultures and hyenas would have finished their work.

The sun did set, and all too quickly the darkness was total.   The pilot, a few of the warders and I sat, by the light of a lone paraffin lamp surrounded by the black of the African night; a vacuum of silence was invaded by the flitter of the moth and the twitter of the bird; an infinity of place on land and space amongst the stars was ours, as too were some avocadoes. The talk was of the beast, yet not an echo was heard for every sound could bounce and rebound only upon itself.   Suddenly, the calm was pierced by a howl and a half and another falsetto staccato hell of a howl.

- What the blinking blank was that?   I asked.   The hyena.

The harbinger of death.   I began to understand the African's
justifiable fear of the scavenger.   I needed no persuasion with
regards to the scorpion, but the one we saw was only a little
feller.   Here endeth the second commercial.

The Warthog, as seen sometimes in game parks....and often on postcards

The next day,   another group of us pretended that the world
was   at peace,   that this boat was ship-shape and that this book
should boast of the beast for the third time.   Off we went for a
pleasure cruise.   Here, there, on either bank all the way up the
river,   were little families of big hippos.   Two nostrils,   two
globular eyes and two tiny pig-like ears were just above the
surface,   as was the broad back of its bulky body.   They didn't
seem to like us very much,   and most submerged and waited for us

to pass by before re-appearing with a snort of the nostrils and a flap of the ears.   Others, however, did do what we wanted, opening their enormous guitar-shaped mouths of pink, or standing up out of the water to prove that not only oil comes in barrels. And pretty was the baby, a mere eighty pounds at birth.   Further up-stream were those beasts whose skins some people prefer to see in hand-bags and high heel shoes - it is surely they who buy and sell who are just as guilty as those who poach and kill.

The crocodile.   What a magnificent brute.   Under a tree, a group of them were asleep, each fanning out from the trunk like the spoke of a wheel; their bodies didn't move, yet their mouths were wide wide open - a sign of a low IQ, they say, but crocodiles are strong, and strength has always been the fool's substitute for intelligence.   The crocodile was camera shy. On waking because of the noise of the boat's engine, the mouth slammed shut, up went the body like an instant hovercraft, and four or five metres of majestic monster slithered into the water.

The boat hove to.   Astern, the Nile was calm, a mirror to the banks and hills beyond.   But ahead, bubbling and foaming from the rocks and stone, the falls - the same mighty falls so beloved of the tsetse - a wonder of nature adopted by the state to be preserved in prestige and flogged at ten bob a time to the rest of the world.   It was wonderful;   and to think that this was the very same sight that had greeted so many Africans before and after a certain European came along, just one hundred years ago, searching still for a wee small stream he wished to call the source. Unfortunately for him, this the White Nile came from Lake Victoria, a full 1,000 metres above sea level, an inland sea only three times the size of all of Northern Ireland, and into it flowed a thousand streams, each one waiting to be controlled by the he who did control Egypt. As mentioned earlier, from Kabalega Falls to Karuma some sixty kilometres upstream, the river was constant confusion as waves upon waves spilled over themselves and each other amidst a scattering of rocks.   On a day removed by a week from my visit to the lower falls, I stopped on the bridge below the upper ones, for a lunch of bananas and inspiration - the latter always the gift of such powerful perpetual motion.

Later I learnt that this was the bridge from which the murderers of Amin had hurled thousands to their deaths.   None could have survived.

But I'll talk of war (and the avoidance thereof) in the final chapters, when I've finished talking of the weaknesses of our peaces.   Once more in the game park, I came to Chobe Lodge, one of those very touristy places with a superb view over a stretch of river littered with little islands, forever making patterns of green white and blue - (a sensible choice of colours).   Again, because of the political situation, there were no tourists.   I did, however, bump into the anti-poaching pilot who, in the course of my one day visit, gave me a bath (my first since Tobruk), a sausage {my first for years, despite the

fact that they contain so much bread and stuff(ing) that they may
well be one of the purest vegetarian foods on the market},   and a
flight in his aircraft (my first since the time when, as they say
in the Irish parachuting club, I'd jumped out of a perfectly good
aeroplane).   He wanted to do an air drop to a patrol out in the
bush,   so he took the passenger door off and asked me to hang on
to the goodies.   This machine was certainly no boeing;   rather,
'twas the sort you get free with ten packet tops of what-nots:
hand-operated, hand-starting, handy.

We took off like a grasshopper.   Oh this was fun,   but I
decided not to congratulate him until after we'd landed   - I
didn't want to encourage him.   As it was, we were twisting and
turning all over the three dimensional place,   flying over the
tree tops,   watching the warthogs and gazelle flee from under us,
the centre of all this commotion in motion.   We flew over the
river,   up over this island,   down again,   in,   along, round that
one,   up and down and on and along over one of nature's best
movies, the Victoria Nile.

Back to work: there were the birds, picking at a carcase,
all that was left of the poacher's prize.   Too late.   And
yonder was the patrol: one wagon,   a tent or two and some maize
meal in the middle of the African bush.   One young Englishman
and half a dozen warders formed the patrol   - yes,   the
previously-considered-extinct species from the colonial era,   the
bwana, was still at large in East Africa.

At   the   lodge I met various officials of different
departments in the Ugandan administration: game park wardens,
district commissioners and police officers.   A bottle of beer
was my second of the year (not counting Tobruk where I lost
count, but I'll tell you about that soon enough) and a second was
my third.   We spoke of animal conservation in the comfort of
materialistic consumption.   I couldn't help feeling,   however,
that we will only really begin to save the elephant and the rhino
when we've learnt to use ALL of the world's finite resources
wisely.

The morning of my departure was pleasantly overcast, and in
such coolness, animals tend to be a little more active than later
in the day.   During the night, the hippopotamus had been up for
its night feed of grass.   They were very noisy eaters,   these
overgrown pigs, and my night had been disturbed by many a raucous
grunt.   The track was now littered with their droppings,   the
food of flies and butterflies.   Again,   many a warthog and
gazelle were spending every hour of their day eating;   and here
too was another buffalo herd,   quietly a'taking the tropical cud
on either side of the track.   I decided it would be politic to
wait.   Each one turned .... and slowly walked away;   oh every
body and thing was most cordial,   the monkeys a mongoose and me,
and thus I left the park with,   just to round things off,   a bit
of a bite from a tsetse.   Sure enough, the park appeared to be
devoid of elephant.

*   *   *

The modern form of wild-life sport, in which shooting is done only with the camera, is better by far than the days of yesteryear, when our parents went to kill and for the kudos of the kill. Have we grown up, or is such a past-time simply a preserve of the prosperous, and perhaps we just can't afford it anymore?

The last quarter of the twentieth century sees many an excessive concentration of wealth now in the Middle East. One particular day of those 25 years saw an excessive absence thereof riding his bicycle into the deserts of Algeria. Earlier in the day, I'd left the Atlas hills behind me, and the last signs of life had been that non-deserted industrial zone and a few lonely tents of the bedouin. I was soon surrounded by a seemingly unlimited horizontal horizon of sand. Just one more sign of life remained, one singular light in the darkening dusk of a moonless night. I left the road and headed for this solitary sign of life. And life indeed there was; not just one light, but a good dozen were fed by the power of a generator. A central canopy was surrounded by jeeps and lorries and marquees of every make and mark. The huge tents had full size doors and windows of canvas, and each pavilion was decorated with, as it were, canvas wallpaper in designs Arabesque. It all added up to a scene most suitable for some medieval Moslem pageant - yet here it was, in 1980.

- Welcome to the Saudi Arabian foreign minister's hunting party.

- Oh.

And welcome indeed they made me. The minister himself was not yet present; this was just a merry band of men preparing everything for him. Some were Saudi Arabians, as was to be expected; others were "Moslems of convenience", from Africa and Asia, for many had gone to Arabia to make money in a land where it flowed like water - wrong metaphor for the desert, but no matter. Around the fire we sat, eating Arabian dates and drinking Saudi coffee; what bitter stuff that was too, coming through the long curved spout stuffed with a filter of camel hair.

- What's that? I asked, pointing to a jeep with an enormous, well-padded, finely embroidered armchair still on the back of it.

- The minister's hunting car. Therein the armchair was obviously going to stay.

- And that? A container lorry with container attached.

- Oh, that's his air-conditioned bedroom. (For his pre-conditioned harem?)

Everything was there. So, just as the English, on safari in East Africa, had taken even a bath into the bush, the servants carrying the damn thing prior to filling and heating it ready for their white master and mistress (in reverse order, of course, not together; afterall, they were British), so now their Arabian successors went a'hunting in an equally ridiculous and extraordinary manner. The Algerian government actually forbade

its own nationals to hunt game;   more the pity that it had
another rule for the rich.   My own appeals for conservation were
met with the usual hypocrisy:
    - Oh but we only shoot the male gazelle.
    Amidst such magnificent hospitality, with food and drink
coming at me from every angle, I'm afraid I found it hard to
criticise.
    Sitting by the fire, his head resting under one of those
superb red and white tasselled head-dresses, his eyes deep set,
his nose finely pointed and his features firm and fixed - oh
these were Arabs of stature, most unlike their distant cousins of
the Maghreb - my Arabian host asked,
    - Tell me, why can't you Europeans entertain properly?
Always, you entertain only for as long as you, the hosts, want
to; never for as long as the guests desire.

                        *   *   *

    As you might have gathered, it is a European who is writing
and I'm again going to do what I want to do: to question the
whole business of tourism and to ask whether it is just another
commercial project more to do with pomp, prestige and pounds, and
rather less to do with progress.
    If you're clever and rich, (and perhaps you're not quite as
one as you are the other, for 'tis impossible to achieve the
superlative in both), then you might decide to go on holiday, to
Kenya, to Egypt and elsewhere.   You could then nip down to the
(American owned) travel agent to book a flight on the (American
owned) American built boeing, for a holiday in the
intercontinental hotel in Nairobi which, despite being thousands
of miles away, bears a remarkable resemblance to the hotel by the
same name in Cairo.... or even, at a guess, to the one in New
York!   Indeed, such are the achievements of the multi-national
hoteliers that it is now possible to go right round the world on
a grand luxury tour without seeing anything different except the
postcards.   For the more adventurous, of course, there are the
(American owned) safari cars outside the foyer, and you could be
driven to and conducted round the game parks, and even stay
there overnight, in the (American owned) game lodge. A pleasant
evening could be yours, drinking scotch, eating the very best
French and Italian cuisine, and taking photographs on your
Japanese camera of the African African African wildebeest.
    If you were still clever but not so rich, you could say you
were giving jobs to Africans;   drivers to drive you, waiters to
wait upon you, and porters for to carry your luggage. Yet most
of these people, to get that employment, have had to forsake
their African ways, to learn a European language and adopt
European habits.
    If you were still rich but not so clever, you could say
tourism was bringing foreign exchange into the country.   But

because so much of the business is foreign owned, much of that
money goes back from whence it came or, via the package tour
agreement signed in New York, it might never get to Africa in the
first place.   In the meantime, Kenya has had to import cars and
petrol, whisky and wines, caviar and cornflakes, just to cater
for the European taste.

        If you were still either, what you probably would not say
is that the very heavy influx of tourism forms a sort of semi-
colonialism;   that it deters from the creation of a homogenous
and self-reliant community .... rather, that it tempts the many
towards the excesses of materialism so prevalent among those
human migrants;   that it causes the economy of the capital city
to be far too orientated towards the visitor who is rich rather
than to the resident who is not; and that tourism is just one of
the reasons why Nairobi, still so high on the foothills of Mount
Kenya, is simply upside-down.   Before this tourist is accused
of hypocrisy - or am I already too late? - I'll change the
subject.

                    *   *   *

        The most excessively wasteful projects of the prestigious
variety are the most lethal.   Just as we in the industrialised
north are tempted to national pride, so too is the modern
African nation which has inherited our ways.   And just as we
spend pounds and pounds on arming this to defend that, so too the
states of Africa have thrown away fortunes on importing arms and
weapons systems with which to defend those most unAfrican lines
called borders, and with which to uphold existing state
structures no matter how decrepit or corrupt they are.   In fact,
the worse they become, the more such force is employed, and the
more is the profit of the European dealer in the arms trade.
But more of war in chapters four et sequitor.

        In the meantime, let us cast a glance at the log in our own
eye, the log of British rhubarb, the log that clogs the brain of
the Brit abroad.   In the UK, folk are English, Scottish and/or
Welsh.   Abroad, they all suddenly become British.   The word
is a figment - it really is time it faded.   Yet I am not
allowed to forget it; my passport is British, my embassy is
British, and everytime I fill in some piece of paper, I must tell
the world I am what I am not.

        It was a bit odd, to put it mildly, in a world where one
saw far too many people, especially students and others who
should have been more objective, almost worshipping their leader
Gaddafi, their President Moi or their King Hassan deux, one also
saw extreme nationalism among British export Britons.   There, on
the wall, was a picture of .... er .... oh yes, Elizabeth, Queen
Elizabeth, along with all the other relatives and corgis who
somehow qualified for a large slice of the British taxpayers'
budget.

To a certain extent, the habit of extolling one's leader was a reaction by many a third world citizen to the propaganda they'd been subjected to during so many years of colonial rule, which had said the white man was superior. Now, their country was independent; their country was going to stand up among the nations of the world; their country was an equal member of the world community of nations; therefore, their leader was as good as any other president or prime minister .... if not better. The English, who think they are so superior, go through exactly the same sort of rituals and thus prove they are not. But why do we all, be we nationalists, party political activists, ayatollah wallahs or pope fans, why do we always attach so much importance onto just one individual?

*   *   *

Every nation, be it in the first or third world, is tempted by projects prestigious. It is a facet which appears to link all races and, as a quick glance at Egypt would confirm, all ages. The pharaohs of old have been criticised for their obsession with death and with themselves. I think the criticism a little unfair.

First of all, we all tend to be children of our age, thinking as others of our era and not as those of previous times, and thus we find it easy to condemn our ancestors. Secondly, where's Buckingham palace? Thirdly, the human race is still building large structures "to the glory of God", though the cathedrals temples and mosques of to-day are less grand than those built for Him when God was a He called Amon. (God, I suspect, may not care very much for any of them, for 'tis better to love some one than some brick, and it's better to love the creations of God than those of ourselves. Only a primitive God would want glory, so perhaps, in time, humankind will outgrow this passion.) Lastly, the pharaohs gave us temples and tombs. What are we building? We are not obsessed with death; no; we're obsessed with life, our own lives, and to hell with those of others. We build blocks of little aesthetic value; we build nuclear power stations although we know they'll only last for a mere forty years and that then they'll have to be concreted up for generations, mausoleums not of mummies but of the daughter products of radioactive fission; we build everything for our own immediate consumption; and just in case someone disagrees with our way of doing things, we build bombs by the dozen which might mean the very death of the planet. Ramses or Reagan? Cheops or Chernenko?* Oh Amon, give me pharaohs any day!

A combination, then, of modern civilisation with the leaders of old could, in fact, be a more wholesome way of life

* ooops - Gorbachev.

than our present dangerous situation. Through the centuries, humankind has progressed, not least through the benefits of science and education. At the same time, however, the corruptions of power have tended to get worse. While we, the powerless, are less powerless than our forbears and more able, therefore, to exercise some degree of restraint on the powerful; they, the powerful, have become more and more powerful and so corrupted the more. Indeed, the evolution of our species would tend to indicate that in some respects to-day we are better, in others worse. Would it not be fair to suggest that those of us without an excess of power are progressing reasonably well, while those who lead are alas deteriorating badly? And thus, the very future of this planet is imperilled. If nowadays the leaders are sane, there's a chance; but just one George III, Hitler or Amin could cause the end of us all. Is the answer, perhaps, a world with no leaders; a world wherein there is no ultimate power, only ultimate responsibility?

*   *   *

Unfortunately, we're a long way from that at the moment; the world is still gripped by the powerful, governed by the nation state, geared for war. Where, pray, is all this leading us, the arms race, this process of centralisation, this craze for the prestigious, this thing called progress, this development of cities roads power-stations things and things always things? There must, obviously, be limits to our 'progress'; for the developing nations to follow blindly the policies of growth advocated by the industrialised north is at least not the best policy; and in the countries of Europe the limits are becoming more and more obvious each passing day:-
*   the unemployment which continues to rise in both boom and recession;
*   the pollution which one day will seek its revenge;
*   the mounting levels of (high grade) radioactive waste in the seas and oceans;
*   the destruction of the rain forests and the excessive use of the motor car leading to higher and higher levels of atmospheric carbon dioxide;
*   the exhaustion of mines and oil-wells; and
*   the southward march of the Sahel belt.
The problems are all man-made or man-exacerbated. They are all aspects of our current economic system, and they will all lead us to a crisis .... if we don't change .... which is what we'll have to do after the crisis anyway .... if anyone's still here.
A further reason why the world must change is simply because it is working under the system of economic growth and clearly, in a limited world, we can not go on growing for ever.

So even the advocates of growth should believe in change.   Alas, in the councils of Europe, in the state houses of Africa, and in the banks which connect the two, people are more interested not so much in the future but in the immediate short term and in a policy of economic national capitalism.   It is the latter which runs that education system to feed the policy of centralism which in turn consolidates the state.   Hence the regressive progress of urbanisation;   hence the mad race to the prestigious;   hence the armies of the state.   Oh the world is beset "by a thousand ills", but do they all stem from but one?

CHAPTER 4

ECONOMIC NONSENSE

This will be a fairly short chapter, for I would not wish to write a lot on nonsense. But just to ensure there is at least some sense in the words that follow, may I first talk of my own fiscal flirtations in Uganda?

Needless to say, in the aftermath of war, the economy was in a totally collapsed state. Whole sectors of it had ceased to function at all let alone properly, and inflation was the only item recording growth .... and rapid it was too. Everything there was not, but anything there was was both scarce and expensive. At the official exchange rate, a mug of tea was Ł1, a plate of rice and one small hunk of meat Ł3, a packet of twenty a fiver. Less than ten years earlier, a mug of chai had cost the equivalent of one penny.

Now my conscience at this stage was a little torn. Was it better to go to the banks and change my travellers' cheques at the official rate? Or should I operate on the black market which was higher by a factor of 10 or 12!? Well, I am in favour of the individual earning a living by the unexploited sweat of the unbowed brow; it is good for the soul, the mind, or whichever word your belief would prefer. The Ugandan or Ulsterman who plants and harvests her/his food deserves respectively her millet and his crispy crunchy nutty flakes. But they who make money by smuggling or speculating, betting or broking, theirs is not such a wholesome career.

Uganda had suffered an almost complete breakdown of its society. She would find it impossible to survive economically until, via a devaluation of the currency or suchlike, she stopped the smuggling. Prompted by entrepreneurmanship and/or selfishness, individuals were taking everything produced in Uganda over the border, to Kenya, Zaire or The Sudan, and there they were getting in effect ten times the official rate, or 1,000% profit! In a country that was starving, people were even smuggling out food! Market forces in a market collapsed!

Well, having written all that, it's as well that I chose to opt for the official exchange rate and to leave the blackblackmarket well alone. So, when I got to Arua, I went to the bank. Behind their desks, young men in smart clothes sat smoking and drinking tea; what contrast with the little farmsteads I'd passed and stayed in on the way. Over the counter went Ł100 sterling, and back came 1,600 Ugandan shillings; the official exchange rate had not changed since 1972 when Amin had come to power. (In the back streets of town, I would have got up to 20,000 shillings!) As a result, then, of my being a bit of an idiot, Uganda's holdings of foreign exchange had gone up. And that was a good thing. The UK's reserves had gone down, and that too was a good thing, for it was and still is one of the world's richest countries. But who had really gained? Was it the Ugandan peasant? Or was it the bank clerk? Was it the country? Or was the bank some subsidiary of some multi-national so that whatever gain there might have been, went straight back to the West from whence it came? I didn't know. I gave up, and went to have a cup of tea instead. One pound please.

Wouldn't it be nice if money couldn't earn money, if only people could earn the stuff? If the world operated according to Islamic principles such that money could never earn interest, such that banks could never charge or pay interest on overdraft or deposit, then I reckon inflation would be almost defeated, at a stroke. Or, if the world operated according to ancient Jewish codes under which all profits were re-distributed at the end of every fifty year season, life would be more than tolerable. Or indeed, if civilisation was Christian, and all soldest what they hadest and gavest to the poorest, then again life would be quite pleasant. Unfortunately, all too often, the Christian misses out that bit and quotes instead the parable of the (fiscal) talents.

*   *   *

Right; let us now have a look at economic nonsense.

Planting trees is uneconomic. Planting trees may be natural and sensible; it may be far-sighted and wise; it may be all sorts of adjectives from Roget's thesaurus; but it's just damn well not economic - that is the logic of our system of finance. In the words of the economist: "due to the absence of returns on capital costs in the short and medium term, interest charges on capital expenditure are unlikely to be offset by long term income." If, therefore, you want to make a quick buck, don't put your dollars into poplars.

A young tree, sitting in the dried up river bed, can prevent soil erosion come the rains, it can re-convert the oxides of carbon once more into oxygen, it can aesthetically enhance the desertscape, yet it can generate no income whatsoever. But it could earn a penny or two if it was cut down and sold for firewood!

Another example could be this: a lot of oil, sitting doing nothing in the North Sea or the Sahara desert can only earn money via speculation and change of ownership (though, as we discussed earlier, the 'right' of any one person or group of persons to own a natural resource exists only in the minds of those involved). Leaving much of that oil, therefore, in reserve for future generations, who have just as much right to the stuff as us lot, would be utterly sensible .... and downright uneconomic! For to extract it, exploit it, export it and exhaust it all is, apparently, good for the economy. Up go production figures and, after some good advertising and/or government promotion to boost demand, up go sales and so too do the profits. Everyone who thinks on a short-term time-scale will then be happy; the business managers, the financial experts, the shareholders, the workers perhaps and the government, oh most certainly, for it will mean direct benefits in the form of company taxation and VAT, and indirect ones like increased levels of employment, better trade figures .... and more votes!

In the **shambas** of the tropics, on the banks of the Nile, and on the desert plains, where folk with little resource to or use of money struggle to survive, many are the instances which in the eyes of the fiscal are financially unsound. Their ways of life are, of course, far from perfect and far too close to poverty; can I first dash backwards and forwards across the continent to describe what I saw, and then we'll return to the economists and their logic.

* * *

High high in the Atlas mountains, deep in the wildest winter on the wide and wind-swept plateaus, there lived a bedouin peasant. Only the lone nomad said this was no no-man's land; it was a quiet part of the world, with little to view and less to comfort. There was I and there was he and there was the horizon - such was the scene. After a good eight weeks in the Maghreb, I was now able to speak more than a few words of Arabic; and this Algerian nomad, uneducated perhaps, illiterate certainly, seemed to understand my Belfast dialect of the local tongue and he bid me welcome.

Intent on tea

Home consisted of two tents, one for himself, and one for the missus and kids. Each was made of the most thick and heavy wool, especially strengthened by strips of extra material for those parts which rested on the wooden supports. The edges were tied down, fairly close to the ground, by large wooden pegs, and loose straw was placed around to stop the breezes. Inside the tent, tall enough only if you were sitting down, lay the wool to wool wool carpets and rugs. There we sat, he crossed legged for hours, me cross legged for minutes .... until my knees started aching. A little fire was prepared and food was cooked. And I really quite impressed myself and no-one else when I was actually able to read the Arabic writing on his packet of sugar; not bad at all really. For this most pleasant shepherd, that packet was one of the few contacts with the great big outside world .... beyond the great big plateau. When the time came for bed, the two of us just covered ourselves up in blankets and rugs and he then kicked away the two supports so that the entrance part of the tent also lay close to the ground.

His property was minimal: a herd of goats and sheep, about 40 head, was his running source of income. Two horses provided the transport for when the time came to move to greener, or less yellow, parts. And three fierce dogs provided protection from the beasts of the night, whatever they might have been. That was virtually the lot; a few carpets and rugs with which to keep warm and a few utensils with which to cook. Life's pleasures were few. One goat sold equalled much sugar and mint and grain, and thus the family survived. The big problem was that such survival was tenuous; the slightest tragedy or illness could have spelt disaster; that commodity so common to our western way of life, security, is rarely found in third world countries - hence their high birth rates.

Under such conditions, where resort to the resources of the state could well lead to no benefits no help and nothing, a belief in a God is perhaps a wise investment; the constant worry was that God and/or nature would not provide that which It/she had provided previously. Those of us who live in the West, where food is always plentiful (even if we've had to import it from the third world to get it), tend to think that natural disasters occur in the poorer countries of the world - droughts, floods, earthquakes and hurricanes - and that whatever God might try and do in Europe will be financially compensated for. All you need, therefore, having acquired or inherited a fair measure of property, is a suitable life savings scheme. The conclusion would seem to suggest that either you believe in a deity or you believe in an insurance policy; you may, perhaps, believe in neither .... but you cannot, surely, believe in both.

*   *   *

I believe ....'tis time to recall a simple scene. Tunisia, on the outskirts of the capital: one middle aged man held on a lead what was probably fifty per cent and more of his fixed-cum-movable assets, one cow, and this he grazed by the roadside, and that was his occupation all day. What joy there was when the cow did calf; the joy was celebrated, and the kous-kous of supper was dressed in the resulting liquid asset, milk.

*   *   *

Still in the Maghreb, I return to Morocco. In the steep and rocky foothills of the Atlas, arable land was hard to find. Where the stones were too many, the olive did grow in olive groves as too did the almond and other nuts. Where it was a little clearer, even on the steepest incline, the land was ploughed and cereal was grown.

In the absolute quiet of a sunful dawn when not a breath of air did rustle even the lightest leaf, the oft repeated cry of a farmer exhorting his mule to pull the plough did carry and rebound tofrom the valley beyond. To replace the mule by the tractor would in theory be economic .... but on these steep slopes, happily impossible. The farmer may continue his music; not yet and not ever will it be drowned by the diesel, high-frequency-farting.

*   *   *

At the time, I thought the road I travelled was the worst in the world, for it was little more than a linear collection of stones and rocks in an otherwise random setting thereof; it really was suitable only for something with independent suspension on all four, something .... like a donkey. Two days later, while still in the southern Atlas of Morocco, I decided that this had not been the worst road in the world.

What was only the second worst road in the world led to a somewhat isolated cobalt mine. All around was barren and bare; all inside the home was still a little bit basic, for the manual workers had been given only the simplest accommodation, though all the basic necessities of life were available. For the mine to be mined and for the miners for to mine, a number of essentials had been imported, the most important of which was, of course, water. For kilometres and miles, a huge pipe went up and down, along and around, following the contorted contours wherever they went, to carry the precious liquid from somewhere to here. It was, obviously, economic so to do, and the cobalt covered the cost. But to carry water only for people, for plants, for trees .... ?

In similar vein, the deserts of Algeria and Libya were littered by the sparkling aluminium of tubes, tubes that twinkled in the sun, tubes and tubes that twisted and turned their tortuous route to the whateveritwas that began with a 't', in the sea, ah the terminal.   To transport one liquid this a'way was, they did say, a wise use of resources, a sound investment and other clichés.   To transport a different liquid that a'way, from the de-salination plant out into the desert to the young sibling plant as part of the re-afforestation programme was just one of them - uneconomic.   Oil could go one way, OK, but water could not come the other.   To consume in the present is, while to invest in the future is not, apparently, economic.

While on the subject of oil, perhaps it is worth comparing two liquids in Europe.   One of them, oil, is sought after, drilled for, piped in, pumped ashore, refined up, blended with, distributed away and sold out, often with the most expensive devices like off-shore rigs and super-tankers and oil refineries and special business accountants to work out how best to reduce the companies' tax bills.   And this thick black oil, once it's been reduced into petrol, is at the time of writing and has been on and off for a number of years, almost exactly the same price as a different liquid which comes from that other remarkable machine called a cow: petrol, £1.80 a gallon, and milk, 23p a pint. The price of each depends oh of course of course on economic considerations .... whatever they are.

I called in to see an oil refinery one day, a huge complex on the Libyan Mediterranean coast, and therein worked over twenty two different nationalities, each of them living in mono-linguistic villages of monolithic portacabins of monotonous plastic - and only the British and the Irish liked each other, while everyone else kept to their own.   The Libyans enjoyed the spoils of the oils, but they imported others to do all the work.

And in they came, for the money.   The Americans and western Europeans worked something like this: 28 days on, 28 off, all accommodation and food on site free, all leave on full pay, all flights to and from home paid for, and salaries paid in any currency into any bank account in any country of their choice.   Sounds all right, doesn't it?   Must be quite nice to work in a socialist state.   For such conditions of work, even you might be prepared to go into the desert for a whole four weeks without the pleasures of a daily dallas.   So much for the revolution.   A small few got the benefits of capital intensive technology, while others worldwide remained unemployed.

Almost every Libyan job, or so it appeared, was done by the expatriate.   The East Europeans - believe it or not, Libya had hired a brigade of Bulgarians (atheists) to build a mosque! - tended to live a rather segregated existence, barricading themselves into work camps of communist conformity just as soon as the work bell tolled.   The Japanese contractors worked and worked and worked building anything anywhere until the job was done;   only then did they collect their huge pay packets and go

home for a quick week-end before the next assignment.   Despite
the Libyan/Egyptian breach in diplomatic relations and the closed
border,   the educated Egyptian was still allowed to come and
teach,   as long as he came via Greece!   And the Tunisians and
the Turks were at the bottom end of the wages scale,   running the
cafés and restaurants with the superb foods of their   native
lands - those Tunisian sandwiches of fish and egg and vegetable
and an olive were my cold favourites.   The only Libyans I saw
working, apart from many a farmer, were either policemen or
border guards or soldiers or officers of the special branch.
Oh and a few bureaucrats.   Only by the importation of foreign
peoplepower was Libya, a land of but two million or so, able to
maintain a vast armed presence.   The economies of multi-
national companies I blame for many ills;   but only in Libya do I
blame them in part for the militancy of their host government.

                        *   *   *

      In just as long as it takes to write in just as long as it
takes, I takes you back to war weary and worn out Uganda.   Where
poverty was widespread .... where self-sufficiency was   survival
and where not all were successful, nor in the circumstances could
they be .... and the poorest suffered, as always, the most.   A
lonely **shamba**, some maize, some bananas, a goat, a chicken, some
nuts;   life was hard.   There was no way to earn money and
therefore none to spend; with the shirt of one old boy, my host,
there was literally more of what there was not, and less of what
there was.   If to live without hope is merely to exist, then his
indeed was simply an existence.   Yet how much worse off would
he have been if he had not had that patch of land?   And what was
the fate of his cousins in the slums of Kampala?

                        *   *   *

      My   last example of a way of life,   typical only in certain
parts of the world,   demands the European reader's imagination to
travel only as far as the back door.   For beyond it, perhaps,
lies a little vegetable patch, where the occupier can plant a
parsnip and reap a reward.
      Now, after all that, let us look at life with fiscal logic,
at the Moroccan peasant, the Ugandan farmer, the Algerian nomad
and the European pensioner, all a'quietly cultivating the cactus,
crushing the cassava, cuddling the kid and collecting the
cabbages.   In so doing, they are all helping to increase their
own standards of living.   As a result of their labours, the
world will be a better place.   Yet the national measurement of
betterment, those tools of the economists called gross national
products and gross domestic products, will not measure these

improvements because no money was involved.   GNP is measured in moneyed terms,   so it is incapable of recording an improvement if such has not involved financial transactions.   If, however, the cactus the cassava the kid and the cabbages were grown by somebodies   elses,   specialists   -   folk   educated   in   a compartmentalised academic system, with 'O' levels and an 'A', and with bits of paper to prove it - and if these people then sold to the peasant,   the farmer,   the bedouin and the pensioner, then   a   change would indeed be recorded,   even though the four concerned would be worse off as a result.

Take   another example.   Think of the Arab who travels to and from market by donkey,   and of the European who commutes   by car   to   the desk in the city.   In   the   correct   environment, donkeys   cost   little and pollute not a lot,   and even then   only naturally   so.   Yet the measure of standard of living has   no means by which it can record the use of this fixed asset,   nor of its   replacement   by the new '85 model.   In using   the   merc, however,   the European executive or the third world   government minister affects the situation drastically.   The car is purchased,   petrol is bought,   insurance policies are taken   out, government taxes are collected,   police officers are employed and the nation,   according to the economist, is a happier place. Fewer   finite resources will be available for future generations; more lead fumes will be likely to affect the brain development of children and more oxides of carbon will be present in the atmosphere to accelerate the southward march of the Sahara.   But the GNP will say the life of the nation has taken a turn for   the better.

Now,   drive faster and think harder   -   take a turn for   the worser -   have a disaster.   Crash!   An accident could mean another car will have to be built,   another   lamppost installed, another   coffin   buried,   another ambulance serviced,   another investigation   policed   and   another   court   case   judged. More resoures will be gobbled up.   Money will be spent in many directions   at   once and,   while we weep o'er   your   grave,   rest assured,   the GNP will be recording yet another healthy upturn in the economy!

To be fair,   it does also go up if a new school is opened or a new house built and so on.   It does not go up,   however,   if the Ugandan refugee flees to neighbouring Sudan and,   from indigenous resources of mud and straw,   builds a new **shamba**;   it does not go up if the bedouin nomads,   from the wool of their own sheep,   make a new collapsible home;   forever,   it can never go up or down if people act self-sufficiently.   The economic thermometers,   by their own definitions, are totally incapable of recording many of the economic activities which take place in the self-reliant sector of the economy.

*   *   *

It would seem, then, that the system of economics currently in use is actually incapable of measuring that which we want to achieve; and indeed, it may even suggest we want what we don't. There are those who will disagree with the above arguments which have been expressed in many a paper elsewhere, and some of them might be economists; but they, like so many others, are specialists, educated and qualified of course, and utterly dependent on the system of which they are a part.

Let us return to that lonely farmer, 'oarsely ex'orting 'is 'orse on the slopes of the Atlas mountains. It could be said that the present methods of farming, in which small holdings are tended by individual families, will be unable to provide the agricultural infrastructure necessary for the development of the industrial base. On the plains, the machinery associated with high production techniques could be, and was being, introduced. Thereby, one person could produce more than was necessary for one family; thus could others leave the work in the fields for a different career, on the factory floor 'creating wealth' or in the city feeding from it. Such economic forces tend to infer that the small-holder hill-farmer will never be able to acquire the material trappings of the blue-jeleba worker on the plains. So it is that, in a world of hunger, fiscal factors are saying certain lands are untenable; in the rocky valleys of the Atlas, where olive and almond trees grow, current economic forces do not fit. Just as here at home, where these same economic forces have been allowed to predominate, there has been an exodus over the years from the Western Isles; so too in Africa a similar effect could cause depopulation of the more remote and barren areas, and yet more problems in the shanties of the cities.

In the not so flat or fertile lands both here and abroad, the economist is often wrong. He/she was not a little wrong, as well, in the granaries of Ouzoud and Marakech. Again, in the wide open desert, the Sahara, the land that once, many years ago, had been a forest, the land that, to-day, could be a forest, the financier has got it wrong and for two reasons: one, he is not planting trees; and two, while the land is dead, the horizon is littered with derricks from which he burns 'excess' gas - because in a world of limited resources but not yet, it would be uneconomic, he says, to collect it.

The first reason concerns not so much the industrial, more the natural plant. As we saw above, planting trees may be sound and sensible, it might help to restore both the local and the continental ecology, it might ensure the well being of generations as yet unborn, but it just happens to be uneconomic. In the more right-wing countries of Tunisia and Morocco, there were very few attempts at re-afforestation; indeed, in places, they were cutting them down at a frightening rate, and all those avenues of eucalyptus planted by the French because they were so très très français were fast disappearing .... and the only things being planted, in lines from here to everywhere, were telegraph poles. Only in Algeria and Libya, where not only

financial   factors   governed   government   thinking,   much   tree
planting   was   taking   place ....   and the world was   not   without
hope.

Where the multi-nationals held sway, the trees did not, and
only   the metallic derricks reached for the cloudless sky.   It
was   not   the roots of trees which   silently sought   the   elusive
moistures of the sands,   damp just a little from the dew of dawn;
rather,   it was the drills of diamond which were thrust downwards
in   their   search for what would become the bank account   in   the
Bahamas   and the barbeque in Bermuda.   Once all this expensive
machinery   had been installed,   the economist would recommend   it
should be worked 24 hours a day   so as to more easily off-set the
interest charges on the capital costs involved.   He would advise
the   maximum extraction rate in the hope of increased sales;   and
he would infer that levels of consumption should increase.   What
the oil is used for matters not to the economist;   but that it is
bought   and   sold   is all that   is   financially   important.   If
production is 90% capacity and if the national demand is for just
a little bit more, the board will be content.

'Tis just the same at home;   the UK is currently extracting
oil   from   the North Sea at such a rate that the   entire   reserve
will be depleted within the space of two generations.   Now that
is   just   downright   immoral ....   but it's   very   good   for   the
economy!

In not planting trees,   in not conserving resources for our
children's children, in extracting those reserves   as fast as the
demand will allow for,   and in building huge motorways for   their
gross   gross products,   the economists are doing damn all for the
poorest   of   the poor who barely come into the   economic   picture
anyway, and they are doing only harm to the future of us all.

Economics,   as   practised,   are primarily interested in the
short   term;   the   future   is merely   of   secondary   importance.
Therefore, the survival of this planet may indeed need a complete
restructuring   of our economic systems,   and not only because   of
all the above.   But consider   this: just   as   an   economy   can
'improve'   by cutting down too many trees,   by killing   too   many
elephants, and even as the result of a motor accident,   so too it
can enjoy a veritable boom ....   if there's a war!

It is sad to see that while economic considerations seem to
dominate   in a way   that they should not, so   much   of   so   many
nations' political decision making,   they do not have any   weight
at   all in the one field where they damn well should   -   defence!
Railways and shipyards have to be viable;   schools and hospitals
have to be cost-effctive;   but aircraft carriers and atom bombs?

War   may be good for business,   military   expenditures   are
easier   on   the conscience not least via the use of   that   'nice'
word "defence", and the export of arms is one of the world's most
lucrative   trades.   In countries throughout the world, north and
south,   east and west, huge sums of money are being diverted away
from the needs of the poor .... into preparations for war.

As   per the current definitions of what is and what is   not economic, it is seen that certain sensible activities are not, while senseless and even suicidal ones damn well are - in the short or most immediate term only.   Our present methods of recording the economy are just totally incapable of measuring a totally self-reliant one; they constitute, therefore, one of the obstacles to be overcome before a move towards even partial self-reliance can be started.   In opposing self-reliance, the system promotes both itself and centralisation, as each of us is made utterly dependent for 99% of everything on others, i.e. the system. And the system is both promoted and perpetuated by its products, the specialists, the economists.

A change in the way we define 'standard of living' and the way we equate that with happiness are perhaps two of the greatest requirements of the future generations who, as yet, have neither voice nor vote in the debating chambers of to-day, yet they must surely have a right to the world they will inherit .... perhaps.

War will be avoided, not only if we ban the bomb, not only if we dismantle the super-power-nation-states, but also if we change the very laws of economics which so encourage that process of centralisation which causes them to exist.

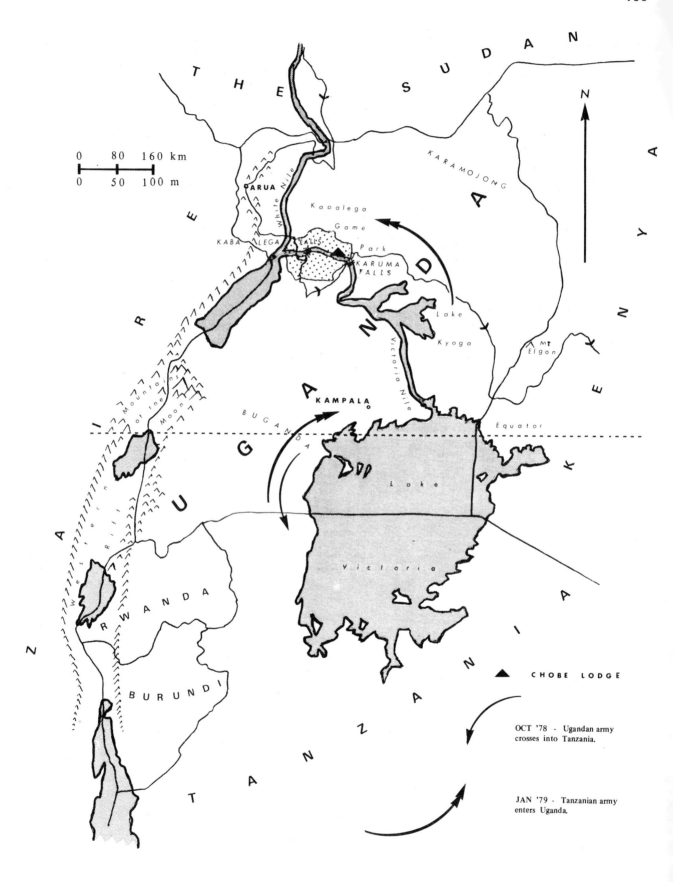

0   80   160 km
0   50   100 m

THE SUDAN

KARAMOJONG

K E N Y A

N

ARUA

Kabalega

Game

Park

KABALEGA FALLS

KARUMA FALLS

White Nile

U G A N D A

Victoria Nile

Lake Kyoga

Mt Elgon

Mountains of the Moon

BUGANDA

KAMPALA

Equator

Z A I R E

Western Rift

Lake Victoria

R W A N D A

BURUNDI

T A N Z A N I A

▲ CHOBE LODGE

OCT '78 - Ugandan army crosses into Tanzania.

JAN '79 - Tanzanian army enters Uganda.

CHAPTER 5

A BIT OF PEACE

- I want peace, said one Egyptian, but I hate the Jews.

Is the cause of war the mismanagement of peace, for has not every peace the world has ever known sooner or later collapsed into war? Yet if the present 'peace' fails, the result could be world war III, and that could well mean the end of all life on this planet. While conflict may perhaps be inevitable, armed conflict need not be so; indeed, in this nuclear age, it must not be so.

Well, the peace of the world was and is in a desperate state. My own little meanderings saw many a military aspect; and no look at a patient is worthwhile unless it offers either consolation or advice as to a cure. May I start, therefore, with a little theorising before once again leading you to where I led myself, adrift astray and under arrest amongst the armies of Africa.

*   *   *

The premier or president of a nation is, as often as not, interested in maintaining usually his and only sometimes her position of supreme power. To do this, he/she will have to woo an electorate or placate a politbureau or whatever, for rulers can only rule for as long as the ruled so tolerate. If the retention of power is important, then it will always be the most immediate short term which will matter the most, and most policies will be orientated thereto. In Europe, all political thinking is usually based in terms of the next general election, but communist and emerging countries also work on the short term, on five year plans and such like.

Well, if policies are so geared to the present, they are ipso facto not good for the future. In the old days of here, and still in these days of there in the third world, those country people who were and are not gripped by the claws of poverty, tended and tend to plan for their succeeding generations. But nowadays, and especially in the cities, the inter-relationships between the generations have weakened, and the short term interest predominates, especially in those democracies where politicians woo the more selfish instincts of the electorate. Democracy, therefore, as presently practiced, this primitive centralised two-party majority-rule stuff, is ecologically unsound; and there is a certain logic, perhaps, in

the one-party states of Africa.   Indeed, seeing as democracies
are more tied to the immediate short term than are dictatorships,
it   could   even   be said that the survival of the species   is   more
threatened   by the former than the latter;   wow,   that's   saying
something and a half, so the other half I'll say on page (145).
          Should we go further? In concluding that our democracy is
tied-in with the concept of the nation-state,   that democracy is
governed by factors economic, and that economics, as   currently
defined,   are   bad if not downright dangerous,   do   we   therefore
decide   that   the   world would be a much better place if we no
longer   divided oursleves into nations?   It could be that   the
world   would   suffer   less if more people had more   control   over
their   own affairs;   if power were devolved back to   the   people
from whence it came;   if power, then, was no longer concentrated
in the hands of a few;   if competition, if exist it must, was not
seen   always   in a nation-versus-nation context;   and if,   when
nations do conflict,   some form of international or supranational
arbitration was possible.   In a word, the world could well be a
better   place if we diverge in the dispersal of power but if at
the   same time we converge in accepting ultimate   responsibility.
Let us now,   then, view just some of the nations of Africa, those
political   states   which,   almost   as   a   consequence   of   their
existence, have become states of war.
          Algeria   was   fighting   Morocco,   Egypt had   fought   Libya,
Uganda   had   suffered   a civil war and so   too   had   The   Sudan,
Tunisia   and   Libya were in confrontation,   Kenya was cued for   a
coup,   (Europe has been designated as the theatre of conflict for
the   third   - and last - world war) and I live   in   Belfast.
Well, I'll start with the worst of 'em:

                          *   *   *

     - Uganda?   You can't go there!   Amin only deposed after
their   civil   war two years ago.   The country torn by   tribal
division,   riddled by lawlessness,   covered in road-blocks   and
tormented by poverty and hunger.   Thus spake the Sudanese, the
Kenyan and the European,   all of whom were resting in the one and
only   doss-house in Juba.   (And therein too I also passed   the
time, doing nothing in a town where there was nowt to do,   slowly
recovering   from the diarrhoea of the cow-pee, with occasional
walks into town .... and frequent runs to the loo!)
          The Ugandan,   however,   said welcome .... until the Sudanese
authorities   arrested him for no reason,   imprisoned him without
charge or explanation,   and deported him at gunpoint.   It   was
often more   difficult for Africans to travel their own continent.
          Well,   I   listened to the news.   There had just been the
military   coup of May 1980 which had caused the third change of
government   since Amin.   Life was obviously most   unsettled.
But   I   thought,   just as life in Belfast is not half as bad   as
outsiders   imagine,   so too did I feel that all the press reports

were, of course, reporting the bad side of Ugandan life and not the good.   The parallel with Belfast went further: just as a sectarian murder gets so much more coverage than a killing motivated by lust or greed, so also the political killings in Uganda were getting far more publicity than the pitiful and painful deaths through starvation up in Karamoja.

Even before the border, there were many signs of the sadness that had hit this land, this so-called pearl of Africa. The occasional Sudanese villages were outnumbered by many a Ugandan settlement, readily recognisable by two factors: their **shambas** were highly productive, with many a plant prospering while only a few goats rummaged for morsels amongst them;   and the Ugandan women boasted the most colourful brassières.   These Ugandan families were all refugees.   Africa has thousands.

From '65 to '72, the Sudanese fled south across this border, seeking refuge from their civil war.   From '72 to '80, others fled north, escaping from the ravages of Amin, and in the last couple of years from the excesses of Obote.   Now, in '84, the Sudanese conflict is starting again!   Looking at the situation in a broader context, Uganda has recieved refugees from The Sudan, Zaire and Rwanda Burundi .... while refugees from Uganda itself have sought shelter there and elsewhere.   There is no peace for the poor.

Uganda, at first, was desolate.   Villages lay empty, the huts that had been homes were wrecked.   Life had left. Further inland, of course, such an escape from the brutalities of Amin's armies had not been so easy for those with few possessions and next to no money.   The first border town was a good thirty kilometres from the frontier, and here were the first signs of the recent fighting.   The story was repeated all over the place: some homes survived, but public and commercial buildings like police stations and garages were left wrecked.   As always, the human victims of conflicts were buried, but the material ones were left, bleeding.   Just like Belfast.

Under Amin's racialist policies, most Asians and many Europeans had been deported, and this and other factors had caused the economy to just collapse.   The resulting inflation and chronic shortages in almost every commodity had, as always, wrecked most havoc amongst the poor.   We have already discussed those desolate shops, devoid of stores save for a box of this and a packet of that.   Some people were wearing rags because for eight years they had not been able to afford more clothes.   But yet .... jambo, karibu .... so warm was their greeting.   The humanity of people in adversity is amazing.   Again, just like Belfast.

Since leaving Juba, the huts had been changing slowly in design.   (And like so many others in Africa, the Sudanese/Ugandan border bore no relationship to the tribal make-up of the area.   A cousin of the same tribe could easily be a citizen of a different nation.)   At first, the round mud sides were topped with a thatch that extended way beyond the walls to form a verandah supported on wooden poles. Where gradual development had been in progress, the walls were now being made of brick. Further south, the homes became squarer, the thatch still extending way over the edges in order to keep the seasonal but torrential rains well away from the mud walls. These were often coloured with earth dyes, both inside and out. Meanwhile, the waters pouring off the roof formed little streams of mud around the house; as the years went by, so much of the soil was washed away to The Sudd and Aswan, and thus each house stood on relatively higher and higher ground.

The Shamba

Signs of pre-Amin were everywhere; in some shambas, the main house was definitely rectangular, its roof of corrugated iron. Behind stood the more traditional hut, the kitchen and the tiny little granaries - little hollow cylinders of mud on raised platforms, one for the maize seed, another for groundnuts. Entry to these larders was made by lifting the 'Chinese hat' of thatch and in you climbed. The few homes with many granaries had had a good harvest.

I spent one night in a mission; it was sad to hear of their lives during the years of Amin. But it was good to see a (mission) school that actually believed agriculture should be part of the syllabus, (and not only because one way of getting to know God is by getting close to Its earth). It is of course easy to criticise the missionary, the way so many Africans suddenly acquired the name Patrick; the way Christ was, or had been, depicted as a white man; the way English aspects of Anglicanism had been exported lock stock and barrel amen; the way Christianity had been so closely associated with the colonial powers, their imperialism and materialism; the way missionaries on the whole continued to enjoy a standard of living far higher than that of their flock; and the way they lived a very European way of life, eating European foods and so forth. But, looking at Uganda, there wasn't anything better. All the businessfolk and others who could speak so altruistically about job creation and world development and so on .... oh, they had all disappeared long ago, claiming expenses as they went. Not that I blame 'em for leaving. At least some missionaries had stuck it out, and not all of them had survived. Of those who had died, some perhaps had defended the faith; but others had died defending property, the mission car for example. If the missionaries had been as poor as the people they'd ministered to, such deaths as did occur might never have happened. Now, should the missionaries have been more outspoken in getting rid of Amin? Could an institution as conservative and established as the church have been the advocate of reform?

*   *   *

In the years immediately after independence, Uganda had been ruled by a sort of dual system (of power sharing) under which Obote, a son of the tribes near Lake Kyoga, had co-operated with the Kabaka, the king of Buganda in the south west of the country. The system had been under strain from the start, not least because the Bugandans were Bantu peoples, well settled folk who had long since cultivated the arable foothills of the western rift; while those in the north east lived in a dry and parched land, they were Nilotic nomads who dug for water in the sands of dried up river beds and who scratched a living from their goats and cattle. The extremes were total. Uganda, in theory, was one country; in practice, it was a mixture of peoples more different than those of Ulster and Austria. The colonial 'settlement', then, could only have lasted for so long. In 1966 Obote sent his army under the command of a certain Idi Amin into Buganda; many died, the Kabaka went into exile, and Obote assumed total power. It was a bloody act, made no less bloody by the bloodier acts of his successor, and its bloody repercussions are still being felt to this day.

Obote in his turn was deposed by the same Amin, an ex-sergeant, British trained, from a tribe in the north-west near Arua.   There was a certain logic in his evil thinking, and just as the seeds of fascism were laid in Hitler's head during the first world war, so the source of Amin's hatred of so much lay in his background: a Uganda under British rule, an Africa of small consequence in the corridors of world politics.   His racism deteriorated into tribalism, his fanaticism into violence, and this last reached epidemic proportions.   Too, too many died. Ugandans most immediately, and the citizens of the world only less so, were confronted by a major problem.

*   *   *

I pause.   There are some thoughts which rack my brain. The removal from power of the perpetrator of violence is the most serious challenge anyone could face;   that perpetrator could be illegal or legal - he could be the paramilitary who intimidates and kills, he could be the bloody dictator who creates internal strife, or he could be the democratically elected ruler who threatens the very annihilation of this planet.   To the pacifist, such evils cause almost insurmountable problems. Only almost.
Perhaps, then, it would be easier to consider the simpler situation first.   If A beats up B in my presence, I am morally bound to do something.   If I do nothing, I aid and abet A.   The pacifist must, therefore, intervene.   To not do so - in other words, to do nothing - is to be violent.   If I intervene with no force, then B may escape unharmed.   Minimum force, in a one to one conflict, need not involve killing, but it could mean being killed; under such circumstances, those of us who are not exactly saints could be forgiven for deploying and employing guns, shooting only to maim.   (Don't worry, we're just at the theoretical stage at the moment; in practice, guns are too risky .... and in pacifism, unnecessary.)   But could, in theory only, the application of minimum force involve killing?
Well why is it that whenever good people try to kill bad, on a rather different one to one basis, when the pacifist directly seeks confrontation with the baddy, why do they often fail?   Twenty times they tried to kill Amin - damn it, one grenade actually bounced off the brute - yet all attempts ended in failure.   They tried to kill Hitler too, but again, in vain. But when a different they tried to kill the good Mahatma Gandhi or Martin Luther King for example, they succeeded, and often at the first attempt.   When the good try to achieve good by means bad, they fail; but when the bad try to achieve bad by bad means, they do indeed succeed.   Fate would appear to have a certain logic; and the positive good may only be achieved by the means positive .... which might still involve the use of force.

In the more serious cases of conflict, where numbers confront numbers, what is required of the pacifist is less obvious. Some sort of holding ground policy in the "no-man's land" area is possibly the best, but it is difficult to generalise. Nevertheless, such a ploy I would advocate in the event of a riot, a shoot out or even a war. As long as those who don't know what to do keep out of the way; and as long as those who do, actually get in the way ....

*   *   *

The situation in Uganda, then, was more than serious. The bloody Amin was assisted in his bloody tyranny - as Gandhi said, no tyrant can exist in isolation - by his bloody army of bloody soldiers and bloody civil servants. If the principle of minimum force was to be able to succeed against him on a one to one basis, killing might not have been necessary. But if such a principle was to be followed in a crowd-versus-crowd or in a nation-versus-nation (army-versus-army) scenario, then some killing would be almost inevitable. At least such killing as there had to be, could be, as it were, under a code of minimum force chivalry. To fight a war under such pacifist instincts is not a total contradiction in terms; the old chivalry of war demanded the rescuing of survivors from the ship now sunk and the feeding of prisoners now captured. (Only nuclear war is unable to follow any civilised codes of uncivilised behaviour.)

What, then, was the world to do, given the desperate situation which everyone suspected of evil in '72, which everyone knew was evil by '75. The former colonial power had not only helped to organise the political structures for a post-independent Uganda, it had also been instrumental in drawing up the borders of that country in the first place. Britain, therefore, was responsible at least in part for the sadness that had followed its departure. Yet the British showed minimal interest; they did eventually break off diplomatic relations in '76, but they continued to supply Amin with arms and whisky, for .... economic reasons. The other countries of Europe cared little, while even the Organisation of African Unity did nothing.

And the missionaries, in the main, also did nought; they continued to do their daily tasks of course, but they did not mess around in politics which is how they say they did not criticise the state. Even when murder and mayhem were the norm, they took very little direct action. Two or three spoke out and, as a result, one or two died; but, if I may generalise, they tried to steer clear of stormy waters .... even in the hurricane!

Only Tanzania didn't do nothing. For years, Nyerere was virtually alone in his outspoken criticism; he lost friends, he gained enemies, but he stuck to his principles. He sheltered the now exiled ex-bloody Obote, and he bided his time.

In '73, the world would not have tolerated a Tanzanian invasion of Uganda.   Six years later, Amin actually sent his army over the southern border and this gave Nyerere every excuse for what, at least in its initial stages, approximated to the minimum use of retaliatory force.   He persisted both on the diplomatic and military fronts, his forces were joined by ever increasing numbers of Ugandan soldiers, and Kampala was soon liberated.   Mopping up is a ghastly military term used to describe the next phase, when Amin's forces were pushed further and further into the north-west.   Violence became the norm. Excesses were committed, if not at this stage, then certainly in the years that followed; if not by Tanzanian soldiers, then certainly by the Ugandans who replaced them.   In late 1980, thousands of citizens in West Nile province were killed by the Ugandan army, a bloody act of revenge against the tribes-peoples and the guerilla army of Amin.

As a military operation, the first phase of the Tanzanian incursion into Uganda was a success.   Whether or not exactly the same ends could have been achieved by more pacific methods of international, non-violent action is debatable.   Personally, I believe the answer is yes.   But in the absence of any such acts by anyone, civilian or governmental, national or international, then I will give credit to the ones who did do something, even if the cost was in blood.   The Tanzanian army, in going into Uganda, caused people to die.   But if that army had not entered Uganda, many more people might have died, and Amin could perhaps still be there.   The Tanzanian army, therefore, was less violent than those African or European pacifists who did not intervene.

The more pacific solution could possibly have been achieved in a number of ways, all of which might have involved risks, many of which could have involved bravery and sacrifice if not indeed martyrdom.   If the British had not been so constrained by diplomatic protocol, they could easily have staged the reception to achieve the incarceration.   If folk had felt less afraid, then by sheer force of numbers they could have imprisoned him in his palace or whatever.   And afterall, if Gandhi was able to get rid of the British Empire, surely all things are possible. (Even the solution to Northern Ireland ....?)

*   *   *

We all know that fighting wars is altogether different from keeping the peace, so why does the world ask the same people to do both jobs, while only training them for the former?

The Tanzanian army, in 1979, was a successful army of liberation.   Within six months, success turned to sadness - it became an army of occupation.

The British army, in 1969, was welcomed to Belfast. This is a limited operation, said the Home Office.   Alas, it wasn't; and within a time scale of only months, that which had been merely a symptom became a part of the problem.

Uganda, in the immediate post-Amin phase, was a country longing for peace. Yet only just under the surface were animosities and bitter memories. I, being white and therefore foreign to all local conflicts, was welcomed everywhere; but a stranger from even the next door village was often treated with the utmost apprehension, and if he was of a different tribe, suspicions would be deeper, and if members of his tribe had in the intervening years committed some crime against this village, then he'd have been wiser to have stayed at home.

The drought in the drier regions of Karamoja was starving hundreds to their deaths every week, food everywhere was in short supply, the economy was chaotic, smuggling was endemic, stealing was commonplace, and the traditional inter-tribal cattle raids, even against the Karamojong, were frequent. Society had indeed collapsed, and the desperate state of affairs could not be over-emphasised: guns were everywhere, the army had made the police almost powerless, the civil war had wrecked so much. The country, under Amin, had witnessed the murder of hundreds of thousands of people. It really was umpteen times worse than Northern Ireland where tribal tensions exist between the two communities; in Uganda, the tensions were polygonal, between any one of many tribes and perhaps all of its three or four neighbours, each one of which had similar problems.

To have expected the Ugandan peoples, in '79, by themselves, under such conditions of mutual fear and mistrust, to have sorted out their own problems would have been to expect too much. Some form of international help/intervention was bound to be required. That fact was proved beyond all doubt by what did happen and what did not: no help came, and the problem was left to the Ugandans. And one of the first things they did, in 1980, was to ask directly and specifically for international help.

That's the proof.

And still no help came!

In '79, we should have offered our services; in the following year, we should damn well have answered Uganda's requests positively and with enthusiasm. We didn't. We did *NOTHING*.

In this one world, every problem is everybody's; and nearly every conflict demands some form of intervention.

- I wish the British were back, said one police officer.
- The British in Northern Ireland are so impartial, said another.

In '79, the Ugandan A was beating up B. In '69, the Northern Irish A was beating up the Northern Irish B (or should I say, in a rather special way, the Northern Irish B was beating up A?) Intervention, in both cases, was absolutely imperative. In '69, in Ulster, the British did not allow anyone else to help; in '79, in Uganda, the Tanzanians were the only ones willing to and, despite the cost, they stayed on.

In theory, Nyerere could have used his army to just re-install Obote and that would have been that.   In practice, a more democratic process was essential.if peace was to have any chance at all.   At an earlier conference in Tanzania, a small group of Ugandan exiles had elected a certain Lule to be the interim president.   But in that coup of May that I spoke about earlier, the person who had couped Lule was in turn couped by a coup mark two led by Muwanga who now headed the so-called military commission.   This was to be the new interim rule.

Elections were still to go ahead, perhaps in December 1980, perhaps under international supervision.   The latter had been asked for.   Indeed, the British government had been formally requested to provide assistance in a number of ways.   To a great extent, the Ugandans looked back on "the good old days of colonialism" with affection.   Who wouldn't, if the intervening years had been under Amin?   The British, afterall, had always been damn good administrators; and as adjudicators, they'd always been frightfully frightfully fair on the one condition, namely, that they'd always remained on top!   Undoubtedly, however, a major British colonial weakness had been an inability to prepare to leave; a second defect was that, once they'd left, they washed their hands of ALL responsibility. Amongst other things, the Ugandans asked the British to help administer their police force.   This again had been refused by the diplomatic technique of offering a useless alternative, namely, that Ugandan police officers should be sent for police training .... to Sussex!

Muwanga, then, was rigging I mean organising the elections. He rigged them.   Obote, as one of the contenders, looked as if he was in with a good chance.   Tanzania had looked after him during these nine long years of his exile; to the objective observer, therefore, Tanzania appeared to be partial.   To the political opponents of Obote in Uganda, to those who had suffered under Obote's bloody rule in former years, Tanzania's partiality was EFFING OBVIOUS they contended, and with every suspicion utterly justifiable.   Such feelings were exacerbated by the inevitable story of bored young soldiers, untrained for peace, getting drunk, and ....

The Tanzanian forces, if only because of their proximity to the problem, could not be impartial.   In similar vein, the British could and can not be impartial in the Northern Irish conflict which was and is, at least in part, a British/Irish one. Likewise again, the marriage guidance counsellor least suited to the task is the mother in law!   International politics are only human problems writ large.   The principle of minimum force demands, as it were by definition, maximum impartiality.   A Nigerian, perhaps, could easily have learnt to understand the problems of Uganda, and he/she could have been, and been seen to be, impartial.   A Swede could have gone to Northern Ireland. And an Irishman did go to the Lebanon to the Arab-versus-Israeli,

Moslem-versus-Jew conflict in the Middle East.   Now that, (if we exclude the Christian militia), makes impartial sense!

If Nyerere had really wanted a peaceful solution to the Ugandan problem, he would have asked for an international peace keeping force.   He did.   He suggested a Commonwealth presence. Britain, the 'mother' country, did nothing.

If Obote had really wanted a peaceful solution, he would have admitted that his previous personal involvement in tribal conflict disqualified him from the role of peacemaker.   He should have stood down to allow fresh faces to contest the elections.   He did not.

If Muwanga had really wanted a peaceful solution, he would have ensured the elections were open to all parties and/or independent candidates;   furthermore, he would have insisted that the electoral system to be used would not allow ALL the power to go to any ONE political party, any ONE tribal group or any ONE person.   (Needless to say, there could be little more inappropriate than the British political system, containing as it does the one all-powerful lot called the government, and that inexplicable illogical and totally unAfrican phenomenon called the "loyal opposition", which remains all-powerless.)   But Muwanga didn't change anything.

As a postscript, I can add that Obote is now in power, that peace has not yet arrived and that Amin still lurks in the shadows of Arabia.   I can also add that suggestions to the British High Commissioners in Nairobi and Kampala, and to the Foreign Office in London, received polite acknowledgements and no action.   The most obvious reasons for official British disinterest were these: involvement could be costly; an interim presence could turn out to be permanent as solutions failed to materialise;   lastly, and most importantly, Uganda was of little or no economic or strategic value.   In 1980, no-one wanted the source of the Nile.   If, but just IF, she had been sitting on an oil field ....

The Commonwealth Secretariat did actually observe the elections;   their report, critical in parts, nevertheless commented that it "believed this has been a valid electoral exercise".   Yet was it not obvious to all that Muwanga had been biased in favour of Obote?   And was this not confirmed when Obote decided to appoint his vice-president, none other than Muwanga!   The tensions remained .... the days ticked by .... the time bomb was bound to explode ....it did.   Just two months after Obote came to power in December 1980, these new wounds in old sores led to renewed guerilla activity in Buganda; else-where, the malpractices of the election caused the Democratic Party to set up its own military wing;   while in the north-west, former supporters of Amin continued to fight a terrorist war.

In January '82, the British did actually send some soldiers to help 'pacify' the situation.   Too bloody late!   By this time, Obote's armies had already committed atrocities, and to help train just one of FOUR armies is hardly going to help the

The Crested Crane — Uganda's national emblem

cause of peace!   Now,   in 1984,   it is being suggested that in
just four years of Obote's rule,   over 100,000 Ugandans have died
either   because of the armies of the state and/or because   of the
government's   failure   to   tackle   the   problems   of   hunger   and
poverty.   The other armies have also committed atrocities, but
how   can   the present government claim any right   to   rule   while
admitting to the deaths of 15,000?   - a figure which is   no
exaggeration and which may well be a gross underestimation!
        An international peace keeping presence could have   enabled
(and   it   still   could enable) Uganda to tackle the rest   of   her
problems.   She needed to sort out her economy.   Before that
could be started,   she needed the re-instatement of an   efficient
police   system,   the   introduction of a (Ugandan) form of   power-
sharing government,   the establishment of a non-tribal system   of
courts   and   prisons   and the rounding up of all those   guns   and
munitions;   then,   and   only then, would she have been   able   to
concentrate   on the biggest problem of them all,   the eradication
of poverty in Karamoja.   Uganda, therefore, needed   -   and had
asked for   -   police officers, political scientists and electoral
observers;   may   I   suggest   she   also   required   judges   and
solicitors,   and   perhaps a few soldiers.   Yet all she got was
soldiers.
        The intervention of some international and impartial judges
and   jurists in Belfast, could have eliminated the   necessity   of
one-person   courts.   Similarily,   some equally international   and
impartial   police   officers   and   solicitors could   have   prevented
some   if not all of the mistreatment of suspects held in custody,
of the practice of strip searching in women's prisons, and of the
use of the uncorroborated evidence of supergrasses.   Furthermore,
the   intervention   of   political scientists could have   put   into
perspective   those myths of sovereignty and of the   nation-state,
it could have laid bare the antiquities of majority rule,   and it
could   have   facilitated   the   way   forward   to   a   politics   of
consensus.
        International   intervention,   in Uganda or Ulster,   should
involve   not only soldiers,   and nor should it involve only   men.
In years to come,   future observers might suggest it should never
include   even a few soldiers,   but a little bit more evolution is
necessary   first,   methinks.   When in the future   our   western
minds are more able to appreciate the eastern philosophies,   then
perhaps   the Gandhian principles of non-violent intervention,   of
satyagraha,   may come to have a place in international   politics.
Roll on the day.

                              *   *   *

        The   underlying   principles of intervention I advocate   for
Uganda must,   because of their very internationalism, be suitable
for universal application or not at all.   After an air crash, a
public   inquiry tries to establish the cause so that the   tragedy
will not be repeated.   After a conflict .... nothing.

If we work on the premise that we all live in one world, then we could say we are all responsible for all the wrongs of this world, though to greater and lesser extents. In Northern Ireland, Britain is deeply involved; and in Uganda, in theory, not much less so. In a world where borders are the artificial creation of man, it is inadequate for one group of peoples to say it has no responsibility for the internal conflicts of another. National sovereignty is a myth; the Tanzanians, while in normal times respecting the rule, refused to be bound by that United Nations dictat which tries to differentiate between the internal and the international conflict. That, then, is another lesson of the Ugandan tragedy; perhaps some good can yet come from that most bitter of confrontations.

Just looking at the rôle of Britain in Uganda, I think two conclusions are clear. Firstly, that she should not have intervened in the way she did (by continuing to export military equipment); and secondly, that she should have intervened in the way she was asked to but did not, that she should have suggested a more international intervention in the form of a commonwealth peace keeping force or a United Nations one. What she could not do was to say she did not wish to intervene (because she was already doing so and) because all countries tend to intervene in the affairs of others, just as all individuals affect and are affected by other individuals. Those peoples and countries which did nothing actually helped the status quo to perpetuate itself, while those which did something, more obviously affected the situation.

But all countries and all peoples, by their very existence on this planet, if only via the collective unconscious, influence all others. To suggest, then, as some do, that no nation should interfere in the internal affairs of another is to talk of the hypothetical and, furthermore, it is to talk from a position of vested interest. The artificial division of the world into nations detracts from the common ties which unite us all; and one cannot help wondering whether or not there may be a basic contradiction in that organisation called the United Nations - the coming together of the very entities which have so divided us.

*   *   *

Senseless as their troubles may appear, neither Kampala nor Belfast need have suffered totally in vain .... and evolution may yet be the gain. In either case, only via internationalism could the indigenous problem be more easily solved by the indigenous. That is the lesson they teach to the world - would that the world would learn.

International conflict resolution is the means by which arbitration may replace argument, by which the impartial can referee the partial, and by which indigenous appeals for help can be assured. International conflict resolution, if it is applied in sufficient time, could be the means by which wars are avoided. Therefore, it is a sine qua non for disarmament, in Uganda, in Northern Ireland, in the nuclear arms race, and throughout the world.

*   *   *

From Uganda, recovering from one and suffering from another war, we'll travel to the Maghreb, where Morocco and Algeria were engaged in yet another. Now the incompetent non-combatant is always a bit of a nuisance to those with that other contradiction in terms called the military mind. They, like their political masters before and after them, tend to draw lines - forward areas, security zones, defence positions and so on. Cycling tourists tend not so much to intervene, more to interfere in such scenarios, and my arrest was, I suppose, inevitable. But first, while I'm still free, a look at the state of the state.

If the eyes are the reflection of the soul, then perhaps the state censored television service is the mirror of the nation. Morocco was run by King Hassan II (Hassan **deux** as they say). He had been just an ordinary Sultan until, one day, in a moment of inspiration, he'd voted to promote himself, and God had abstained. The TV now showed this petty prince saying this or doing that while lots of people, all of them men, ministered to him. Army officers kissed his hand, he kissed the flag, and his little son wondered when all these nice big toys would be his.

Morocco was a democratic monarchy, if you see what I mean. No, I didn't either. Apparently, lots of political parties did sort of exist, or so the people believed and/or thought and/or said, but all decisions and important things like that were made by Hassan **deux**. He, in the eyes of so many, could do no wrong; his word could motivate and mobilise. Obedience is frightening!

The borders of Morocco had not always been so, (despite Hassan's claims to 'natural' ones!) For in days of yesteryear, the Berbers had been the only folk in the Maghreb, though the Phoenicians and Romans had had a considerable influence in what had been the city of Carthage. The most decisive invasion had come from the Arabs, shortly after Mohammed had written a few rabble-rousing rallying cries so that his policy could become a philosophy: jihad. To shroud wrong in a cloak of righteousness is always the most effective way of sustaining a fighting morale - compare the crusades of the popes and the campaigns of Cromwell; or ask any Israeli army officer, protestant paramilitary or NATO army chaplain. The invasion had been amazingly successful - militarily speaking. Not only did they take all of the Maghreb; they also crossed over into Spain and even into France. This had rather upset the good Christians who, for the sake of their goodness, fought their way back again, but only as far as Gibraltar. Then, in thanks to the divine, they built all those magnificent Spanish cathedrals; (building monuments to a deity, that old Egyptian habit, is one of the less offensive abuses of power). But in Morocco, and indeed in all of the Maghreb, the Arabs stayed to share a land with the Berbers who then readily accepted Islam (not least because their variety of Christianity had recieved the wrath of Rome), and all somewhat reluctantly accepted the various Sultans which fate imposed upon them.

In 1912, after several international to-ings and fro-ings, the French arrived to 'protect' Morocco, whether they'd wanted protection or no. And **tous les choses** became French with remarkable speed while **tous les hommes et les femmes** remained somewhat Moroccan. In '56, the winds of change blew France away, and the Arabs and Berbers began to live in peace again; well, sort of.

Over one thousand years of 'togetherness' has not seen much intercourse of any variety between these two peoples. Religion was the only common factor - at least that stopped them fighting - but they remained separated by language, race and tradition. A certain amount of assimilation had taken place, but when a Berber woman married an Arab man, or vice versa vice versa, the wife always adopted the identity of her husband and never vice versa! All sorts of people, therefore, could be Berber - I met one negro, whose forbears had doubtless crossed the Sahara, and he was most proud of his Berber inheritance; and all sorts could be Arabs. But few, in a potentially polarised society, cared or dared to be neither or both. So much, then, for the history of the nation, a basis broadly similar to the situation in Algeria.

Morocco was a country in which the rich were free to become richer, the poor were free to remain so, and the multi-nationals had a pretty free rein for as long as the king who did reign did so deign. So, the West liked Morocco. The latter said it was democratic, because it wished to line up with the former in a mutual back-scratch by which the West got Moroccan phosphates, and Morocco got western weapons for Hassan's wars. What, in the long term, was in the best interests of the country was debatable; but what, in the short term, was actually happening was, one, an exploitation of some finite resources; and two, Hassan **deux**, an eighteenth century monarch with twentieth century armaments, was seeking colonial expansionism.

Short term economics were especially cut and dry when it came to the situation in what had been called the Spanish Sahara. With incredible lack of foresight, the Spanish had decided as recently as the mid-70s to end their colonial control of this place, and they'd decided half could go to Morocco and half to Mauritania.   Spain had then washed its hands,   just as the British had done in Uganda.   The people living in that desert were, apparently, of no Spanish consequence.

They thought otherwise, and Polisario was born.   Under international pressure, Mauritania pulled out.   So Morocco, tempted by all those extra phosphates, decided to take all.   The guerilla war started.   Algeria supported Polisario.   So Morocco began to fight Algeria as well, and to dispute the common border;   hence I found a situation in which one lot of Arabs and Berbers was fighting another lot of Arabs and Berbers over the 'correctness' of a border which should not have existed. Mad.   It was a predicament in which the first world of the North bore not a little responsibility.   Overhead flew American fighters, defending the indefensible;   phantoms for phosphates. Across the 'border' were Russian aircraft;   migs for figs. Such was the trade.   In total, it was almost as bad as that other scene of super-power rivalry, the Horn of Africa.   Here, then, the USA and the USSR were fighting a proxy war over a group of people who were claiming the right of self-determination in a land marked by a line of longitude!

For the moment Morocco was not going to fight Spain which continued to maintain a colonial presence in Sebta and Melilla (because Spain was bigger than Morocco) but it was going to fight the Polisario and, if Algeria insisted on intervening militarily, then it would fight Algeria as well.   Such a state of international tension meant there was quite a strong military presence along the southern part of Morocco;   here stood soldiers by the dozen, ready to argue and fight at a moment's notice, ready to arrest anyone and everyone and me, especially when I was in that military zone, and more especially because, one day, I just managed to get completely and totally lost, somewhere to the east of Zagoro.

*   *   *

If a lorry went across a bit of desert, even a rather stony bit as this one was, it was bound to leave its mark.   Well quite a few vehicles, at some time or other since the days of Henry, had travelled about in these parts, but which of many tracks was the one on my map and which were not puzzled me. And I had diarrhoea.   Again, as I moved further to the east, the tracks got fewer and fewer and the situation clarified itself; the track however did not, for it deteriorated into rock and boulder, while my stomach called noisily for frequent halts.

The road rose over a rise;   the land was barren;   the distant hills showed no sign of life;   I was alone.   And here was a sort of junction.   The hypothetical coin was tossed - I went this a'way. Then that a'way. What a way to go.   I found myself lost.   I reckoned there was a village fairly close though.   There was a small ridge of rock to the west .... I'll just climb this to see what's what, I thought.   One dark and rocky ridge was followed by another, the sun was setting, the track was getting weaker, twilight dusked .... ah, was that a village?   Did I see a light?   I walked on.   Darkness was approaching.   Where was venus?   Ah yes, sinking fast, and not without good reason.

Under such conditions, one could be forgiven if one started talking to oneself.

- Ouch! I said, for there, in the sole of my foot, was a damn great thorn sticking down like an Australian flag-pole. It was time to check my tyres.   Both flat.   OK.   That was it. I called it a night and pitched tent.   Problems were shelved until the morrow.   First of all, though, I climbed the sand-dune behind me, just to see if I could see or hear any signs of life. My cries - confound it seemed to be a suitable oath - received only echoes in reply.   Nothing was near, but in the far distance were some lights.   Those over there seemed to be the nearest, so that was my direction for the morning.   Where was the north star?   Right.   And before zipping myself up in my tent for the night, I arranged a little pile of stones so that I would know the direction to aim for, come the dawn.

It was time for some food.   It could have been my last meal.   While occasionally it is good to think about death and the ethics of it all, the actual practicalities are always a little discouraging.   So I ate and drank to my fill.   If I was going to go, there was no point in dragging out the agony for a week or more.   Eat well to-day and die well ....

I slept unconsciously well.   On getting up, I drank some more water and started to replace my inner tubes.   The pump had chosen this moment to resign, so I had to take some grease out of my pedals to rejuvenate the damn thing.   What a sense of timing.   Just about all packed up and ready to go, I was, in the direction of my little pile of stones, when .... hallo? .... what was that?   An engine?   God-damn-it, a diesel pump to suck up the waters from deep under the dried up river bed was starting-up, barely one hundred yards away, for this was the hour when work commenced.   Thus was death postponed.

- Good heavens good morning.   They were a little surprised to see a lone cyclist coming out of the yellow.

- Have some fruit, they continued.   Time for a date.

And <u>there</u> was the village.   I'd been close.   What I hadn't realised was that these Berber homes had little wooden shutters with which they closed all their windows at night so that the entire village lived, as it were, in a blackout.   Not yet had those twentieth century amps reached the average village of South Morocco.   So, unlike us, they were not dependent on them, and these wooden shutters were far more efficient than many a double glazing.

People.   Well, having thought I'd been pretty close to a lonesome death, it was just great to see people again .... wasn't it? .... well .... wasn't it?

- You're under arrest.
- Sorry, my Arabic is a little weak, what I said was could you please tell me the way ....
- You're under arrest!
- I thought that's what you said.

Here, then, was my first encounter with the strong military presence; I was led away to the army camp for questioning. I hadn't been treated like this for at least six months when I'd been apprehended under the prevention of terrorism act at a time when I hadn't been up to anything more than five foot eight.

I was surrounded on all sides; some were soldiers and some were those funny things called superiors.

- Would you like to make a statement?
- Yes.
- That'll do.   Sign here.

So that was the Moroccan side.   Later on I came across to cross the border (and fortunately, though the exact whereabouts of the border was questioned in war, the site of the border post remained an established fact) and there, on the other side, I also got arrested, but only once.

At least in Algeria, soldiers did a little bit more than just patrol and control; here, the state job creation programme had decided to do something more positive with its youth, and planting trees was the answer.   Right across the Atlas, from west to east across the plateaus of the Bedouin, there was to be a line of conifers.   So, many of the country's youth put down the gun and picked up the spade, if only for a time.

There were two fundamental reasons why Morocco and Algeria were fighting over the question of Polisario.   The first was because both states existed, and had national armies with which to fight.   The second was because of differing ideologies; Morocco, the right-wing monarchy, was poles apart from the socialist state of Algeria.   Looking at the former reason, I wish to question further the wisdom of their existence.

Just like the folk on either side of the Ugandan/Sudanese frontier, the people on this side of the border in Morocco were the cousins of the Algerians on that side; the differences between these Moroccans here and those of Marakech were far greater than the small differences which existed either side of the customs post, as too were the differences between these Algerians here and, to take a rather extreme example, the Mozabites of Ghardaia.

Nations may exist if they want to.   But so too should the smaller counties or regions within nations as well as the bigger units, the Organisation of African Unity and the (as yet non-existent) Anglo-Irish somethingorother, especially if the very existence thereof can help to resolve disputes within the membership.   Ideally, the autonomy of those local regions should not only cover domestic issues like housing and education; for if these peoples on this side of the Moroccan/Algerian, Ugandan/Sudanese (British/Irish) border want to establish closer

ties with those people on the other side,   then no (centralised)
nation state government authority should be so covetous of that
authority as to not allow them to do so.

Returning, then, to the Moroccan/Algerian war, it is
obvious that the dispute should have been at least the subject of
dialogue. Both countries were part Arab and part Berber. Both
countries spoke the same language and shared the same religion.
And both countries had far more serious problems to contend with.

Now for the good news. They're talking. I'm not sure
what they're saying 'cos sometimes Gaddafi visits De Chablis and
then he sees Hassan deux and then he talks with Bourguiba and
then he starts arguing again while Bourguiba sees De Chablis and
De Chablis sees Hassan deux and all the talk is of unity, though
who is to unite with whom is debatable while who is to unite
under whom is downright controversial 'cos who wants to unite
under Gaddafi?   However, at least they're talking, and 1984
sees the Moroccan/Algerian conflict coming to a close.   The
reason behind it, namely the struggle of Polisario for
independence, alas continues unsolved and unabated.

*   *   *

Algeria had started off, after the regulation coup or two,
under Boumedienne. His policies had been socialist, his
leaning towards the east. He died in a Moscow hospital
somewhat unexpectedly, in 1978; the pictures of his successor,
De Chablis, already lined the streets, but nobody yet really knew
what he stood for. Boumedienne appeared to have been genuinely
admired, and I must say it was good to see a country which, as I
noted on page (74), was trying to do its own thing. Algerian
factories made this and that; the thises and thats might not
have been as good as the stuff made by the French companies which
had invented them, but nevertheless, they were Algerian.

Furthermore, it was a pleasant change not to have everyone
orientated towards money ALL the time. In Algeria, the kids
said hallo. In Morocco, one heard give us a shilling, a
cigarette, a something; while in Egypt, of course, the ceaseless
cry was that dreadful **backsheesh, backsheesh.**

While there was this genuine desire of Algeria to stand on
its own feet and be independent, it nevertheless followed a very
French way of life. Umpteen cafés, very much à la français
were invariably full, everyone chatting away over countless tiny
cups of strong black coffee which were so small, you had to stay
for another one; which was why the cafés were full.   In the
town centres, **boulangeries** sold the long French loaf, pâtisseries
their pretty cakes and delicious (Algerian made) French
chocolate. In the streets of the more northern cities,
shapeless gowns and the naked eyes of the Mozabites gave way to
knee length skirts and youthful smiles. The young men too wore
western clothes, but they'd been under the **jeleba** for some years
already anyway.

Some of the various Berber tribes still spoke their own tongue, but elsewhere, French was more often heard than Arabic. It was, indeed, very difficult to improve my own Arabic here for most folk, on seeing I was a European, assumed I spoke French. On hearing my French, they guessed I was English, and often they spoke that too. The only way I could practice the language was by replying with an absolute lie:

Je ne parle pas le français,
- I don't know English

and

.cibarA kaeps ylno I   -

* * *

While talking of Uganda, I succumbed to the temptation to compare it with Northern Ireland. With Algeria, again, there are similarities, this time in their histories. In the space of just two paragraphs, I will attempt a summary of both.

They, the French, the English, came to stay; land was expropriated and political power concentrated in the hands of the settlers. Society was thus divided. And that division was aggravated further because most of the new-comers were of one religion while the indigenous population preferred a different belief. The natives revolted but, against the might of the colonial power, violence was bound to fail. Then, in the second half of the twentieth century, along had come the winds of change. First India and then umpteen countries in Africa were being granted their independence. The wind reached Algeria - before it blew in Ireland, however, it had fizzled to a fart. And violent struggles commenced.

The settlers, like the unionists of Ulster, insisted that they were an integral part of the colonial power. De Gaulle, a military man by training, told the settlers that either they could be French, or they could be Algerian, but that they couldn't be both. The unionist paramilitaries, the settlers' army which contained retired army generals and not just the lads from the shipyard, lost the day because De Gaulle used a democratic weapon, not a military one. A referendum or two sealed the fate: Algeria became independent. The threatened generals' revolt didn't happen. A few 'French' went back to France; a few 'Algerians' stayed where they were. And that was that. And that, a similar that, could perhaps be the end of the troubles in Ulster .... if .... but steady .... I've come to the end of my second paragraph.

CHAPTER 6

BORDERS ARE THE LIMIT

And so, from Uganda of the civil war that had been and is, via the Atlas of the proxy war that was, to the desert .... to the sands of seemingly eternal war; to Libya, a land plagued by the presence and psyche of military might. Libya was a country which in the name of Islamic socialism had managed to fight or threaten wars with almost all of its neighbours save the sea. Secondly, it had shouted much belligerence on the Middle East question. And furthermore, it had even interfered in Uganda, not because Amin was a fascist, the very antithesis of all things socialist, but because he was a Moslem (up to the point of having four wives and not much further).

My own story in Libya is complex and long: it started in the police stations of Tunisia; and, to be complete, I must include a few words on the penal institutions of Egpyt, for 'twas in a jail in Alexandria that I did not, but this tale did, come to an end.

On crossing from Algeria into Tunisia, I immediately realised I was in a right-wing semi- if not complete dictatorship, wherein the president ruled his own as he wished, wherein his actions were subject only to the whims of neo-colonialism and international finance. There, on a billboard in an otherwise delightful little village tucked away in the mountains, was an advertisement for that well-known softdrinkrustremover to be drunk with things. In subsequent and bigger villages, it and other commodities were blazoned everywhere. The multi-national companies of the West were here in strength. Algeria, then, was the socialist centre of the Maghreb sandwich; on either side were the two right-wing crusts, Morocco and Tunisia, the latter ruled by Bourguiba, habib to his friends who, by presidential decree, included everybody.

In earlier days, Bourguiba had been in the vanguard of the struggle for independence, along with another leader, Beni Yusuf. The French had then said:

- OK, you can have independence .... like this. Bourguiba had responded positively if that's the right way to describe the one word "yes"; but Beni Yusuf had replied:

- No; that's only half independence - it's still economic colonialism.

The two leaders argued and split; Beni Yusuf went into exile where he was mysteriously murdered, and since then, Bourguiba has done virtually whatever he's wanted to. After a few years in power, he too became convinced of his own importance and he had himself declared president for life. For the average Tunisian this was unfortunate, for the old boy seemed to have but the one talent, longevity.

In the city, the more sophisticated spoke freely of the country, its ageing president and the corrupt system of government he'd imposed. Too often, however, the conclusion was empty, for the organisations of state - police, military, "public sûreté", gendarmerie - each, in their different uniforms, uniform in their obedience to habib - kept a close eye on even the tiniest of subversive coughs. Freedom of speech did not exist. Freedom to make money was here, by definition a freedom not everyone can enjoy; and there was also complete freedom of dress, religion and way of life, for no strict ayatollah was forcing religion down unwilling throats. Every so often, of course, most political leaders in predominantly Moslem countries made suitable noises in order to keep the imams happy; but they, like the bishops of Christendom who serve both God and state, were remarkably easy to keep quiet and content. And Bourguiba hoped that in allowing everyone freedom to do anything but criticise his dictatorial capitalism, no-one would do so. Just in case they did, however, his security forces were everywhere.

He, then, was the one person who decided what was, and what was not, to be. He was ministered to by his ministers of state, all of whom were highly paid for saying yes, and he was, like so many politicians of his position, drunk with the power vested in him, the power political. The power economic was not his; it was French. Indeed, a large slice of the French way of life had been imposed-cum-imported, and French customs were many. Even wine, upon which the average imam casts his wrath, flowed liberally in cafés of coffee and cakes. Those who could afford it liked it - and their politics moved to the right as vested interest did demand.

Now it just so happened that I was abroad in the northern part of the country when, unbeknown to myself, your man the president addressed the nation. In third world countries, some people actually believe their political masters; and throughout Tunisia, in town and country alike, little transistors cracked and crackled his every word.

- Beware, said he, the stranger, the foreigner, the architect of plot and ploy, the subversive harbinger of confusion and intrigue.

Apparently, as they say in Belfast, there'd been a bit of a riot. This one had been down in Gafsa, which just happened to be the birthplace of the late Beni Yusuf. Former supporters of his had attacked the civil authorities in a revolt which, after but a few days, petered out. But that was not what Bourguiba said; no, he was saying it was people from Libya, inspired by that monster Gaddafi. Like so many statesmen, the Tunisian leader was finding the external cause of his internal problem.

Now barely had this peasant farmer switched off his radio when along came one Belfast bicyclist who wanted to stay the night. Decisions .... I was chatted up by many but, round the corner, serious talk was under way. I, of course, still

knew nothing about the broadcast, the revolt or anything else.
I soon learnt.
    - You're under arrest.   Over me stood a policeman.
    - Oh.
    On the spot, I was not, for Gafsa is in the southwest of
the country;   but in a spot yes I was.   The farmer had cycled
all the way to town to tell the special branch especially of me;
and so I was taken awayawayaway.   But it was all quickly sorted
out, and after the usual round of unusual questions, I was
returned to the village and allowed to rest in peace.
    Back in the capital, life was settled enough though news of
Gafsa was uncertain.   Apparently, Bourguiba had asked France for
military protection.   France, always keen to defend someone
else's freedom if it coincided with her own economic interests,
dispatched a few warships.   The nineteenth century was alive
and well.
    Now remembering that Russia had just sent her troops into
Afghanistan on the vague pretext that she was defending the
freedom of some of the Afghani people to be communist, one could
be forgiven if one thought it was wrong for France to defend the
right of some Tunisians to be capitalist.   Just in case,
therefore, the British ambassador had sort of forgotten what
freedom was, there, outside his embassy that very morning, was
the French ambassador's car.   **Mais alors,** he had no cause for
concern: British ambassadors ne'er forget what they've never
learnt.
    The foreign policies of most countries are governed by the
one and only 'principle' of vested interest.   Right-wing
countries support right-wing regimes and vice-versa.   That, of
course, is a bit of a sweeping generalisation, not least because
it ignores all the variations on the themes of -isms which each
and every nation, under each and every government or regime,
tends to impose on the -isms it adopts.   Nevertheless, it is
fairly true to say that the West usually supports the very status
quos it helped to create and in so doing, therefore, it hinders
progress;   while at the same time, the East supports those
countries which are either pro-marxist or simply anti-west;
either way, their thinking as a result often gets stuck in a
1917 groove.   In theory, western countries, upholders of
freedom and things, never interfere in the internal affairs of a
foreign state;   in practice, however, they're just as bad as the
rest, and they'll do whatever is expedient.   The foreign
policies of Britain are just as bad as those of France, they're
just a little more timid about it, or they were until Thatcher
rejuvenated the long lost days of jingo.
    Meanwhile, of course, the international situation between
Libya and Tunisia was, to say the least, tense.   (There was
nothing unusual in that, really, for the international situations
between Libya and everybody were pretty tense some time or
other.)   There were many bad reasons for this friction. Libya
was a socialist state, it said.   It wasn't, actually, but it

said it was. What people are is usually of far less import than what they think they are. And Tunisia, as I'd discovered, was of the right-wing variety. That did not mean, though, that Bourguiba and Gaddafi were poles apart in their political thinking - heavens no - both of them believed in at least minor dictatorship and both enjoyed disguising that fact. But there, most similarities ceased.

So Bourguiba, in his lack of wisdom, blamed Gaddafi for the riots in Gafsa. Gaddafi, in his void, denied his involvement in what he said was an internal affair. But then, from the radio and television roof-tops, he did shout to the Tunisian peoples, urging them to rise up in revolt, to follow the Gafsa riots to their leftful conclusion, to overthrow Bourguiba and to declare Tunisia to be one, socialist, Arab state. Not a very wise message, really, when one recalls that many a Tunisian was a Berber and none too fond of his Arab neighbour (though here, both were closer than in other parts of the Maghreb). And the second reason why this act of Gaddafi's was not as wise as it might have been, was because he was now interferring in the internal affairs of Tunisia, thus changing what had been the lie of Bourguiba into a truth. The plot, and its participants, were thick.

At this time, I was in Tunis, keeping a close eye on the invisible situation in so far as I could; the British embassy official told me as little as possible with the excuse that such riots were only to be expected from such unpredictable people; it was obvious that she'd been in the British foreign service for so long that she'd long since forgotten the whereabouts of Notting Hill and Brixton, let alone Northern Ireland. So I waited for the Libyan consulate to give me a visa and, as soon as that was cleared, I was off. My fear was that the border would shut. Knowing the vagaries of international frontier posts, I ventured towards the more southerly one, thinking that perhaps there the position would be a little less formal.

Life was terrible. Everywhere I went, I was a stranger, a foreigner, an architect of evil and whatever else everyone was wary of. Therefore, the loyal and upright citizen, of which Tunisia seemed to have a most high proportion, did apprehend and arrest me. I tried the lonelier trail, but thereon my presence aroused even more suspicion. The upholders of no law and far too much order were polite enough but, as I said under oath, the purpose of my presence in their country was not to pay umpteen cultural visits to just so many bare-walled multi-faced police stations. On another occasion, when I demanded reasons for his actions, the army officer replied that I was the first person ever who had doubted his wisdom or questioned his authority. So I asked him another question.

My first attempt at crossing the border at the more southerly post was in vain. That area had been declared a military zone and little cyclists were just not allowed therein. The main border post, however, was still open though business was

not "as usual" for a certain tension was in the air.   Thus I
entered Libya.

That all sounds pretty easy really, but in fact there
weren't that many travellers who actually managed to get there.
Come to think of it, there weren't that many who wanted to, but
what the hell. When in London, I had visited the Libyan consulate
only to find that I'd chosen one of those days on which Libyan
students demonstrated support for the revolution and opposition
to the imperialist lackeys of whatever was not in vogue.   Of
such days in the average year, there appeared to be over three
hundred and sixty.   I was told I was a friend of the Libyan
people and all that, but as far as a visa was concerned, well, I
was advised to just go away.
      - But ....
      - Eff off.
      The only chance, then, had been for me to have another go
at that Libyan consulate in Tunis.   By that time, I could speak
a fair bit of Arabic as well as write my name in its script.
I was damned if I knew words like immigration control and
passport, though .... but still ....along I went for the crack.
After only ten days, during which time I visited some Carthagian
ruins and many Tunisian chief constables' offices, a Libyan visa
was all mine.   **Hamdullah.**

Gaddafi did not like western imperialists, or that was what
he said.   He hadn't liked the way King Idris had been a bit of
a puppet to western interests, so, in '69, he'd had a revolution
to depose the guy.   One of the first things he'd done was
remove all the 'filtee' English road signs - everything was
Arabised and, as a result, the immigration officials were
conspicuously unable to understand words like "no" and "non". He
also Islamised most codes of conduct and nationalised the oil
companies so that the profits from 'Libyan' oil could be shared
amongst the Libyan people.

He, like Bourguiba and Hassan deux, was also pretty
convinced of his own importance.   Inspired by Chairman Mao's
little red book, Gaddafi wrote a little green one; green it was
for he wished to cultivate the desert, a noble goal at which to
aim; green it was, his first attempt at a philosophy; and
little it was, in every sense of the word.   But it was not
without logic, and underlying his every utterance was a hate of
capitalism and its many manifestations, especially as expressed
in Israeli zionism.   His knowledge of western democracy centred
on the British system of politics, and his criticisms thereof
were many and justified.   To describe our system as imperfect
was fair enough; to describe his answers thereto as fantastic
would be not a little rash.

His domestic policies I'll come to later.   Suffice for
the moment to emphasise that he simply loathed any form of
western imperialism.   (The Russian variety of same did not
receive so vehement a criticism; it was ignored.)   And the
situation in the neighbouring country of Tunisia was that the

capitalist French were supporting the regime of a semi-senile dictator just at the very moment when it looked as if a popular uprising could have caused the overthrow of that right-wing neo-colonialist administration and its replacement by a left-wing one.

French troops were reportedly on Tunisian soil. French ships were definitely in the bay off Gabes. This was too much. Right. Ring for a riot. And many a loyal student came into Tripoli to sack the French embassy - great sport. (If only the Northern Ireland office had that same, mad, adventurous spirit!) The French ambassador was expelled. In the circumstances, such was fair enough. But, only a few days later, when the ships were still in the bay bobbing up and down with excitement, the French were allowed back in again. All most odd. Well, was it? No; politics are never inexplicable. And my guess is that the French just squeezed the Libyans a little, telling Gaddafi that if he wasn't going to be a good little boy that then they, the French, would withdraw all their personnel and logistical support from the Libyan air force to thus render the entire fleet of supersonic mirage jet fighters useless. Er .... oh. So Libya played ball. And France managed a two-faced foreign policy, maintaining, in Tunisia, 'freedom' (and her own economic interests), and in Libya, je ne sais quoi (and her own economic interests).

And that was the end of that little episode .... well .... almost. At the time, I just happened to be wearing a pair of Tunisian shoes, not because I am an inveterate collector of the souvenirs of the sole for the mantlepiece back home, but for the very good reason that my previous pair, with some 6,000 kilometres beneath them, had ceased to be. A Tunisian in Libya would thereby know whence I'd come, and a conversation in French would follow - French, the language of the imperialist, the colonialist, the capitalist, oh, the list of -ists was endless. For Arabic was the language of the socialist, or so said Gaddafi, though how a socialist could be such a nationalist was beyond my comprehension. Anyway, Libya was a socialist Arab peoples' state; and Tunisia, in the eyes of Libya (and quite a few Tunisians) was the very opposite.

Gaddafi believed in socialism; what's more, he believed all Libyans should also believe in socialism, so just in case any refrained from such beliefs, he had his plain clothes police but everywhere. In a café, then, I did sometimes have a delightful little conversation in French. Ah's, mais oui's and bien sûr's abounded.

Immediately, the little ears of the listless -istless intelligent services pricked up. And beady eyes, befogged, begad, behind their special branch see-through sunglasses, did wink a blink. Notes were noted, plans were plotted, and I was arrested. Here, then, was another similarity between two diametrically opposed regimes: both, totalitarian in style, were utterly dependent upon the forces of the respective state. The

Tunisians were also arrested, and the treatment they received was worse by far, for they were suspected of being .... well, I didn't know really.   I thought this Libyan behaviour to be somewhat extraordinary;   they sought the Tunisian up-rising and the spontaneous peoples' revolt, but any person of that nationality working or travelling in Libya itself, was harassed and hounded from pillar to police post.

*   *   *

So getting into Libya was not without its difficulties, and getting through Libya was not exactly eventless; but getting out was a real problem.   I came to Tobruk.   I did in fact travel fairly quickly across Libya, partly because my Egyptian visa was only valid for one month, partly because I was only allowed one month in Libya anyway and I thought getting out might pose a problem or two, and partly because I was having a spot of bother with the bike.   Both hubs were bent on being bent and, in Libya, with everyone driving cars, there just weren't any bicycle repair shops.   How travelling faster was going to ease this particular difficulty was uncertain.   Tobruk, then, was the last town before the Libyan/Egyptian border which, I knew, was officially closed and had been since the 1977 mini-war between the two countries.   I met an English couple and their friends:
    - You haven't a hope in hell!
    - Any chance in heaven?
    - Well, if anyone can get through, it will be the lonesome cyclist; good luck.
    - Just in case you have to come back, my home is up this a'way, said Mano.   The pessimist.   The realist.   Three days later I was back.   The soldiers at the border, frightfully polite perhaps, just would not let me pass.
    - You must have a letter of authorisation from Tobruk, they said.   I visited them all: the civil authorities, the police, the army, the military police and finally the secret police. Not one of them, not even those with more pips than a tangerine, had the guts to oppose the ultimate authority, the state. Arguments about freedom and Allah's one world held little sway. Outside, high in the sky, another flock of migratory birds were on their way to immigration control and spring in Europe.
    I thought a thought.   First of all, I would not tolerate the intolerable.   I had come to go to Egypt and that was where I would go, come what may.   On the face of it, there were two alternatives.   If I couldn't go through the border post, I would just have to go round it, either by going into the desert or by sailing out to sea.
    I went to look for a camel.   A friend of a friend squared said the bedouin took little notice of each and every government, no matter what its leanings, and that they continued to travel in their camel caravans as they had always done, ignoring borders

and other imaginary lines which tried to say that this grain of
sand was different from that one.   But a visit into the desert,
many miles south of Tobruk, was inconclusive.   Not a camel for
miles around, they said;   instead, there were rumoured to be a
thousand and more Libyan soldiers patrolling the frontier and
they tended to shoot first and ask questions afterwards.
Already, apparently, some folk had died.

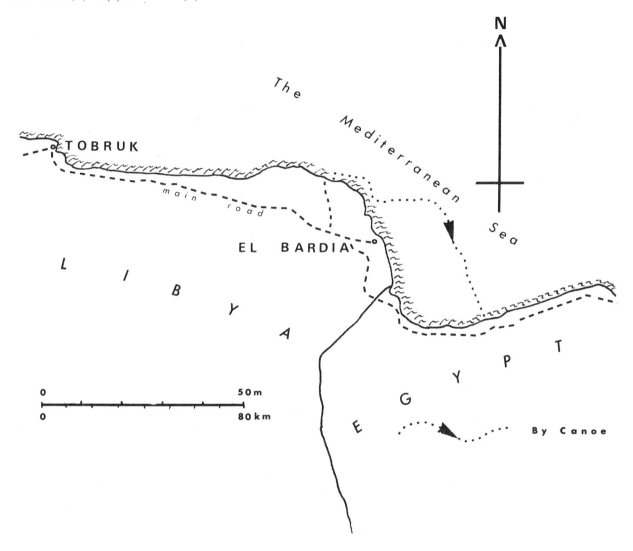

     So, camels were off, love.   It was time to consider the
second alternative.   I visited a lonely fishing village on the
northern coast, but a walk along the shore revealed not a sign of
any little old boat.   That village had lost its second
adjective to remain only lonely, for the entire area east of
Tobruk had been declared a military zone and all fishing boats
that had been were now no more.   There was not even enough
debris on the beach to make a raft.   All I saw were
those dreadful modules of oil, for pollution in the Med was

slowly building up.   Furthermore, all navigational aids, like
the old lighthouse,   had been removed.   The villagers were very
warm hearted - a friendship was soon established   -   but in
hearing of my ideas they warned me no.   They knew the military
mentality of the Libyan authorities and they realised my venture
might be completed only posthumously. No joy there.
        In Tobruk,   there were some Russian missile-carrying boats
which, like the warships of many modern navies, seldom went to
sea;   and of course there were all the oil tankers taking away
the black gold while other ships returned with consumer goods for
the consumptive.   But of fishing boats,   not a thing.   The
nearest one was found fifty miles WEST of Tobruk,   and that was
rather a long way from Egypt. However, it could be hired .... it
was a nice little job,   the size of a rowing boat .... with a
sturdy pair of oars ....
        Thinks ....
        The imagination   contemplated a journey of two hundred
miles ....
        The brain said that was over three hundred kilometres ....
        The conscience ruled that a cheque would have to be left
in exchange for what would be the equivalent of a hijack ....
        And that small part of the head called the intelligence
pondered .... for a moment .... and then exclaimed:
     - TWO HUNDRED MILES?   YOU MUST BE BLOODY JOKING!
        So that idea fell through as well.   Days were passing and
cause for optimism was minimal.   Until Mano and I went and had
a drink with this friend who said why not go by canoe?   Why not?
Umm .... good question.   Have a non-Islamic beer.   He just
happened   to   be   the   former   British   junior   lightweight
underwater canoe champion or something and he said he'd make me
one.
     - Have you ever canoed before?
     - Well once, when I was fifteen, I went canoeing on ....
     - Yes, I see.   Er .... have another beer.
        And so it came to pass that he did not make me one, for we
couldn't find the right materials.   But what did come to pass
was something else that was just able to pass as a canoe.
Specially designed for taking the kids out on a FriSunday
afternoon it was: an inflatable bubble.   Different bits were
blown up,   not by the Libyan security forces,   and sure enough,
there it was,   one little,   ten-foot canoe.   The very thing,
just as long as you were only going out for the day onto the
Lagan.   Have another beer.
        Time   to   think of other thoughts.   Where was   the best
place for launching?   How far off the coast would I need to go?
What look-out posts and radar stations did the Libyans have on
their cliffs and out to what range did they operate?   How long
could I survive at sea?   What weather conditions would I meet?
Would I like another beer?   I must say,   these expatriates did
seem to be remarkably buoyant in booze.   I had not had one
alcoholic drink since arriving in North Africa,   mainly out of

respect to the Moslem, but here, in the privacy of their own homes, every westener was busy with his dustbin, brewing up another gallon or two of not best but good if not better bitter. Work routines were pretty casual, so generosity and beer overflowed. Meanwhile, whenever a problem of transport arose, the good Mano would say, don't worry, I'll drive you there. Fortunately, he had a government vehicle, and this facilitated our passage through army checkpoints .... but they were pretty casual efforts at the best of times anyway.

Further thoughts revolved around what might happen if I was detected at sea. The trigger-happy habits of the Libyans were well known. We decided that my best hope would be for the first bullet to make a small hole in the main buoyancy chamber because then, as air hissed out of the resulting orifice, I would speed like a rude balloon in an erratic zig-zag unto the blue. Er .... have another beer.

So, the plot was hatched. This was to be the day. The sun had set, our earlier reconnoitres had been successful, and after a long haul over the sand dunes we came to a spot at the end of a long long beach where, in the lee of a small headland, the surf was relatively peaceful. Here, in the faint twilight, we prepared for sea. Into the canoe, we blew exhausted air; and into the canoe, we laid an egg and other food supplies, enough for a good few days. Most things, especially the paddle, we tied to the canoe, and me, with string. My reasons for this were actually because I thought it wise to do so, just in case I was shot at and one or more air chambers were punctured. The dangers, I felt, were Libyan rather than nautical.

The wind had died to a whisper, and with luck would resume from the west shortly. Further down the coast, Russian missiles pointed in all directions. Nearby, French mirage aircraft were on constant alert. All along the coast, West German infra-red devices and radar sets were being built, all to be fed into a central computer at HQ, the army post of El Bardia. Fortunately, this last lot was still under construction, but other radar sets were definitely operational. Mano gave a great push. I was launched. The first thing I did, in this happily gentle surf, was a complete circle. I did not know how or why. Mano shouted advice, but in the noise of the waves, I heard nothing. Somehow, I managed to sail sinuously through these little breakers. I was at sea. I turned to wave good-bye but, as they say in Belfast: there he was, gone. All was dark.

And all was well. Alone, I felt not a little small. Indeed, I was altogether rather apprehensive about the whole crazy venture - hadn't I already used up all my quota of lives? - was the cost of flying via Greece really that much more expensive than a plastic paddle boat? - was I nuts? Heading out to deeper waters, I hoped for the assistance of a God or luck; and perhaps it didn't matter which I received, as long as I realised I couldn't do things just by myself.   So, with a long and lonesome journey in front of me, I was tempted to prayer .... to two prayers, in fact, for my ecumenical deity:

> Patron saint of consolation
> Help me in my desperation,
> From here to my destination
> Grant me constant constipation.

And:
> Guide me, lead me, back from deuteronomy,
> To the book of exodus.
> N-sha-Allah, the soldiers of Libya
> See me not.   Hamdullah.

Up the Poop

The piece of metal called my bicycle I had, needless to say, left behind. There it would sit, no doubt for many a year, until at last Libya progressed into the post-capitalist era. At this stage, I had not thought about my own future; all I was intent on doing was getting to Egypt where, at a guess, I would kiss the soil. What was to happen then, I knew not. I would face that obstacle when, if, I got there. Meanwhile, the immediate problem was to get this canoe under control. It kept on going round in circles. I altered the loads, moving myself to the middle, to the back, anywhere, to try and make it go straight. I even turned right round to make the canoe go backwardsforwards, if you see what I mean, but nothing worked. The only result was that all my bits and pieces, on all their bits of string, were by now in an absolute mess. At least my bailer was close at hand.

Gradually, I got the hang of how to paddle in a straight line. Navigation was fairly easy, for it was a beautiful starlit night, the north star was clearly visible, and after I'd got a few miles offshore, an easterly course was readily set. The wind was perfect. Calm indeed it had been for the launching, and now it was beginning to be a fair and gentle breeze from the west, pushing me from behind. The only thing I knew not was the speed I was making, not least because of the switched-off lighthouse; my only method of navigation, therefore, was that of dead reckoning; in theory, a 1 knot current was urging me forward; in practice, the wind was also helping but to an unknown extent. The half-moon which arrived at midnight gave insufficient light on the subject, namely the headland, and I didn't know whether or not it was time to start heading south-east rather than east. I turned. Better to be closer to the land than further away, I thought, especially as the westerly wind meant there was no danger of a lee shore. That thought was nearly a fatal mistake. Meanwhile, the wind was still increasing, as too was the sea.

The trouble with this inflatable boat was that the damn thing was neither rigid nor ridged. So when a wave came along and hit the stern, the stern did duly rise, and as the crest moved along the length of the canoe, so did the midships section and finally the bow respond to the law of Archimedes, while the stern section then sank into the ensuing trough. For me, sitting, my back resting on my rucksack, my legs straight out in front of me, the sensation was odd. In a small sea, with lots of little waves, it was like working a silent pneumatic drill - a slightly longer sea gave an effect which was little less than erotic - but an increasing wind and rougher seas soon brought my mind back to earth .... which was somewhere .... over there .... on the starboard beam .... perhaps. Where was that headland? Soon the waves were getting quite substantial, rising above my head for the moment or two I sat in the trough. And yet still further the waters swelled, the crests now breaking in their enthusiasm as they sucked and swirled round this blown-up bubble of a boat.

It must have been about three in the morning - the moon was quite high - when suddenly, the silent arm of a powerful searchlight beamed out across the troubled waves .... sweeping .... sweeping round .... and back again.   Thank God or luck, I was sunk in a trough when the beam passed for the first time, well protected in the shadow of a crest of what was now becoming really quite a rough sea.   That crest probably saved my life. Meeeow.   Thank God or luck a lot, I was in another trough when the beam passed back again.   A second crest on an act of mercy. Meeeow meeeow.

The conclusion was obvious.   I'd been detected by radar, doubtless as a faint echo, and 'they' were searching for confirmation. "They". They presumably were bored radar operators, sitting in front of a circular screen which rotated with a monotony which could only mesmerise .... until .... at last .... bleep!   A little echo twitched the tedium of the ops room.

- Contact! New contact Sir.   Echo, bearing zero five seven, range five thousand metres.

- Switch to searchlight!   All positions to standby!

I immediately turned tail and crouched over my knees so as to present as small a radar target as possible, and I headed further out to sea.

- Echo faded Sir.   Lost contact.   Searchlight operator reports no sighting.

- All positions, relax.

Empty boredom returned to the look-out post, Libya was not going to be invaded, not this night anyway, and thus the middle watch passed.

- One small contact, but it was nothing.

How wrong they were.   It had not been nothing;   it had been me, it was me.   And me was it.   And it me I did manage to get a quick compass bearing, so at least I knew exactly where I was.   It was a near escape, though; saved by the rough weather.   Perhaps it was also just as well my canoe was a soft and circular inflatable.   Anything else more solid or of squarer cross-section would have given a more positive radar echo.   And I would have been shot or bombed or missiled or otherwise unable to write for the rest of the night, I headed east.   Only when dawn confirmed that I was well off the coast did I start once more to turn to a more southerly course.

My big worry - or one of them - was the wind.   As long as it was from the west or north, I would be OK, ish, but if it backed southwards and blew me out to sea, well .... again, I would be sunk.   (If after eight days there was still silence, Mano was going to initiate an air-sea search;   perhaps;   for how, he knew not;   but it was good to know that somebody was worrying about me.)   At the moment, however, the wind was a little confused, sometimes from the north-west, sometimes the south-west, but always fresh to strong.   Thus also was the sea in a mixed up state, with waves coming from many westerly directions, while a bigger more persistent swell still originated from the mid-west.

Anyway, so far so good. The sun was now shining. The crests of the waves were a'tumbling down in excited white horses. The sea was a brilliant blue. The breeze still fresh to strong. It was, altogether, perfect after-shave weather. Knowing the height of the cliffs at El Bardia, I reckoned I was now about eighteen miles off the coast. A bit too far for nautical comfort, perhaps, but at least I was safely out of sight of militant radar or eye. And the wind, on the whole, was still pushing me in the right sort of direction.

Lunchtime; ri'ht oh. I laid the paddle alongside my legs. Up .... and down .... went the canoe. I hadn't eaten much so far, not least because of my lavatorial problems. Up .... down. Peeing was OK; I just pee'd into my bailer and then threw the contents over the leeward balloon. Up .... down. More serious operations .... up .... well, I'd prayed they wouldn't be necessary. Down. Now, what would I have? Up. A cheese sandwich? Down. Or jam? Up. I leant forward to have a closer look. Jam I think. Up. Like Pooh bear, I buried my head in my sack of food. Up. Up? Three ups? What about a down? Ooops. Ooops? What's ooopsaaaAAAAGH!!? Over! Splash! Capsize! Downdowndown, down and out and downunder.

Up .... down. Upsidedown. Upset. Wet. Still the crests came and crashed their blessed baptisms upon me. What had been a good force 6 protecting me from the military eye of the searchlight was now a bad force 7 protecting me from everything save only itself. I held the bubble close to my bosom and trod water for a while in my own get-away corner of the Med.

N-sha-Allah. Everything, well most things, were tied to everything else by those ex-infernal now precious pieces of string. The main item on the agenda was to get myself back onboard by first righting the canoe, and then by pulling myself up and over one end of it, and hence into it. I grabbed the stern, an appropriate end. Heave. And again. Bit more. Nearly there. Another heave. Ah shit - capsized again. OK, lad, take a rest. I was puffing heavily, and I thought a little pause would do no harm. Again, I thought of death. But I couldn't die yet; damn it, I hadn't even written 'me' memoires! And I thought of all those others, whatevertheyweres, who could see me. My own deceased relatives and ancestors, were they enjoying a free farce? What a fool I must have looked.

If life is full of dangers, as sometimes it is, then I would far rather face the dangers of nature than those of my fellow man. To be caught at sea, in a desert or on the mountain top can easily be fatal, yet somehow such dangers cause less fear. To die of natural causes in a natural world of which one is a part would not be such a bad thing. To face the dangers of man, however, to be confronted by hatred or jealousy,

it is that which makes me shake in trepidation.   Natural pain I
will accept;   the scourge of cancer, if such is to be my fate, I
will struggle against;   even the wrath of a wild animal I will
if necessary submit to;   but the violence of another human being
I dread, with every fibre of my being.   In all such cases, if it
is only I who am threatened, I will forever run away.   If
someone else is the victim, God give me strength to intervene.

        After a suitable rest thinking about holidays in Bangor, I
made a second attempt at getting myself back into the canoe.
Another heave .... steady now .... slowly .... keep your legs
low ....   I was in!   I laid down, just for a moment or two,
and then started to pull lots of bits of string to get everything
back onboard.   Some things were gone and gone for good.   My
hat!   One bag of food - all of it - loaves of bread, fresh
fruit by the kilo and even a tin of cheese - had all gone to
feed the fishes which perhaps would now also believe in miracles.
I'd lost my diary and a book or two, those little things which
are so important to only their owner;   the book, James Joyce's
Ulysses was not so much a loss, and I happily joined the ranks
of so many who have failed to read it in its entirety.   (Damn
it - you can't say that - you'll never get a review in the
Irish Times!)   But all the addresses of folk I'd stayed with
throughout the four countries of North Africa were now up wind,
down stream and down below;   that was serious.   I'd written to
quite a few from Tunis, but I knew there were many Europeans who,
in return for hospitality, promised to write and never did.
Now here was I, and I was going to be another one.

        But grave was that loss of food, though grave it was not to
mean.   My desire to reach Egypt became more urgent, if only
because of hunger.   Thank the Lord and bits of string, I still
had fresh water;   needless to say, in my capsize, I had swallowed
a fair percentage of the Mediterranean, and my thirst was now
noticeable.   I had but one option in front of me: keep
paddling.   The wind was now, in fact, subsiding a little;
anything else would have made life impossible, if the positive
can be rendered negative, or death possible, the negative
positive.   Yet this was no time for philosophising or playing
with words which all too often is what philosophy is all about.
Paddling was resumed, due south, straight, ish, for Egypt.   The
afternoon was quiet enough ....   and by early evening the entire
surface of the sea was amazingly calm, save for a long and gentle
swell.

        Dusk.   Listen.   I could hear the noise, the roar of
surf crashing onto a distant shore.   What joy was mine.   I did
not at this stage know what size those breakers were, nor their
range from my present position - but that was because I now
didn't really know where I was anyway;   my navigation out of
sight of land was subject to error.   But like a French
lieutenant heading for the Nile, I knew I was going to literally
hit Egypt .... somewhere.   So I kept paddling.   Sometimes, I
rested; I even tried while the seas were so calm, to catch a wink

or two of sleep, but that was impossible.   I was, afterall, still soaked to the skin, and quiet slumbers were just not on. The one trouble with these calm waters was that there was no way of knowing from which direction the wind would start again.   For a while, it began to blow from the south - I was already paddling! - but it faded.

At last, the dawn.   And there it was: the land of Egypt! An undulating line of solid ground, silhouetted in the first faint light of day, was visible only when the swell held me on its crest.   As each in turn rushed towards the shore, so I sank back into the long deep trough which followed, and all was hidden from view.   The wind was still calm but for some reason, this enormous swell was forever rushing in from the north-west to concentrate and strengthen itself in this slightly concave bay before cascading down onto what was obviously a very steep shore. As the twilight pushed the darkness away, I could not only hear the breaking surf; I could now also see great plumes of spray as so much kinetic energy was so abruptly smashed to a halt.

I began to think of how best to land.   The slalom champion in Tobruk had told me exactly how to do it, but I couldn't remember whether he'd said head-on or sideways.   It struck me that there was a pretty fundamental difference between the two.   Ach, what the hell.   I decided I knew nothing.   I would just paddle as hard as I could, hoping to start after the last wave and to arrive before the next one.   Naïve fool that I was.   For a time, I sort of went up and down, not just vertically now, I mean horizontally, looking for a bit of beach where the surf was not so menacing.   Alas, no variety in its ferocity offered itself.   I was also a bit worried about the possibility of landing on rocks but, as I got nearer, it looked as if these were few and far between.

So, that was OK.   I would just have to keep my fingers crossed.   Right.   Good luck.   Let's go.   Or good God. Paddle, son, paddle.   A wave caught my stern, lifted me up, hurled me forward, cast me down and sucked me back a little while it itself sped on forward to roll over itself and crash onto the beach, sending feathers of spray whipping across the surface of the cascading crest like a dying sailfish on its tail, fast and fierce in its flight from fear!   It was all very beautiful.   For God's sake, lad, you're not writing your memoires yet, PADDLE!   Another wave put me through the same routine, uplifting my stern my midships my all till I was almost in a standing position, up up over down - ah, my penultimate wave - and the breaking foam careered forward with suicidal speed to smash itself to death with deafening noise on the steep and stubborn sands of land.   The next one would be it.   Head-on or sideways?   God?   (It was no good asking luck.)   I paddled as fast as I could.   Faster.   FASTER.   Oh hell ....

The wall of water arose and lifted me once more into a semi-vertical pose, while its curling surf loomed over me for a moment .... pause .... and then the froth came crashing forth:

I was sitting;   I did stand;   I was off;   it was over;   all was under,   rent asunder,   in the thunder of the surf.   Capsize!   I'd done it again.

SWIM!   Swim, splatter, splash.   The shore was sheer indeed; just   three   metres   in   and   I   was   out   of my depth.   I   swam   and scrambled,   for an undertoe could very easily have sucked me back to where I'd just been.   That I write these words is proof that it did not.   A couple of strokes and I was there,   touching the firmament,   terra firma,   dry land.   Success .... just. Meeeow meeeow meeeow.   I struggled for a time, heaving canoe and goods up onto the shore,   safe from subsequent waves.   My paddle had broken   -   glad it hadn't done that out at sea.

A lonely figure,   a man,   was over there.   He was running away.   Oh, cheers. No. He stopped. He was coming back. Good good.   In a babble of Arabic,   he greeted me warmly and thrust a cigarette   into my mouth.   Immediately,   he started to   rummage through   my   baggage.   I didn't care;   I was   too   tired,   too exhausted, too hungry to care.   Soaked and shivering, I was just glad to be alive.   But I did not kiss the soil of Egypt;   there was none;   it was all sand,   just like Libya.

Pchiaow!   Pchiaow!   (Wow,   another meeeow!)   Pchiaow! Sorry,   dear   reader,   I'm just trying to write of rifle fire; and in the still of the dawn on this open beach,   the noise shattered the silence.   Pchiaow,   pronounced with a capital pch,   fits the calibre.   The soldier took his head out of my rucksack, waved a ceasefire to his companion and resumed his search.   His comrade in arms,   not such a friendly fellow,   spoke with his   gun.   Now hand-signs   were   often   a form   of   inter-racial   inter-national communication;   gun-signs,   more limited in scope,   were far more readily   understood.   OK,   so I stuck my hands up and OK,   so I stood   over   there and .... well ....   I suppose if you were   an Egyptian soldier,   forever posted on bleak and lonely shores,   then you   too would have been quite surprised if somebody from Belfast suddenly arived,   unannounced,   in a little red bubble boat.   Come to think of it,   I was quite lucky the Egyptians didn't shoot   me on sight.   Fortunately,   and it was pure luck,   or something, I arrived   at   the   very hour of sunrise.   They had not   seen   me coming.   I just, as it were,   appeared, and it was then too late to shoot me 'cos they were already talking to me.

*   *   *

Here   endeth my on the spot inspection of the Libyan   armed forces;   and   here beginneth my look at the Egyptian ones,   and their   look at me.   Having searched all my belongings and changed me   into a dry set of my own clothes   -   quite chuffed by that   I was;   two capsizes yet all the clothes in 'me' rucksack were still perfectly dry   -   they escorted me down the beach to their little army look-out hut.   I could hardly move!   Both legs were stiff, and my right arm had just seized up;   I couldn't rotate my wrist at all, and any attempt at so doing made a horrible noise of friction from somewhere amongst my ligaments.   The wrist straps I'd worn had only eased the pain, for nothing, I suppose, could have prevented some damage from thirty-six hours of near-constant paddling.   It was amazing, though, that apart from a little stiffness in the thighs, I'd noticed none of these ailments while I'd been afloat.   After I'd landed, after the main worry had gone, only then did I realise that, damn it, I was only in agony!

I hobbled slowly along, using the half paddle as a support, while the soldiers carried all my gear.   In their tiny hut, a radio buzzed and burped messages of me, but at least I was given some food.   Beans.
- More?
- Please.

Then an army jeep rolled up, out stepped an officer or two, out poured a question or many.   In between beans, I provided what answers I could and, once my story was known, and believed, they all seemed quite happy.   Though yet again, everything was searched.

By military escort, I was taken to the main army camp. More senior officers were called, more searches were initiated and more questions were asked.   It was all a repeat performance. Within a disciplined force, everybody is frightfully good at doing what they've been told to do, but helpless at doing something which requires unprecedented procedures, and my case had not been covered by book reference one rules and regulations army soldiers for the use of.   {Initiative is only allowed, a), if it's successful, and b), if no-one more senior is present.}

By this stage, I was with the colonels and the brigadiers. They, fortunately, were a little longer in coming, so I had a little sleep.   I was out like a Tobruk power cut.   But not for long.
- Are you a spy?   The temptation to be frivolous I subdued. Compared to the sophistication of the Libyan army, the Egyptian forces seemed to be a motley, medieval crew.   Not that there was merit in either, of course.   It was just so very obvious, right from the outset, that Egypt was the poorer country.   The villages were more sleepy, the donkey was back in prominence. And army camps, in which most of my sight-seeing was conducted at this stage, were just loose collections of old huts, a few empty oil-drums, and the odd loop of barbed wire.   Such military posts were placed haphazardly all over this western part of the country, and in them soldiers were abandoned for months at a time. People sometimes ask others, what do you do?   And if the other replies, I'm a soldier, he thus absolves himself from the responsibility of having to do anything.   He just has to be, here, there, or way out there, somewhere in the western desert.
- I'm intelligence, he said.   The disguise was convincing. I'd been promoted, and I was now being questioned by all sorts of people.   Not just army brigadiers and police inspectors but

also intelligent .... whatever they have in intelligence; I didn't know - that was secret.   Needless to say, however, the questions asked were just the same ones regurgitated; I must say, these officious officials had a very nasty habit of repeating themselves themselves themselves.   And the net result of all these questions was that I was going to be taken to Alexandria.   What for?   For questioning.   Ooh, that would be nice.

Now during all these searches, I'd lost really quite a lot of stuff - some books and clothes, a penknife and even the broken paddle.   Everything had been stolen either by policemen, soldiers, secret agents or intelligent somethings.   Throughout the other countries of North Africa, I'd had next to no trouble from the thief.   The beggar and the peasant do seldom lower themselves to steal;   everywhere, kindness had been the norm; the exception, I now discovered, was the Egyptian policeman. Well, as I just happened to be imprisoned inside a police station, I decided to report these thefts to the police.   Oh well, never mind;   it was just a thought.

To Alex!   (One of the great things about being under arrest is the almost unlimited opportunities for free travel.) At the crack of a tropical dawn, with the sun no more arrived than it was already warm, I was led away under armed guard, along with a couple of other prisoners, to the railway station, where we were all piled into what was a very socialist train - all third class!   The wooden seats were comfortable enough, and every window had a wooden shutter, ready to keep out the glare of the sun.   At least, that was how the train had been built, many many years ago .... in 1903?   Not everything, in these days of lunar travel and space research, was now in working order.

Off we went.   What a train!   No wonder they used to give these things names like flying horse.   The build up to speed was a little slow and laborious but, ah well, it got there soon enough.   And the build up to resonance was taking place at the same time.   These tiny little carriages, only half the length of the modern luxury-appointed vandal-annointed coaches of the Northern Ireland railway service, started to oscillate - not in a rocking motion from left to right, but in a jerky bounce up and down;   they actually started to gallop.   And what a noise!   How they managed to stay on the rails at all was as mysterious as how the bumble bee doth manage to fly, for all the relevant laws of science were defied.

After many a mile of empty desert, I was really quite relieved to reach Alexandria which was, in contrast, full - full to the brim of seething humanity competing with itself.   Buses were forever packed; cars blew constantly at their horns; horses and their two-person carriages had more pleasant but baser hooters;   mopeds were cheeky;   bicycles were everywhere and people too were in the roads 'cos the pavements had been full since long before the sunrise.

But at this juncture my tour of the historic city and its charms was a shade limited; I was dragged off to a police station and dumped therein. By day, I sat in the main sort of question-hall-cum-inquiry-centre and read Dickens; by night, I enjoyed the comforts of a wooden bench. The police were friendly enough, they were just very bad at feeding their suspects. Every day, I had to demand the minimum of sustenance, and the minimum I got - no more. Thereagain, I wasn't taking much exercise, so my hunger was not as bad as it might have been. It was sad, however, to see what might have been reversed racialism. The other prisoners were all crowded into badly lit and badly ventilated rooms such that each had just about enough room to lie down on the floor and no more. I suppose I should have protested to demand equal treatment.

The next morning I was led off, under guard, into the city. A little chat up would be a good idea, I thought.

- Who's that? I asked my escort, pointing to the statue of what had obviously been a pretty important personality.

- Mohammed Ali. Yes, I suppose he was almost bound to be what he had a 99% chance of being. At that time, alas, I had not read my Egyptian history and didn't know that here was a nineteenth century ruler of Egypt just as good bad as the European colonialists who took over the country on the grounds that such rulers had not been good bad enough. So that conversation didn't get very far. Nor did the subsequent interrogation.

On day two, I was pushed into the back of a black moria which was already full of criminals various and off we went to one of those relics of British colonialism, the old courthouse. Down, down we descended, to the very cellars; with a pair of hand-cuffs my wrists were clasped and I was cast into a cell. The door clanged shut. An enormous key turned the lock; and each such noise echoed in the vastness of the vaults.

- Oh hallo. I had company. His crime, like that of so many others, was simply that of having hash. What a tiny offence. What a commotion to deal with it all. Orders were shouted and decisions were yelled; the net effect was nothing. Suspects were continually being taken from here to there; cell doors were opened and shut with the frequency of those in the public conveniences of Piccadilly - a poor parallel, for these inmates looked anything but relieved - and in my tiny cell, I began to look at the little things in life, the different lines on the different bricks, the tiny minutiae of nothingness. What a change it was from exploring in the desert. Come the end of the day, we were all shoved back into the black moria and returned to the police station. A fellow prisoner gave me a sandwich; now why couldn't a police officer do something like that?

To be fair, the policeman in charge of the station - he spoke frightfully good English, actually - was a gentleman. He had learnt from the English not only their language. His manners were exemplary, and his dress tunic was always impeccable; meanwhile, the poor ol' lesser ranks wore thick serge uniforms, the sort the military always give to the raw recruits so that they can never look as smart as their superiors. It was good for discipline, I suppose, if there was always something to criticise.

And I will criticise. The loo in this police station was absolutely revolting. Loos throughout North Africa were pretty filthy for all too often, where once there had been, there now no longer was proper drainage, proper flushing or proper anything. I was perfectly happy using the non-European type loo and I think water is much much cleaner than toilet paper. But in mosques, cafés and hotels, I learnt to expect something to be out of order in the loo. As a Parisian I bumped into commented:

- One is persuaded by the customs and circumstances which prevail .... (she spoke very good English) .... to change one's attitude towards shit. (Pardon her French.)

It really did seem quite incredible that so much effort should go towards the arrest of drug smokers while so little was done in sanitation. The drug takers affected few. The police loo, a pile of festering faeces, was the breeding ground of flies and the sustenance of cholera. It was, literally, a crime.

Still, my crime wasn't dope. My offence was simply the circumnavigation of that fence which the Egyptian defence forces insisted could keep out the offensive Libyans. And little me was telling all of them they were only wrong. In mitigation, however, I'd also proved the Libyan system to be equally useless, and on reflection they were then quite pleased with my exploits. Hence my first and only bottle of special branch special brew.

More black morias, handcuffs, interviews and what in Belfast would easily have been described as harassment but what in Egypt was just the Egyptian way of doing things were eventually followed by my release.

- D'you mean I'm free?
- Yes; we don't charge for accommodation here.

So I picked up my rucksack and my deflated canoe without a paddle and walked out into the streets of Alex. First things first: a meal o' beans, a hotel with a shower, and then a message to Mano to say I was still alive. Altogether I'd spent six days in custody; it could have been worse. N-sha-Allah.

So concluded my fact finding tour of the Libyan/Egyptian border; and the facts were simply that two nation states were wasting an incredible amount of resources in a situation which was, at best, permanent cold war; a sad state of affairs if compared to previous years when week-ends in Alex had relieved the monotony of months in Tobruk. Both states, in theory, wished to uphold principles and things like that, but both states in so doing severely restricted the freedom of their own citizens to move around their own country, and both states gave excessive powers to certain groups and individuals called the security forces. In defending rights, they restricted them. Perhaps it

is as it were by definition impossible to uphold freedom in a
militarist state. Here lies another reason why the world must,
and why the world will, learn more of positive pacifism.

                              *   *   *

        I will return to the politics of Libya, not least because
there are some progressive ideas both expressed and practiced
there. For the moment, however, let us travel not to the most
positive of peaceful states, but to what was, in 1980, a troubled
land, The Sudan.
        In Khartoum lived the president, in his palace. Next door
lived the army, in their barracks. In a land where coups could
and did so easily happen, it was sort of safer that way. Yet
again, a thin veil of democracy covered a virtual dictatorship in
a land too large to be one. In the early years of independence,
The Sudan had suffered a bitter war between the Arab speaking
Islamic north and the more English speaking Christian negro south
- yet another war for which the nineteenth century European map
drawers bore not a little responsibility. Then in '69 -
'twas a very good year for the coup - Numeri came to power in a
somewhat undemocratic but nevertheless bloodless manner, and
three years later he managed to bring the civil war under
control. The south was given a certain measure of autonomy, and
that compromise was the basis of the subsequent peace.
        The emphasis was on the words "certain measure". Come
April 1980, the southern president did something wrong. So
Numeri sacked him, dissolved his parliament and called for fresh
elections. Autonomy, afterall, does have its limits! Trouble
was afoot, and some inter-tribal-cum-inter-racial tensions were
still just below the surface. Now to have declared a state of
emergency would have aroused suspicions and stirred up the
international press; that might have solved nothing. Indeed,
it could actually have exacerbated the situation. Instead,
Numeri said there was a cholera scare. There wasn't at all.
Yet with this one stroke, the movement of peoples was drastically
reduced and the influx of foreign reporters was avoided. Very
clever, really.
        As a result, there were no boats sailing up and down the
river and it was quite likely that the one and only road of sand
would also soon be closed. My own journey south indicated
that I was, indeed, slowly leaving the desert of the Arab north
to enter black, negroid, tropical Africa. The signs were there:
yesterday, a hippopotamus bathed by the banks of the Nile; to-
day, a Christian, bible in hand, spoke of Babylon, of the
apocalypse, of seven headed harlots and of all sorts of things
designed, no doubt, to ensure that any Moslem of any sense stayed
a Moslem.
        The line between north and south Sudan was certainly no
mark of latitudinal whitewash registered in the United Nations

and recorded in public libraries throughout a land without any. Rather, it was the whitewash of the mind which suggested to all in a world or nation divided that they must be either this or that. Just as in Northern Ireland where folk fear they must be catholic or protestant, unionist or nationalist; just as in the world at large where we are told we are either of the east or the west; so too in The Sudan one was either Arab or Negro. Yet here was a land where, via a series of small villages, discernible trends from one community to another, between one tribe and the next, gradually culminated in a considerable difference between he who said he was an Arab of the north (even if he was part-negro which he almost certainly was) and he who claimed a purely negro birth-right.

Now the President had decreed that elections there would be, so elections there were. And in the land to the east of The Sudd, where miles of flat and barren scrub separated one lonely village from its distant neighbour (and where at one stage I travelled on 'me' bike for well over two days by myself, in a land of no people, no water, no relief from a scorching sun, no punctures, no hyenas, a few passing onyx and a packet of biscuits), democratic principles were put into practice. The promised election was in full swing, and this was the chance for the people to choose a new administration (as long as it was more suited to the wishes of Numeri) and thus to stop 'the cholera scare'. Schoolteachers and suchlike were the presiding officers, and each village was visited in turn. Where adult illiteracy was so high, symbols were used as well as names, so the voter could choose his or her own candidate, if not by his name, by his insignia. Such included the spear, the bicycle, the aeroplane and the bed .... but what the political significancies were remained obscure. After each had voted with his or her little 'x', he or she would have the index finger daubed in ink so that there would be none of the intimidations and impersonations that you get in Belfast's elections.

Too often the commentators of the west dismiss the 'democracy' of the third world as empty. They criticise and rightly so those presidential elections in which the sitting president is the only candidate standing; the choice therein is, of course, none. They also complain about the use of symbols and again, not without some justification. Perhaps the nicest incident was in a two-cornered contest in which the incumbent used the symbol of the lion, inferring strength, power, might and all that; while his opponent was only allowed a picture of the hyena, that most hated scavenger of the savannah. Oh, by the way, the hyena lost. Lastly, many a European finds fault in the way most African 'democracies' have evolved, if that's the right word, into one-party states.

*   *   *

Before too much abuse is hurled at the African adaptation of the Oxbridge adoption of the word democracy, perhaps a closer examination of the Westminster model would not be inappropriate. Let's look at it this way. Prior to any election in a two-party system, the party in power will be tempted to do one or two things. Like it might give a tax-cut or two; it might extract some more of that oil, just to boost the economy a little, and so on. It could be worse: it might even fight a skirmish in The Falklands, raise the temperature on the question of the north, invade Grenada, or whatever, just to whip up patriotic fervour and national chauvinism. The two-party political system, then, can prompt some to violence - and not only in Northern Ireland has it done just that - and others to economic abuse.

In total, the two-party system can and does tempt the government of the day to put short term economic gain first, and the long term, a very poor second. The present is given priority, and the future is put at risk. Either it's the fault of the political parties who promise those who have, that they will continue to have .... or those who have less, that soon they'll have more; or it's ourselves who are wooed by such selfish motivations and who then vote 'em in!

The two party political system - those very institutions which control all that is economic and whose interests are best served by extracting the oil and cutting down the tree etc, - that whole structure which we call democracy, in effect risks the future for the sake of the present. Therefore, the party political system is a major threat to the ecology of this planet and the survival of our species! It's not that I'm not democratic - no no - 'tis just that our democracy so called, this 'x' every four years or so and in the meantime shut up, deserves not the name.

The two party system suffers from many deficiencies; let me talk of just two more. In this technological age, the job of prime minister is about the only one for which no formal academic or professional qualification is required. In theory, therefore, the British people for example could elect any one person of the forty million sane sober and sensible adults domiciled therein. In practice, however, the party political system allowed them to choose, if we take the year '83, between Thatcher and Foot, and perhaps Steele was in with half a chance. The British, therefore, had a choice of 2.5; the Irish one of 2; while the Sudanese had one of 1 - Numeri; and the Russians also had a choice of 1 - Gorbachev. But is 2.5 much of an advance on 1 along a scale of freedom measured from 1 to 40,000,000?

Just as a one-person presidency limits an African election to just one candidate, so too the party system of politics restricts our choice to one of two, or thereabouts. Furthermore, in almost every democracy, there is this disease, this plague, this tendency for each and every nation to divide itself into two. America has its Republicans and its Democrats; Britain

for years has suffered under alternative Labour and Conservative
administrations;   Ireland   has its Fianna Fail and Fine Gael,
(and while the differences between the two are not always
apparent, they are nevertheless keenly felt);   and so on, in
Germany, France and elsewhere.   {And it was not by any
revolutionary process that the Russians split into the bolsheviks
and the mensheviks!}

Now to export that two-party-political system to a country
like The Sudan, already divided between its Arabic and its Negro
peoples, was at least unwise;   as it was to send it to Uganda
which we've discussed already;   or to Kenya where the Kikuyu
tribe of the central region has a small but nevertheless real
numerical predominance over the Luo tribes in the west of the
country. In such circumstances, the two party system was bound to
provoke inter-tribal conflict and perhaps even violence.   In
such lands, councils of elders and so on would have been and
would still be much more appropriate - and much more
democratic!   The one party systems of Africa might actually
warrant some consideration.

The two-party system in Britain for example, means that the
British politicians are always squabbling amongst themselves ....
unless they're united in a major squabble against someone else,
like Hitler.   The party system, in effect, is almost a recipe
for disaster.   In Northern Ireland, of course, it was and is
just that.   The one party states of Africa do most certainly
have logic, and they might, afterall, be not such a bad idea.

Alas, they probably are.   If the president was Amin,
there was no chance.   If 'twas Gaddafi, there was little.   If
Bourguiba .... well the old boy has just swung backwards-forwards
into a multi-party state, after years and years of one party
rule.   Is it a reform, I wonder, or is it merely the senile
stagger of one close to his grave?   Ummm .... the latter, I
suspect, especially when in the '81 election the national front
got 95% of the vote!   Let us continue;   if the one party
president was Moi or De Chablis, there was a ray of hope, and if
it was Numeri of The Sudan ....

Well at least he was able to bring an end to that civil
war, a war which by its close in '72 had killed almost a million
people.   Unfortunately, like most politicians around the world,
he knew not when to step down or how to devolve power.   The
very civil wars he helped to stop have now, eleven years later,
started again.   And all the elections were merely the tools by
which he hoped to retain acceptability and thereby the
presidency.

The average southern Sudanese voter, however, believed in
democracy and in the system his/her country had adopted.
Happily, they did all go and vote for the local candidate of his
or her choice.   None of them belonged to any one particular
party or faction (or politicised tribal and/or religious
grouping) - such are the advantages of one party politics.
Each of them was standing on his - they were, unfortunately,

almost   inevitably   all male   - own ability,   each with his   own
policy and philosophy,   and I suspect the guy with the double bed
was the winner.   'Cos that's what politics is all about.
        Meanwhile,   in   the   'advanced democracies'   of north-west
Europe, people wave their symbols of red white and blue and green
white and orange,   and they forget that all this cotton came from
The Sudan.
        Alas,   whoever   was   the winner mattered little,   for Numeri
dissolved this assembly as well,   not many months later,   and he
then   tried to divide the whole southern province into many small
regions.   Good ol' British ploy, that one.   Like most things
in life, the politics of the place were complicated by subtefuge
and   intrigue,   and   the   situation at the   time of writing   is
affected   by   a number of factors: 1,   an American oil company has
found   oil   in   the   south   -   at last Numeri has   a chance of
clearing his national debt,   a debt as big as the gross national
product!   2,   the   south want their share; 3, America is playing
dangerous   games   with   its rapid deployment force;   4,   Libya   has
decided it's time to hate its Sudanese neighbour; 5, Numeri has
gone all Islamic to try to placate the Moslem Brotherhood; 6, the
southern rebels are attacking the American oil companies; 7, the
USA   supports the Islamic state of Numeri while Gaddafi helps the
southern rebels and even drops a few bombs on Omdurman .... and
8, I for one am confused! All in all, however, suggests that the
democratic   process   is merely a therapy for the public at large,
while behind closed doors abroad,   plots are planned, plans   are
plotted ....   and principles give way to pragmatics.   Of such is
politics, worldwide.

                              *   *   *

        Now   let's   look   a little more closely   at   that European
tendency   in   which every political question is viewed as one   of
only two alternatives.   Happily,   it is a tendency not employed
in most   domestic circumstances,   so the rate of   separation of
couples   is   still considerably less than that of   their   comings
together.   Compromise   is in the home,   and arguments of   the
youcan-youcan't/youcan-youcan't   variety   don't   afflict   our
personal relationships too often.
        In politics they do.   It is this-or-that, for-or-against,
youcan-youcan't;   it is a system which allows for the most simple
of   voting   procedures to be employed;   it is called   democracy;
it   is enshrined in the 'principle' of majority rule;   it really
is all very childish;   and it allows every nation which practices
it to   suffer from this disease of "national   schizophrenia",
dividing   itself   into   two,   allowing the two bits   to be made
manifest in two political party groupings,   and living in a state
of   permanent   cold confrontation.   The very buildings of   our
democracies   have been designed especially to allow this   process
to be   institutionalised into perpetuity;   and   one side,   the

government, confronts the other, the opposition, in every chamber, in every debate, in every sense of the word.

This European habit has also affected the politics of the international scene, partially because in the two super-powers a European influence is strong, and partially because the world has evolved to the stage where super-powers dominate everything and where there are, for the most part, just the two of them. The communist-or-capitalist, this-or-that argument threatens the very survival of us all. It is interresting to note, in passing, how much more schizophrenic each side gets when a third super-power enters upon the stage. Is China on this side or that? And if it's neither will it soon be either? And do we prepare the banquet or the bomb? The very uncertainty of it all are the horns of the diplomatic dilemma. All the anti-communist 'principles' were, are and will continue to be thrown overboard, as the Americans first fight, then woo, then arm, and will they soon argue with and fight again the peoples whose culture was the very foundation of their own European civilisation?

In time, however, the world will, might, get better. Of sanity there are signs, not least among the nations non-aligned, neither this nor that.

In the meantime, everything on the scale writ large remains us-versus-them, left-or-right, east-or-west. "As one dictatorship of man and tyranny of state after the other take over new and larger segments of the international scene, it would seem as if the world itself (has) gone insane. All the signs of an international schizophrenic seizure are multiplying." (Van der Post in 'Jung and the story of our time' - The Hogarth Press.) In external affairs, the world is divided into two; and within our western democracies, everything is again divided into two. The first division is called the cold war, and this we all fear; while the second is described as party politics, which many revere!

So is not our schizophrenia itself schizophrenic; and is not our schizophrenia preparing to defend itself by fighting itself? Verily, the world is contemplating schizophrenic suicide!

It is more often than not quite right for us in the West to criticise the abuses of power which take place in most one-party state democracies in Africa. But we are quite quite wrong if we think that there is something better about our own systems of government. Different, yes; but better, not necessarily. Both systems are primitive tools, and the evolution of our species both demands and depends upon their reform.

*   *   *

Institutionalised schizophrenia under its jingoistic title of majority rule was transported by the British to various corners of the globe, not the least of which were in Africa. As a political system, it has been used and abused in Kenya, and totally rejected in Libya.   They are the two more obvious examples, so can I just look at these?   A combination of the good points of both the two party system of government and the one party state method could result in human progress; a confrontation between the two could be world war III.

*   *   *

Kenya, yet another country where borders were drawn by the courtiers of nineteenth century Europe, was a land wherein prior to that time tribes had lived in what only some historians would describe as anarchy.   It is an oft used word;   the only thing definite about the time and place to which it refers is that little is known.   Perhaps the tribes did fight, perhaps they enjoyed some peace.   But who is to say whether or not that existence was better or worse than the chronicled conquests of chronic civilisations established by the descendents of those (anarchists) who founded the empires and kingdoms of history?

Kenya, then, was a land with an uncertain past.   Before looking at its certain but doubtless dubious present, I want to take a brief look at its recent history, and I start in the foothills of the western escarpment, on the northern slopes of Mount Elgon.   There the land was not so flat and, therefore, not so good for white men to draw straight lines on, to plant by the acre and own by the estate.   So the agriculture was more traditional, the **shambas** smaller, the labour more intensive. And therein sat a village, where once there'd been a jail.   It was a perfect setting for such an imperfect institution;   nature at its best, as it was here, was surely ideal for the purposes of rehabilitation.   The point was made because one of the former prisoners later turned out to be president: Kenyatta. Not a perfect argument, because in that position he had still been a bit of a crook;   he had done a lot for his country, true, but his bank balance showed he had done even more for himself and his family.   And just in case a crisis could cause chaos, he had bought a little nest-egg in the form of a farm in Sussex.   It's a habit not confined to the powerful of Africa, of course   - Paisley has his bolt-hole in Canada.

Kenyatta's wealth had originated from the UK (and a lot of the UK's wealth had originated in Africa, of course, but not all of it from Kenyatta's shamba).   Without the process of decolonisation, he would have remained comparatively poor; without continuous supplies of government finance, he would have been unable to amass the financial bonanza that was soon all his. His wife came to own a few companies, he bought a couple of farms, and a myriad of friends and relatives were able to do very nicely thank you.   Such were the 'benefits' of 'freedom'. Amidst such blatant misappropriations, petty corruptions were commonplace.   Meanwhile, disquiet about his conduct mounted, especially in circles outside his tribe or outside his particular family within the tribe.   But **Mzee**, as he was affectionately known, was as the name implies an old man.   He had a certain charisma   -   his power of oratory was strong   -   and he would be allowed to die naturally.   Perhaps.   Certainly he was not going to be disposed of in his absence;   he made sure of that by never leaving the country.   And certainly he was not going to suffer at the hands of his main rivals, the Luo - their leader,* his old pal in the struggle for freedom, he imprisoned. Another Luo and a most talented politician, Mr Tom Mboya, was gunned down in Nairobi in broad daylight.   The resulting riots left 43 dead, and Kenyatta never again visited those lands in the west.   But who was to be his successor?   As the years went by, interest and intrigue intensified.

In the latter phase of his presidency, one promising MP** from a minority tribe near the coast died somewhat mysteriously in a (sort of) road accident.   He would have been acceptable to most people, being neither Kikuyu nor Luo, but therefore he had been a threat to the Kikuyu succession.   He died, almost certainly at the hands of the GSU, the General Service Unit as the tough boys were called.   Later, a young Kikuyu MP who spoke honestly and frankly about corruption in high places, a certain J.M. Kariuki, was also disposed of.   Before concluding that African countries have terrible politics, it should be recalled that one of the senior police officers reportedly involved in this murder was a white man, a certain Mr Shaw, whose other work was with the Save the Children Fund at a school called Starehe.

Kenyatta, everyone knew, was to die soon.   Just in case the Luos planned a little something, the Kikuyus had their people ready - a force, known as the Ngoroko, was in the hills, ready to take over Nairobi at a moment's notice.   But then the in-fighting amongst the sub-tribes of the Kikuyu was a further complication, those from Nyeri favouring one of their own in preference to the Kiambu nominee.   The plot thickened.

Then Mzee - damn it, he wasn't meant to do that, he only went to Mombasa for two weeks in every year, why did he? .... he was dead.   Hasty phone calls, quick manoeuvrings by Moi and Njonjo who rushed to state house to then broadcast to the nation and .... done.   'Twas all over.   And the moment many had feared passed peacefully enough.

Moi, whom everybody had thought was a bit of a yes-man, figurehead type vice-president, took over with vigour and vim. Njonjo, whom we first discussed on page (61), was an establishment Kikuyu if ever there was one, the very chief of the **wabenzi** tribe, and he backed Moi in his efforts to stop the corruption which had been almost endemic in Kikuyu circles. Meanwhile, the lungs of multi-national companies were able to breathe more easily once more.   With millions invested and millions more in turnovers, they had been worried that the

* *Mr Oginga Odinga*
** *Mr Ronald Ngala*

'stability' of the Kenyatta regime would not last.   Moi, or so
it   appeared,   was   going to offer a more acceptable face to   the
unacceptable façade of capitalist development and so Kenya - like
Egypt, Tunisia and Morocco - again qualified for   the   western
press adjective of 'stable'.   All the company bosses   brackets
white   had   to do was to re-appoint an adviser brackets   black   or
reshuffle   a sales manager brackets black in accordance with   the
ethics   I mean tribalism I mean pragmatism of big   business,   and
the   world of finance could then sit back,   continue trading   and
await the collapse by death or coup of the next presidency.   Of
political stability, there was all too little in Kenya.
        Kenya,   at the time of independence, inherited from Britain
that two party system of politics, that democratic schizophrenia.
It was bound to and indeed it did lead to the Kikuyus of Kenyatta
being   in   one   political party while the Luos were   in   another.
Unfortunately   for the latter,   the former were the   bigger,   and
thus   it became possible for the majority tribe to   dominate   the
smaller ones.   The two parties received voting support based on
tribal   affiliations;   to   move   towards   a   one   party   system,
therefore,   was   essential for the   unity   of the nation   (though
whether or not that was essential was and is not   clear;   still,
we can't change history).   So Kenyatta banned the other lot and
said   his   organisation was   from henceforth to be   <u>the</u>   party.
Since then,   all parliamentary   candidates have had to belong   to
this,   the   one   and only registered party which happily   became
multi-tribal,   and   such   as put themselves forward have   had   to
swear allegiance and that sort of thing.   In theory, within the
nation, within the party, all opinions could be expressed without
fear of factionalism and friction.   In practice, well,   it just
didn't quite work out like that,   and party loyalty all too often
demanded an obedience which was silence.   In theory,   electors
were   still   able to choose between candidates of these   policies
and those of those;   but real politic has seen Njonjo and others
invent   that   perfect   tool   which so   neatly   combined   all   the
principles of democracy with all the pragmatics of   dictatorship:
the uncontested election.
        In moving to a one-party state,   Kenyatta did succumb to   a
bit of the heavy stuff;   just like the two party system,   it's all
subject   to abuse.   The one advantage of the latter is that it
is   usually possible to swing from tweedledum to tweedledee every
5 years or so,   whereas in the one-party state,   the president is
as immovable as a bishop!
        Nevertheless,   at   the   parliamentary   level,   one   party
politics can work,   and work well.   In the first elections after
the   death of the first President,   740 candidates contested   158
seats   -   that's pretty good;   nearly half the sitting members,
cabinet ministers and all,   the electorate rejected in favour   of
some new blood   -   and that's excellent;   and of the MPs elected,
all   the   main   tribes were represented as were racial   minorities
like   the   Asians   and the   Europeans   -   and that's   bloody
marvellous!   Meanwhile,   Britain's ancient two party system   has

yet to produce one black MP!

Kenya's second ruler was not yet as bad as the old man had been, but a few years of power soon dulled his reforming zeal, and yet again the very maintenance of his presidency was becoming a prime objective.   Those of his subjects who dared to voice objective criticism were at best subjected to verbal condemnation, at worst, with all objections over-ruled, sentenced to a spell inside.   In the name of freedom, free thinkers were being confronted by that same heavy hand of the forces of the state.

In the last couple of years, Kenya has had a bumpy ride. An attempted coup in '82 didn't get very far, but popular dissent rumbled on.   In the following year, Moi decided to make Njonjo the scapegoat;   words like traitor were aired, deeds like resignations followed, and in '84 the blackwhiteman par excellence was put on trial.   At the time of writing, however, it seems the tactic may have backfired a little, for while all know Njonjo was not a little corrupt, they also know that Moi is no better.

Kenya, as it is, will not survive very long.   Nor, in theory, should the right-wing regime of Hassan deux;   nor in fact did the presidency of Sadat, so convinced was he that those soldiers were his accolades and not his assassins (though he, of course, was killed by extremists more religious than political); and perhaps the biggest certainty is Bourguiba who even at this late hour, will still be lucky if he dies in his bed.   Alas, everywhere, power has corrupted the powerful, the politics of the one-party state have been introduced for pragmatic reasons only, and the principle of vested interest predominates.   On balance, it is probably fair to say that Africa is a better place as a result of one-party democracy;   a mixture of political and tribal schizophrenia would have been too much.

*   *   *

A younger man by far comes from the opposite end of the political spectrum: Gaddafi.   With much good reason, he sought to replace the old monarchy with something better than the over-centralised politics which Europe pretends are democracy; instead he sought a system of participatory government in which even the villages could play a no less important part.   Let another curtain rise:

On the flat open plains, where drops of rain did seldom fall, where the view was of yellow and blue that was all, life was simple enough even if the blessings of the revolution had given everyone the radio stereo video.   The houses were flat-roofed, single-storey affairs, designed to keep in the breeze and out the sun, and each was in its own compound, the garden of dust and no green surrounded by a wall and a large metal gate.   Yet from this separation all did come together.   The local shop was small perhaps, but all the products of civilisation were there, and all the profits stayed where they were for it was a co-operative; the villagers were justly proud of their achievements in the shop, in the school and in the field, and perhaps not least because they recalled the bad old days of the king.   Under straight capitalism, the bonanza of oil would have led many to the get-rich-quick entrepreneurman-thisword·is·already·long·enough without·adding·woman·person-ship and it would have left others to remain poor.   Under Gaddafi's socialism, the benefits had reached just about everybody.

His philosophy, as expressed in his writings, suggested that every village could and should and indeed would conduct its own affairs.   Each was to elect a committee to be responsible for the shop, the establishment of works and health clinics, the running of the local school.   Excellent.   I did indeed witness clear signs that this policy of self-reliance was actually creating positive results.   Each little village committee then elected one representative to go to the regional chamber, and each regional one did the same for the national council.   All very democratic.   Different from our democracy it indeed was, but democratic it remained and, at least up to this stage, it was actually more democratic than our own version. The national committee then elected its own chairperson and thus was the system complete.   Now we all know that power corrupts and that politicians have already, by virtue of their position, been corrupted.   To ensure the Libyan interpretation of the democratic spirit would not founder on the same rock, Gaddafi decided that the chairperson should only stay in that position for a limited number of years.   Again, the theory appeared to be sound.

Here we come to the crunch.   If everything was to be so frightfully democratic and fair and things, how come Gaddafi was still there, ten years on.   What was more, it seemed as if he was there to stay, that was if **Allah** didn't mind.   There was, then, this slight contradiction between his permanency in a land of constantly changing democracy.   Ah - a genius stroke; he was not the president or chairperson or anything like that, such politicians being elected - he was merely an adviser.   Oh. Was that all right?   And an amazing number of Libyans, happy in their material well-being, replied yes.   An increasing number, however, did not agree.   Gaddafi's time was limited - as long as the CIA didn't try to interfere.

Indeed, in this Orwellian year of writing, the first attempted coup has just taken place.   It failed.   Perhaps all future revolutionaries would care to read page (106) before planning the next attempt.

Apart from the predominance of your man, then, Libyan democracy seemed to be established on a good basis.   It was not a case where the two-party system had been replaced by the one; rather, it was a land where no centralised party existed, and

where each local region could do and did do many things, just as
it liked .... (for as long as the special branch didn't mind).
There were also, of course, certain guidelines under which
ventures were to be co-operative, but that afterall is really
only another way of saying democratic.   The value of the system
basically depended on the degree of local autonomy granted to the
local committee, and certainly this seemed to cover all aspects
of domestic concern - apart, that is, from security.

Under the guise of socialism, Gaddafi's constant cry was
for the revolution.   The ploughshares were placed alongside the
sword or the gun in the posters which were everywhere.   The
revolution was to be armed, fighting the forces of zionism and
imperialism, colonialism and capitalism, revisionism and
ismism .... all of which were everywhere .... apparently.   Under
such a philosophy, easily blessed according to the Moslem
tradition of jihad, the army and secret police were in control.
Only those left behind were constantly urged to do the other bit:
work, work the land.   Libya, to be politically independent, had
to be self-sufficient in food.   In the two islands of
fertility, Tripolitania and Cyrenacia, the farmer was encouraged
to greater efforts.   Elsewhere, the land was sand, in the sand
was oil, and in that oil enough wealth for every Libyan to enjoy
both the basics and the luxuries of materialism, most of which
were imported (from countries of schismism).   Within the time
scale of but one generation, an entire population had moved from
poverty to excess, and they were already begining to suffer,
just as we in the west have done, from twentiethcenturyitis.

*   *   *

While it is fair to criticise the excesses of Gaddafi's
militarism, it is also true to say that, of the countries I
visited, only Algeria and Libya had attempted any form of
decentralisation.   The former was distinctly the more pacifist,
yet both had managed to give local communities a fair measure of
autonomy.

The logic of local autonomy, of community development, of
regional self-reliance is more than reasonable, and can even be
looked at from a centralist view-point.   For when each part of
the nation is self-sufficient in food production, then so too
will be the whole.   Furthermore, the whole world must be, as it
were by definition, self-sufficient.   Only in the West, where
the future has been sacrificed for the sake of the present, do we
find political philosophies at variance with that fundamental
truth.

Unfortunately, the argument for self-sufficiency is seldom
carried forward to its obvious conclusions, namely, that each
region should be self-sufficient not just in food, but in energy
creation, health provision and so on.   Similarly, each could
look after its own schooling, policing and caring functions.

When each community is not totally self-sufficient but at least reasonably self-reliant (and this might only happen when each have seen the need for a more broadly based, both academic and practical, education), then at last will we all be more developed. And each community will be a whole, for therein will be both the doctor and the plumber, both the lawyer and the labourer; with the philosophy of self-reliance lies the ideal of a classless society.

All too often, those who have campaigned for that goal have abused the priveleges of power, and they have attempted to force the people into what they the leaders thought would be good for them the led, and in so doing they have restricted freedom; in Algeria not much, but in Libya far too severely. But that ideal will surely only be achieved - and will surely be only worth achieving - when people of their own volition want to achieve it, and when they seek to achieve it peacefully; which means individual regions and communities should have more freedom.

*   *   *

There may still be a need for a level of administration called the nation-state. It is, however, quite wrong for the world to suffer under the illusion, which is very much the case in the more centralised countries, that the nation-state is the sole demarcation by which we establish our differences.

Both in Europe and in Africa, a policy of small-is-beautiful could lead to a safer and happier world. The nation-state should be put into perspective, firstly by the granting of autonomous powers to the regions that comprise the state; and secondly, by each nation acknowledging the right of all to be concerned about all, by submitting part of that mythical stuff called national sovereignty to a supranational authoroity of which the best so far constructed is the United Nations, by abiding by rules of international arbitration for whenever internal or external disputes occur at a dangerous level, and by complying with international declarations of human rights to which every individual and every region as well as every nation should have access.

At the moment, the human rights conventions which do exist would be unable to prevent those abuses of centralisation which caused the problems they try to prevent. In time, however, they will improve. Before long, methinks, they will stipulate that all of us have a right to the tenureship of some land, and none of us the right of its ownership; that in this finite world there are limits to the accummulation of wealth or power to which anyone may aspire; that generations as yet unborn also have rights to the finite resources of the planet, and so on. These conventions and courts of human rights will be part of the machinery of our collective responsibility, telling nobody what to do, telling everybody what not to do.

This combination of devolution and evolution, where power is decentralised and responsibility collectivised, could mean, for instance, that the circumstances which caused the Algerian/Moroccan war cold never recur; that those which split The Sudan no longer had The Sudan to split, and so forth.   In a word, it could lead to a much more peaceful Africa.

In Europe and the world at large, the problem is not just "the bomb", it is the very existence of large, over-centralised, super-power-nation-states which make the deployment of the bomb almost inevitable.   Throughout the world, therefore, a small-is-beautiful policy/philosophy is not only an ideal - it is an absolute pre-requisite of a durable peace.

There is, of course, a major obstacle in the way; how are we going to get the centralised governments of nation states to decentralise both government and the nation-state concept?   As I hinted on page (114), it won't be through the United Nations.   No centralised structure will achieve the change.   It could, however, be the indirect result of a world-wide ecological disaster, like the excessive build-up of atmospheric carbon dioxide.   Umm - interesting theory; someone should write a book about that.

Just as people everywhere emerged into nations, so people everywhere could both demand and get regional autonomy within looser collections of federations of regions and nations.   And one day, when a six or nine county Northern Ireland is self-reliant and semi-autonomous within a federation of these islands, the world will be a safer place .... and the province will be merely bending to a new, more lasting, less farting, world-wide wind of change.

*   *   *

There is a problem, however.   On a small wart of rock which sticks to the Spanish mainland, on an isthmus which some hiccup of history made British, there stands Gibraltar.   Now what happens if the local population want for themselves the adjective derived from a noun one thousand miles away? What if Gibraltar, or rather the people who lived there, wanted to be British.   And in Sebta, a tiny little corner of the vast continent of Africa, there was a church, a villa and a bull, and the people who lived there said they wanted to be Spanish.   Two decentralised communities wanted to be combined with distant centres.   Two tiny contradictions stared at each other across the straits, telling themselves they were right, telling the world it is crazy, and telling me I've got it all quite, quite wrong.

It was in Sebta that I first set foot onto this enormous land-mass; it was here that I first glanced at the wonders of nature called Africa and the blunders of men called politicians. In Sebta my journey began.   Extraordinary.   This must be the end.

LINGUISTIC GLOSSARY

ARABIC	FRENCH & Other	SWAHILI	
Akbar			*great*
Allah			*God*
	alors		*then*
	bien		*well*
bismillah			*"for what we are about to receive ...."*
	boulangerie		*baker*
		bwana	*mister; it is often used when refering to the white man*
bucksheesh			*a gift, or something for nothing*
		chai	*tea*
	chose		*thing*
chott			*dried up salt pan*
	deux		*two*
dhorra			*wheat*
	dieu		*God*
	eau		*water*
fad'dr			*welcome*
	femme		*woman*
	français		*french for french*
	gendarmerie		*police*
habib			*friend*
hamdullah			*".... thanks be to God"*
		harambee	*a patriotic cry meaning "pull together"*
	homme		*man*
Id al Fitr			*the Islamic feast which celebrates the end of the month long fast*
	ipso facto		*by that very fact*
		jambo	*hallo*
	je		*I*
jeleba			*the overall tunic of the North African man*
jihad			*the belief that he who dies in battle goes straight to heaven*
		karibu	*welcome*
kisra			*the basic meal in The Sudan, made from dhorra*
		kiswahili	*swahili for swahili*
kous kous			*the staple food of the Maghreb*
Mahdi			*Saviour*
	mais		*but*
		matatu	*general taxi*
		mbuzi	*goat*
medinah			*town*
Mes'r			*Egypt*
	mon		*my*
mussulman			*a follower of Islam*
		mwalimu	*teacher*
		mwiko	*a large spoon or a small spade*
		mzee	*old man, used as a mark of respect*
N-sha-Allah			*if God so wills*

ARABIC	FRENCH & Other	SWAHILI	
	sûr		*sure*
	sûreté		*safety*
		ugali	*the staple diet of East Africa, made from maize meal*
		wabenzi	*blackwhitemen*
		wakamba	*people of the Kamba tribe*
		watoto	*children*
	objets d'art		*art treasures*
	parfait		*perfect*
	pâtisserie		*cake shop*
	quoi		*what*
Qur'an			*the holy book of Islam*
	sais		*know*
	(et) sequitor		*(and) following*
		shamba	*farmstead of a hut or two, and a wee plot of land*
Shi'ite			*a sect of Islam*
souk		sokoni	*market (sokoni is derived from souk)*
Sunni			*the other sect of Islam*

INDEX

Gaddafi, Muammar   was 27 years old when he first came to power in Libya, so he might be around for a long time yet.

Gandhi, Mahatma   was leader of the Indian nationalist movement; he was most esteemed for his doctrine of non-violence.

Gaulle, Charles de   was the architect of France's fifth republic and President from '58 - '69.

Gorbachev   according to western media, has a lovely wife; he is also General Secretary of the CPSU, (USSR).

Gordon, Charles   was Governor General of The Sudan under the Khedive of Egypt, returning to evacuate Egyptian forces because of the rising of the Mahdi. But he was killed by the rebels and decapitated.

Haile Selassie   was Regent from 1916 and Emperor of Ethiopia from 1930. Mussolini's Italy invaded in 1935, and Haile Selassie led the resistance and was exiled. He only regained power with the help of the British during World War II. He ruled as a progressive autocrat in a feudal land, until deposed after a fair innings at the age of 82.

Hassan, King, II.   In 1961, at the age of 32, he succeeded his dad. He has changed a constitution or two, survived the occasional coup, and he led the "green march" into the somewhat yellow former Western Sahara.

Hatshepsut, Queen   was Queen of Egypt over 3,000 years ago, somewhat before the advent of contemporary feminism, so to be the fake pharaoh, she donned a false beard.

Idris, King   the first and last of Libya. As a leader in Cyrenacia he resisted the Italian colonialists who rather belatedly entered the fray. He went into exile into Egypt until the British occupied Libya in '42, and shortly afterwards, they made him king.

Kabaka.   Sir Edward Mutesa II, the Kabaka, the King of Buganda, was affectionately known as Fred. He was deposed by the British in 1953 'cos they didn't like his separatism. Later he was re-instated as a sort of constitutional monarch, soon to be President of the newly independent Uganda, and then he was deposed by Obote. He died in exile, in London.

Karamajong,   one of the tribes in North East Uganda.

Kariuki, J.M.	was an anti-corruption political campaigner (and businessman) who criticised the ill-gotten gains of politicians and businessmen. He was a Kikuyu from Nyeri .... whereas Kenyatta and Njonjo came from the Kiambu half of the tribe. Kariuki's mutilated body was found outside Nairobi in March, 1975.
Kenyatta, Jomo,	was taught by the missionaries in Africa before studying in the universities of Britain. In the '30's he became a communist; in the '50's a terrorist; and in the '60's and '70's, an out and out capitalist!
Kikuyu	The numerically largest tribe in Kenya; their traditional lands are the agricul-turally rich foot-hills of Mt Kenya, upon the summit of which sat their God.
King, Martin Luther	was a black civil rights leader in America, much influenced by Gandhi; he was assassin-ated in '68.
Luo	The numerically second largest tribe in Kenya; their lands are in Nyanza district, on the shores of Lake Victoria.
Lule, Dr Yusuf	became President of the National Executive Council formed in '79 from the Ugandan National Liberation Front.
Maghreb,	The three countries in which stand the Atlas Mountains: Algeria, Morocco and Tunisia.
Mahdi, Al	was known to those who could pronounce it as Muhammed Ahmed Ibn el-Sayyid Abdullah. He was "the right guided one", (another one), a religious ruler of a vast empire in The Sudan a hundred years ago ... until, by jingo, the British wrought their colonial revenge.
Mao-Tse-Tung	was the great big man who wrote the little red book.
Mboya, Tom	was a young and very gifted minister in Kenya's first government.
Mohammed, Ali	was an officer of the occupying Turkish army in Egypt who by popular acclaim became Pasha though still subject to the Porte. However, as Pasha he was able to transform Egypt into a sizeable power, and not least by borrowing from abroad. His sons pursued this habit, and the British creditors pursued his sons.
Moi, Daniel Arap	was a school teacher-cum-self-taught polit-ician who now, as President, began to crit-icise the more objective members of his former profession.

Mozabite,   The original Mozabites were an heretical
                             sect of Shi'ite Moslems expelled from the
                             good lands of the Atlas about 1,000 years
                             ago, since when they've kept themselves pure
                             or puritanical by only marrying their own.

Muwanga   was the chairman of the Military Commission
                             of the Uganda National Liberation Front, and
                             he came to power in the coup of May 1980.

Nasser   organised a coup in '52 against the monarchy
                             of King Farouk. In '54 he became Prime Min-
                             ister and later nationalised the Suez Canal,
                             much to the annoyance of the British and the
                             French.

Nilotic,   those peoples around the Upper Nile, in
                             North and Eastern Uganda, Southern Sudan and
                             Western Kenya.

Njonjo, Charles   was called to the English bar in '54; he
                             hastened back to Africa, failed to get him-
                             self elected, so he got himself appointed
                             instead. Thus he became attorney-general.

Numeri, Gaafer   was actually imprisoned in his palace for 3
                             days during the attempted coup of '71, but
                             his firm belief in Islam and the occasional
                             swig o'whisky aided a rapid return to power.

Nyerere, Julius   was and still is the first President of Tan-
     Mwalimu   zania, and he's still going strong, despite
                             occasional promises about resigning at the
                             end of the next term ....

Obote, Dr Milton   was an ex-labourer and ex-salesman and ex-
                             President when he returned to power in '81.
                             And now he's an ex-President again.

OPEC   The Organisation of Petroleum Exporting
                             Countries.

Paisley, Dr Ian   is reverend, irreverent, but unfortunately
                             not irrelevant.

Pharaoh   one of the five official names for the kings
                             of Upper and Lower Egypt.

Polisario,   The Frente Popular para la Liberacion de
                             Sakiet el Hamra y Rio de Oro was set up by a
                             group of students in 1973, first to fight
                             the Spanish, and then the Mauritanians and
                             the Moroccans after their deal with the
                             Spanish in '75.

Ramses II   was also called the Great; he fought some
                             wars, built many monuments, and via his
                             nocturnal habits could easily have laid
                             claim to another name, the father of the
                             nation.

Sadat, Anwar al — was a former army officer turned politician without much turning. He helped Nasser establish the Republic, and later succeeded him as President in which rôle he continued the wars against Israel until the peace talks at Camp David. Alas, this last was none too popular with the fundamentalists, his future assassins.

Satyagraha, — the philosophy of "truth force", the cheerful, non-violent resistance practised by many who opposed British rule in India, and to-day by several who oppose the nuclear arms race.

Selassie — see Haile.

Shifta — the Shifta wars took place between Somalia & Kenya shortly after independence.

Shi'ite, — a follower of the Shi'ah sect of Islam which predominates in Iran and Iraq. The original split with the Sunni's concerned who should be the fourth successor to the caliphate, but a few religious differences have also crept in since then.

Steele, David — is leader of the British Liberal Party.

Sunni — opposite of Shi'ite.

Thatcher, Margaret — British Prime Minister from 1979 to the sooner the better.

Tut-Ankh-Amun — restored the temples of Amon after some heretical manoeuvrings by his predecessor; well, that was hard work, his god was not grateful, and he died at the age of 18.

Yusuf, Beni — was a fellow member of Bourguiba's independence struggle; having worked with Nasser, he then led the opposition against France's proposals for Tunisian independence. Later, Bourguiba expelled him. He returned to Cairo where later he was assassinated.

GROSS NATIONAL PRODUCT ($ per head)	COUNTRY	AREA (sq km)	POPULATION (millions)	DATE OF INDEPENDENCE	PRESIDENTS & THINGS
2,140	*ALGERIA*	2,300,000	20	1962	*1965 - 78 BOUMEDIENNE* / *1979- DE CHABLIS*
580	*EGYPT*	1,002,000	37	1922	*1952 - 70 NASSER* / *1970 - 81 SADAT* / *1981- MUBARAK*
420	*KENYA*	580,000	19	1963	*1963 - 79 KENYATTA* / *1979- MOI*
8,450	*LIBYA*	1,750,000	2	1951	*1951 - 69 KING IDRIS* / *1969- GADDAFI*
860	*MOROCCO*	460,000	21	1956	*1961 - KING HASSAN II*
380	*THE SUDAN*	2,500,000	21	1956	*1969 - NUMERI*
1,420	*TUNISIA*	164,000	7	1956	*1956 - BOURGUIBA*
220	*UGANDA*	240,000	14	1962	*1962 - 66 OBOTE / THE KABAKA* / *1966 - 71 OBOTE* / *1971 - 79 AMIN* / *1981 - OBOTE*
7,920	*NORTHERN IRELAND*	13,500	1.5	er ...	*n/a, thank goodness.*

.

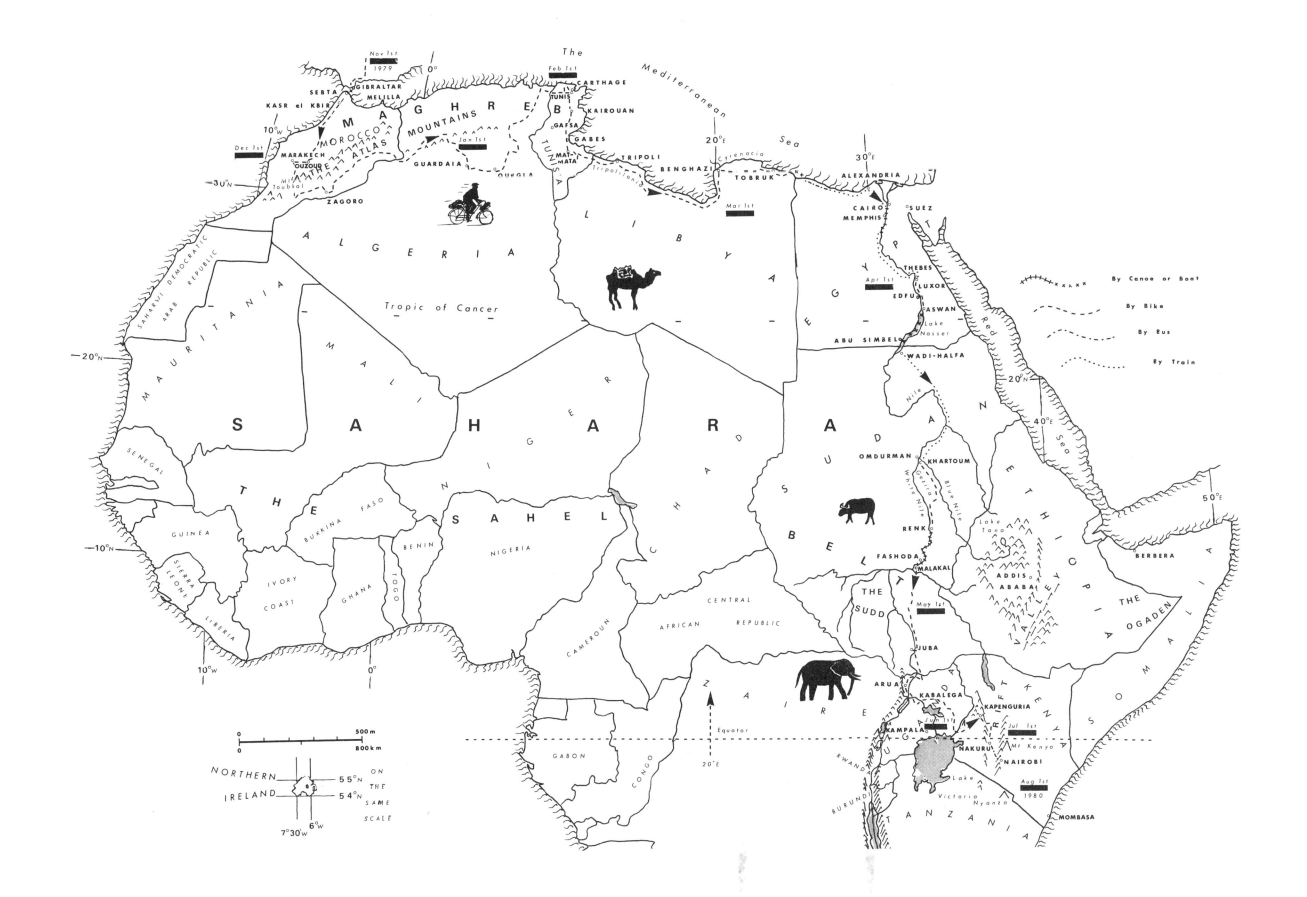

The Mediterranean Sea

Nov 1st 1979

GIBRALTAR
SEBTA MELILLA
KASR el KBIR
MAGHREB
Dec 1st
10°W
MARAKECH
OUZOUR
MOROCCO
Mi Toubkal
ZAGORO
THE ATLAS MOUNTAINS
GUARDAIA
Jan 1st
CARTHAGE
Feb 1st
TUNIS
KAIROUAN
GAFSA
GABES
MAT MATA
OUEGLA
TRIPOLI
Tripolitania
Cyrenacia
BENGHAZI
TOBRUK
20°E
ALEXANDRIA
30°E
CAIRO
MEMPHIS
SUEZ

30°N

MAURITANIA
SAHARVI DEMOCRATIC ARAB REPUBLIC
SENEGAL
20°N
ALGERIA
Tropic of Cancer
LIBYA
EGYPT
THEBES
Apr 1st
LUXOR
EDFU
ASWAN
Lake Nasser
ABU SIMBEL
WADI-HALFA
Red Sea
20°N

Mar 1st

40°E

By Canoe or Boat
By Bike
By Bus
By Train

MALI
THE SAHARA
NIGER
CHAD
SUDAN
50°E

10°N
GUINEA
SIERRA LEONE
LIBERIA
IVORY COAST
GHANA
BURKINA FASO
TOGO
BENIN
NIGERIA
SAHEL
OMDURMAN
KHARTOUM
White Nile
Blue Nile
Lake Tana
RENK
FASHODA
MALAKAL
ADDIS ABABA
ETHIOPIA
BERBERA

0°
GABON
CONGO
ZAIRE
CAMEROUN
CENTRAL AFRICAN REPUBLIC
THE SUDD
JUBA
May 1st
ARUA
KABALEGA
KAPENGURIA
Jun 1st
KAMPALA
UGANDA
NAKURU
Mt Kenya
Jul 1st
KENYA
NAIROBI
THE RIFT VALLEY
THE OGADEN
SOMALIA

Equator
20°E
RWANDA
BURUNDI
Lake Victoria Nyanza
Aug 1st 1980
TANZANIA
MOMBASA

500 m
800 km

NORTHERN IRELAND
55°N
54°N
ON THE SAME SCALE
7°30'W
6°W